Fraud Examiners in White-Collar Crime Investigations

Fraud Examiners in White-Collar Crime Investigations

Petter Gottschalk

BI Norwegian Business School
Oslo, Norway

CRC Press
Taylor & Francis Group
Boca Raton London New York

CRC Press is an imprint of the
Taylor & Francis Group, an **informa** business

CRC Press
Taylor & Francis Group
6000 Broken Sound Parkway NW, Suite 300
Boca Raton, FL 33487-2742

First issued in paperback 2020

ISBN-13: 978-1-4987-2516-3 (hbk)
ISBN-13: 978-0-367-59913-3 (pbk)

Visit the Taylor & Francis Web site at
http://www.taylorandfrancis.com

and the CRC Press Web site at
http://www.crcpress.com

Contents

About the Author

Dr. Petter Gottschalk is one of Norway's leading experts on financial crime and policing. He frequently comments on white-collar criminals and law enforcement in the media and has published extensively in research journals on crime and criminals, policing strategies, and knowledge management strategies. Dr. Gottschalk has conducted extensive empirical research into white-collar criminals and fraud examination reports on which this book is based. He is a professor in the Department of Leadership and Organizational Behavior at BI Norwegian Business School in Oslo, where he teaches courses on policing financial crime and information systems strategy. He is also a visiting professor in the Department of Criminal Justice at the University of New Haven, where he teaches white-collar crime investigations.

Introduction

Dervan (2012) tells the story about Russian authorities raiding Hewlett-Packard's Moscow company offices in search of information regarding an alleged scheme by employees in Germany to bribe Russian officials. The subsidiary in Germany allegedly paid kickbacks in Russia to obtain a contract for delivery and installation of an information technology network. Private investigations initiated by HP into the scheme spread well beyond Germany and Russia, and included the United States, Austria, Serbia, and the Netherlands. It is an example of private investigations into white-collar crime suspicions internationally.

This book is concerned with private investigations into suspicions of financial crime committed by white-collar criminals. Financial crime is illegal possession of others' property; it is crime directed toward values of others for personal or organizational advantage, which is carried out by nonphysical means and by manipulating and hiding criminal activities within regular business activities. It is with purpose, it is a break of trust, and it causes loss. White-collar criminals are persons who carry out financial crimes in the context of their profession. It is individuals who enjoy respect and trust, they have a high social status in society, they occupy important positions in organizations, and they abuse trust and position as offenders. Their financial crime is hidden among legal financial transactions.

This book is about financial crime specialists and fraud examiners who conduct private inquiries into suspicions of white-collar crimes. Private investigations are conducted by a variety of private sector financial crime specialists who can be detectives, forensic accountants, psychologists, or lawyers, all of whom may be supported by investigative analysts.

Criminal investigation is an applied science that involves the study of facts, used to identify, locate, and prove the guilt or innocence of an individual suspected of white-collar crime. A complete criminal investigation can include searching, interviewing, collecting, and preserving. Interviewing is one form of communication used extensively in investigations. Whether used to screen individuals, to elicit information from a witness to an incident, or to obtain a confession, a good interview can have a significant impact on the progress of an investigation. Criminal investigators are supposed to utilize innovative techniques and technological resources to find relevant facts as close as possible to the truth and present them in an objective way.

This book applies a perspective where research, study, investigation, inquiry, and analysis are important to find the truth and its causes in a case. Therefore, this book is more influenced by police science and detective work, rather than laws and legal thinking. It is the private detective rather than the firm lawyer who is a potentially successful fraud examiner when it comes to abuse of power and suspicion of financial crime by the elite in society. But most of all it is successful investigation characterized by a multifaceted and multidisciplinary work, including accountants, auditors, lawyers, organizational experts, forensic scientists, and detectives. Their knowledge exchange and collaboration is needed to solve each financial crime case, which is like a puzzle. If one piece is missing, the puzzle will never be complete.

One of the unique features of this book is that it presents a number of examples of investigations in the private sector, which have been exposed in the media. Presented examples are concerned with investigations into suspicions of financial crime committed by white-collar individuals. Many cases have ended with jail sentences for white-collar criminals after the police got interested in the suspects.

Another unique feature of this book is the policing and detective perspective, rather than the legal or auditing perspectives. This means that information sources and investigative methods are at the core of this book. An example of an information source is people, where the accompanying method is how you get information out of individuals, such as by interviews.

This book applies a project perspective on private investigations, where an investigation is carried out as a project. A project has a defined start and a defined stop, it has a mandate, and it has limited allocated resources.

Last but not least, this book applies a strategic perspective to private investigations, where choice of strategy is the selected path to reach a goal. Strategic investigation is about selection of strategic direction within the following five areas for financial crime specialists and fraud examiners:

1. *Information strategy*: What sources of information are available to financial crime specialists and fraud examiners? What sources are most valuable? How might information be trusted? What information is missing? How do we make sense of information? How is information quality in terms of content, time, and form?
2. *Knowledge strategy*: What knowledge categories and knowledge levels are needed to succeed in this investigation? How are knowledge sharing, knowledge integration, and knowledge creation organized? What kind of culture is created among knowledge workers?
3. *Methods strategy*: What approaches and procedures are followed to obtain relevant information, combine core knowledge, and perform analysis of potential evidence? How are people interviewed? How are documents analyzed? How are intelligent search agents applied in

computer systems? How is forensic evidence collected, stored, and retrieved?
4. *Configuration strategy*: How is the value shop configuration applied to this investigation? What is done to understand potential suspicion of possible financial crime in terms of a problem diagnosis in the first primary activity of the value shop? How do we iterate in the value shop to gain new insights by applying new methods?
5. *Systems strategy*: What information systems are needed to access relevant data for this investigation? What information systems are needed to document this investigation? To what extent are person-to-tools systems, person-to-person systems, person-to-information systems, and person-to-application systems required to succeed in this investigation?

These strategies are described in the middle chapters of this book. Investigation as a project can follow a procedure as illustrated in Figure 1.

Project start is based on a mandate from the internal or external client, resource availability in terms of financial assets and human competence, initial schedule for examination activities, communicated expectations,

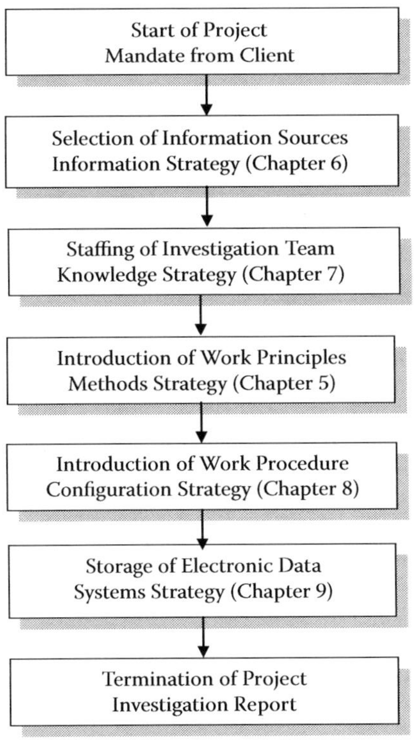

Figure 1 Steps in strategic investigation based on suspicion of financial crime.

identification of critical issues, and information about the project to stakeholders and involved persons. Then work is carried out to identify important information sources, which might be documents, persons, places, and information technology.

The investigation team is staffed with relevant and available experts based on criteria such as competence and representation. Work procedures are introduced in terms of methods strategy and value shop configuration. Collected information is stored in electronic systems, and information technology software is applied to analyze information. The project concludes and closes when the investigation report is handed over to the client and all clarity questions have been answered. This is illustrated in Figure 1.

Strategic investigation can have three parallel paths, as illustrated in Figure 2.

The process path defines work activities to be carried out, how the work is organized, what milestones are to be reached, and how the final report is to be written. The method path defines documents as sources of raw material for hypotheses, analyses, and conclusions. The information path includes all sources of information based on individuals, places, archives, and technologies. The sequence of steps in each path may vary, and so may interrelationships between paths be dependent on the situation to be examined. For example, archives with accounting (Bressler, 2011) and meeting reports might be studied in advance of interviews with individuals in the organization.

An inquiry is any process that has the aim of augmenting knowledge, resolving doubt, or solving a problem. An inquiry may consist of three

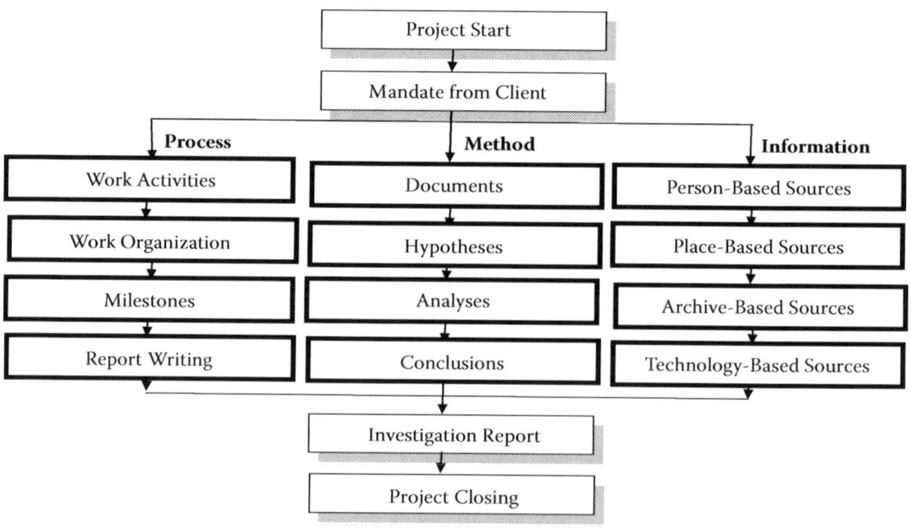

Figure 2 Three parallel paths in the investigation project of possible financial crime.

faces: abduction, deduction, and induction. Abduction is information used to generate a likely hypothesis or an initial diagnosis of the possible crime. Deduction is information used to clarify, derive, and explicate the relevant consequences of the selected hypothesis. Induction is used to test the sum of the assumptions against the sum of the data.

References

Bressler, L. (2011). The role of forensic accountants in fraud investigations: Importance of attorney and judge's perceptions. *Journal of Finance and Accountancy*, Vol. 9, pp. 1–9, April.

Dervan, L.E. (2012). International white collar crime and the globalization of internal investigations. *Fordham Urban Law Journal*, 39(361), 101–127.

White-Collar Criminals 1

Who are the perpetrators of white-collar crime? According to a survey conducted by KPMG (2009), it has become extremely difficult to profile a typical fraudster. They argue that the individual can be of any age group, income level, or tenure of employment. However, they found that most fraudsters are in the age group of 26–40 years, earn a substantial annual income, and have been employed for between 2 and 5 years. Furthermore, they found that men are more typical perpetrators of financial crime than women.

The most economically disadvantaged members of society are not the only ones committing crime. Members of the privileged socioeconomic class are also engaged in criminal behavior (Brightman, 2009). The types of crime may differ from those of the lower classes, such as business executives bribing public officials to achieve contracts, chief accountants manipulating balance sheets to avoid taxes, and procurement managers approving fake invoices for personal gain.

Criminal behavior by members of the privileged socioeconomic class is labeled white-collar crime (Benson and Simpson, 2009). It is often argued that women commit less white-collar crime than men (Haantz, 2002; Holtfreter et al., 2010; Huffman et al., 2010). Suggested reasons for possible gender differences in white-collar crime include lack of opportunity and risk aversion.

Characteristics of White-Collar Criminals

According to Brightman (2009), Sutherland's theory of white-collar crime from 1939 was controversial, particularly since many of the academics in the audience perceived themselves to be members of the upper echelon of American society. Despite his critics, Sutherland's theory of white-collar criminality served as the catalyst for an area of research that continues today. In particular, differential association theory proposes that a person associating with individuals who have deviant or unlawful mores, values, and norms learns criminal behavior. Certain characteristics play a key role in placing individuals in a position to behave illegally, including the proposition that criminal behavior is learned through interaction with other persons in the upper echelon, as well as the interaction that occurs in small intimate groups (Hansen, 2009).

In contrast to Sutherland, Brightman (2009) differs slightly regarding the definition of white-collar crime. While societal status may still determine access to wealth and property, he argues that the term *white-collar crime* should be broader in scope and include virtually any nonviolent act committed for financial gain, regardless of one's social status. For example, access to technology, such as personal computers and the Internet, now allows individuals from all social classes to buy and sell stocks or engage in similar activities that were once the bastion of the financial elite.

In Sutherland's definition of *white-collar crime*, a white-collar criminal is a person of respectability and high social status who commits crime in the course of his occupation. This excludes many crimes of the upper class, such as most cases of murder, adultery, and intoxication, since these are not customarily a part of their job-related procedures (Benson and Simpson, 2009). It also excludes lower-class criminals committing financial crime, as pointed out by Brightman (2009).

What Sutherland meant by respectable and high social status individuals is not quite clear, but in today's business world we can assume he intended to refer to business managers and executives. They are, for the most part, individuals with power and influence that is associated with respectability and high social status. Part of the standard view of white-collar offenders is that they are mainstream, law-abiding individuals. They are assumed to be irregular offenders, rather than people who engage in crime on a regular basis (Benson and Simpson, 2009: 39):

> Unlike the run-of-the-mill common street criminal who usually has had repeated contacts with the criminal justice system, white-collar offenders are thought not to have prior criminal records.

When white-collar criminals appear before their sentencing judges, they can correctly claim to be first-time offenders. They are wealthy, highly educated, and socially connected. They are elite individuals, according to the description and attitudes of white-collar criminals as suggested by Sutherland.

Therefore, very few white-collar criminals are put on trial, and even fewer upper-class criminals are sentenced to imprisonment. This is in contrast to most financial crime sentences, where financial criminals appear in the justice system when typically not without being wealthy, highly educated, or socially connected. White-collar criminals are not entrenched in criminal lifestyles as common street criminals.

What Podgor (2007) found to be the most interesting aspect of Sutherland's work is that a scholar needed to proclaim that crimes of the "upper socioeconomic class" were in fact crimes that should be prosecuted.

It is apparent that prior to the coining of the term *white-collar crime*, wealth and power allowed some persons to escape criminal liability.

Pickett and Pickett (2002) use the terms *financial crime*, *white-collar crime*, and *fraud* interchangeably. They define *white-collar crime* as the use of deception for illegal gain, normally involving breach of trust, and some concealment of the true nature of the activities. *White-collar crime* is often defined as crime against property, involving the unlawful conversion of property belonging to another to one's own personal use and benefit. Financial crime is profit-driven crime to gain access to, and control over, property that belongs to someone else.

Bucy et al. (2008) argue that white-collar crime refers to nonviolent, business-related violations of state or federal criminal statues, and they make a distinction between "leaders" and "followers" in white-collar crime.

White-collar crime can be defined in terms of the offense, the offender, or both. If white-collar crime is defined in terms of the offense, it means crime against property for personal or organizational gain. It is a property crime committed by nonphysical means and by concealment or deception (Benson and Simpson, 2009). If white-collar crime is defined in terms of the offender, it means crime committed by upper-class members of society for personal or organizational gain. It is individuals who are wealthy, highly educated, and socially connected, and they are typically employed by, and in, legitimate organizations (Hansen, 2009).

One of the most famous white-collar criminals was Bernhard Ebbers, chief executive officer of WorldCom (Wagner, 2011: 978):

> To answer why Bernard Ebbers did this, one must take a look at his personal finances. Bernard Ebbers was extremely wealthy by the time WorldCom began to experience difficulties in 2000. Unfortunately for Ebbers (and ultimately for WorldCom shareholders), his desires exceeded his income. Ebber's purchases included an enormous ranch, timber lands, and a yacht-building company, and his loans totaled over $400 million. To secure these loans, he used millions of shares of WorldCom stock as collateral. Any time the price of WorldCom stock went down he needed more cash or assets to maintain his collateral. At one of WorldCom's financial meetings, Ebbers told his employees that "his 'lifeblood was in the stock of the company' and that if the price fell below approximately $12 per share, he would be wiped out financially by margin calls." Bernard Ebbers could not allow WorldCom's stock price to fall even if it was realistically inevitable that this would eventually occur. As Judge Winter stated, "The methods used were specifically intended to create a false picture of profitability even for professional analysts that, in Ebbers's case, was motivated by his personal financial circumstances."

A study in the United States concluded that two main characteristics of white-collar criminals are irresponsibility and antisocial behavior, as compared to other white-collar individuals (Collins and Schmidt, 1993). The common theme running through their study was conscientiousness and positive attitudes toward responsible and pro-social behaviors and activities, suggesting that the discriminating factor between offenders and nonoffenders might be conscientiousness. A study in Germany concluded that two main characteristics of white-collar criminals are hedonism and narcissism, as compared to other white-collar individuals (Blickle et al., 2006).

Bookman (2008) regards Sutherland's original definition of white-collar crime as too restrictive and suggests that white-collar crime is an illegal act committed by nonphysical means and by concealment or guile, to obtain money or property, to avoid payment or loss of money or property, or to obtain business or personal advantage.

In summary, a white-collar criminal is typically a member of the privileged socioeconomic class in society (Sutherland, 1940, 1949) who behaves illegally (Hansen, 2009) in nonviolent acts committed for financial gain (Brightman, 2009; Bucy et al., 2008). The criminal is a person of respectability who commits crime in a professional setting, where criminal activities are concealed and disguised in organizational work (Benson and Simpson, 2009; Bookman, 2008) by law-abiding behavior (Abadinsky, 2007). The criminal has power and influence (Kempa, 2010; Podgor, 2007) and enjoys trust from others in privileged networks (Pickett and Pickett, 2002). White-collar crime incidents are offenses committed by those in professional occupations conducting dishonest activities, by themselves or their agents, for financial gain (Coburn, 2006).

Furthermore, the criminal is often independent and irresponsible, dishonest and antisocial (Collins and Schmidt, 1993; Listwan et al., 2010), and lacks integrity and social conscience (Price and Norris, 2009). The offender is likely to exhibit narcissistic behavior (McKay et al., 2010; Ouimet, 2009, 2010) and psychopathic traits (Ragatz et al., 2012). The criminal belongs to the elite and is often wealthy and higher educated (Heath, 2008). The criminal may be subject to strain (Langton and Piquero, 2007; Piquero et al., 2010) and have low self-control (Gottfredsson and Hirschi, 1990). The offender has legitimate access to the location in which the crime is committed, and the offender's actions have a superficial appearance of legitimacy (Benson and Simpson, 2009).

Finally, the white-collar criminal does not consider his or her own actions as crime (Dhami, 2007; Siponen and Vance, 2010) and has no guilt feeling (Stadler and Benson, 2012). When the criminal is detected, often media coverage follows. The criminal has resources to hire a top white-collar attorney (Weissmann and Block, 2010). White-collar criminals are sentenced differently and possibly milder than street criminals (Maddan et al., 2012; Schoepfer et al., 2007; Stadler et al., 2013), and there is a substantial gender gap (Robb, 2006; Simpson et al., 2012; Steffensmeier et al., 2013).

Characteristics of White-Collar Crime

White-collar crime is a broad concept that covers all illegal behavior that takes advantage of positions of professional authority and power as well as opportunity structures available within business for personal and corporate gain (Kempa, 2010: 252):

> Crimes such as embezzlement, fraud and insider trading, on the one hand, and market manipulation, profit exaggeration, and product misrepresentation on the other, add up to a massive criminal domain.

Criminal opportunities are now recognized as an important cause of all crime. Without opportunity, there can be no crime. Opportunities are important causes of white-collar crime, where the opportunity structures may be different from those of other kinds of crime. These differences create special difficulties for control, but they also provide new openings for control (Benson and Simpson, 2009).

Collins and Schmidt (1993: 296) apply a definition provided by the US Department of Justice:

> Nonviolent crime for financial gain committed by means of deception by persons whose occupational status is entrepreneurial, professional or semi-professional and utilizing their special occupational skills and opportunities; also, nonviolent crime for financial gain utilizing deception and committed by anyone having special technical and professional knowledge of business and government, irrespective the person's occupation.

Blickle et al. (2006: 221) apply the same definition:

> White-collar crime is non-violent crime for financial gain committed by means of deception.

The term *white collar* refers to the characteristics of the occupational position, such as power in the executive position. Therefore, white-collar crime refers to upper-level occupational crime (Collins and Schmidt, 1993).

If white-collar crime is defined in terms of both perspectives of crime and criminal mentioned above, white-collar crime has the following characteristics:

- White-collar crime is crime against property for personal or organizational gain, which is committed by nonphysical means and by concealment or deception. It is deceitful, it is intentional, it breaches trust, and it involves losses.

- White-collar criminals are individuals who are wealthy, highly educated, and socially connected, and they are typically employed by, and in, legitimate organizations. They are persons of respectability and high social status who commit crime in the course of their occupation.

In this book, we apply this definition of white-collar crime, where both characteristics of offense and offender identify the crime. Therefore, white-collar crime is only a subset of financial crime, in our perspective: white-collar crime is violation of the law committed by one holding a position of respect and authority in the community who uses his or her legitimate occupation to commit financial crime (Eicher, 2009).

White-collar crime contains several clear components (Pickett and Pickett, 2002):

- *It is deceitful.* People involved in white-collar crime tend to cheat, lie, conceal, and manipulate the truth.
- *It is intentional.* Fraud does not result from simple error or neglect but involves purposeful attempts to illegally gain an advantage. As such, it induces a course of action that is predetermined in advance by the perpetrator.
- *It breaches trust.* Business is based primarily on trust. Individual relationships and commitments are geared toward the respective responsibilities of all parties involved. Mutual trust is the glue that binds these relationships together, and it is this trust that is breached when someone tries to defraud another person or business.
- *It involves losses.* Financial crime is based on attempting to secure an illegal gain or advantage, and for this to happen there must be a victim. There must also be a degree of loss or disadvantage. These losses may be written off or insured against or simply accepted. White-collar crime nonetheless constitutes a drain on national resources.
- *It may be concealed.* One feature of financial crime is that it may remain hidden indefinitely. Reality and appearance may not necessarily coincide. Therefore, every business transaction, contract, payment, or agreement may be altered or suppressed to give the appearance of regularity. Spreadsheets, statements, and sets of accounts cannot always be accepted at face value; this is how some frauds continue undetected for years.
- *There may be an appearance of outward respectability.* Fraud may be perpetrated by persons who appear to be respectable and professional members of society, and may even be employed by the victim.

PricewaterhouseCoopers (PwC) is a consulting firm that conducts biennial global economic crime surveys. The 2007 economic crime study reveals that many things remain the same: globally, economic crime remains a persistent and intractable problem from which US companies are not immune, as over 50% of US companies were affected by it in the past 2 years.

The percentage of companies reporting suffering actual incidents of fraud according to PwC (2007) were:

- 75% suffered asset misappropriation.
- 36% suffered accounting fraud.
- 23% suffered intellectual property infringement.
- 14% suffered corruption and bribery.
- 12% suffered money laundering.

Schnatterly (2003) argued that white-collar crime can cost a company from 1% to 6% of annual sales, yet little is known about the organizational conditions that can reduce this cost. She found that operational governance, including clarity of policies and procedures, formal cross-company communication, and performance-based pay for the board and for more employees, significantly reduces the likelihood of a crime commission.

There are a number of explanatory approaches to white-collar crime in business from scientific fields such as economics, sociology, psychiatry, and psychology. In economics, the rational choice approach implies that if the rationally expected utility of the action clearly outweighs the expected disadvantages resulting from the action, thereby leaving some net material advantage, then every person will commit the offense in question. One of the many suppositions of this theory is that people generally strive for enjoyment and the fulfillment of desire for material goods (Blickle et al., 2006).

The sociological theory of white-collar crime postulates that managers who commit economic offenses live in a social setting, i.e., culture, in which a very high value is placed on material success and individual wealth. Both economic theory and sociological theory are of the opinion that strong striving for wealth and enjoyment in some way contributes to economic crimes committed by managers (Blickle et al., 2006).

Wagner (2011) puts forward that, counterintuitively, one way to help avoid future accounting scandals such as WorldCom would be the legalization of "fraud-inhibiting insider trading." Fraud-inhibiting insider trading is the subcategory of insider trading where:

1. Information is present that would have a price-decreasing effect on stock if made public.

2. The traded stock belongs to an individual who will likely suffer financial injury from a subsequent stock price reduction if the trading does not take place.
3. The individual on whose behalf the trading occurs would have the ability to prevent the release of the information or to release distorted information to the public.
4. The individual in question did not commit any fraudulent activities prior to availing himself or herself of safe harbor.

Arguing that prohibiting all insider trading incentivizes corporate fraud, Wagner's (2011) article begins by giving examples from recent cases in which insider trading could have been used to avoid significant harm. His article particularly focuses on the two most prominent arguments raised against insider trading:

1. That it erodes confidence in the market
2. That it is similar to theft and should be prosecuted accordingly

Previously unexamined empirical evidence suggests that the confidence argument may be incorrect and does not suffice to justify a prohibition on fraud-inhibiting insider trading. While the property rights rationale is the strongest position against general insider trading, it might be an insufficient basis to outlaw fraud-inhibiting insider trading.

There is a great variety of white-collar crime along the whole spectrum of financial crime. Miri-Lavassani et al. (2009) found that identity fraud is the fastest-growing white-collar crime in many countries, especially in developed countries. In 2008, the number of identity fraud victims increased by 22% to 9.9 million victims since the previous year.

Bank fraud is the criminal offense of knowingly executing a scheme to defraud a financial institution. For example, in China bank fraud is expected to increase both in complexity and in quantity as criminals keep upgrading their fraud methods and techniques. Owing to the strong penal emphasis of Chinese criminal law, harsh punishment, including the death penalty and life imprisonment, has frequently been applied in cases of serious bank fraud and corruption. Cheng and Ma (2009) found, however, that the harshness of the law has not resulted in making the struggle against criminals any more effective. The uncertain law and inconsistent enforcement practices have rather made offenders more fatalistic about the matter, simply hoping they will not be the unlucky ones to get caught.

Fraud is generally defined as the procurement of a private asset or means of advantage through deception or through the neglect of care for the interests of an asset required by duty. In particular, fraud includes heterogeneous forms such as misappropriation, balance manipulation, insolvency, and capital investment fraud (Füss and Hecker, 2008).

Corruption might be defined as the misuse of entrusted authority for personal benefit. Business corruption is defined by the involvement of private companies and is usually motivated by corporate profits. Søreide (2006) suggests that in contrast to the term *political corruption* or the term *petty corruption*, where we focus on the interests of politicians or civil servants, we usually emphasize the perspective and the interests of the bribers when applying the term *business corruption*.

The problem of business corruption can be exemplified by a number of scandals. An example is ExxonMobil in Kazakhstan, where payments were made to Kazakh officials to obtain a share in the Karachaganak oil and gas field. Another example is the Lesotho Dam project, in which eight international construction companies were charged with bribery after they allegedly used bribes to win contracts for a large dam project. Yet another example is the Titan Corporation's unofficial payments to the president of Benin to achieve important business advantages (Søreide, 2006).

Sample of White-Collar Criminals

To identify a substantial sample of white-collar criminals and to collect relevant information about each criminal, there are several options available. However, in a small country like Norway with a population of only 5 million people, available sample size is limited. One available option would be to study court cases involving white-collar criminals. A challenge here would be to identify relevant laws and sentences that correspond with our definition of not only white-collar crime, but also required characteristics of white-collar criminals. Another available option is to study newspaper articles, where the journalists have already conducted some form of selection of upper-class, white-collar individuals convicted in the court of financial crime. Another advantage of this approach is that the cases are publicly known, which makes it more acceptable to identify cases by individual white-collar names. Therefore, the latter option was chosen for this research.

Based on this decision, our sample has the following characteristics applicable to newspaper reporting: famous individuals, famous companies, surprising stories, important events, substantial consequences, matters of principle, and significant public interest. This is in line with research by Schnatterly (2003), who searched the *Wall Street Journal* for several years in her study of white-collar crime published in the *Strategic Management Journal*. Media often pick up examples of companies and their leaders by negative media coverage because of white-collar wrongdoings (Briscoe and

Murphy, 2012). Media coverage is often following individual and organizational wrongdoings (Zavyalova et al., 2012).

Based on the decision to study newspaper articles, we introduce a requirement and criterion to define a white-collar criminal that the individual has fame documented in the news. Thus, media coverage is one of the prerequisites to qualify as a white-collar criminal. The sample thus consists of high-profile and large-yield offenses.

There are two main financial newspapers in Norway: *Dagens Næringsliv* and *Finansavisen*. Both of these papers are conservative-leaning business newspapers. In addition, the business-friendly national daily newspaper *Aftenposten* regularly reports news of white-collar criminals and so was included in the study. Left-wing newspapers such as *Klassekampen* very seldom cover specific white-collar criminal cases, although they do report on the problem of white-collar crime in general.

The use of newspaper reports to assess white-collar crime is, of course, not without potential problems. As a data source, newspaper stories are not entirely independent of the issue under investigation. For example, in a gender perspective, both under- and overrepresentation of women is likely. On the one hand, women criminals, because they are women, may add notoriety to cases, and this may make their offenses more newsworthy than they would be if the same offenses were committed by men. This scenario would lead us to overestimate women's involvement in white-collar crime. On the other hand, a second scenario might lead us to underrepresent women. This could occur if the kinds of cases that newspapers find newsworthy (for example, big, bold, outrageous scandals) are more likely to be committed by men. Furthermore, women are frequently perceived as victims rather than offenders in white-collar crime scandals, which also can contribute to underrepresentation.

Despite such potential bias, we define a white-collar criminal as a person exposed in media after detection and during prosecution in court. Therefore, press coverage is an offender attribute in addition to all the other attributes presented earlier. Examples of newspaper accounts include Dugstad (2010), Haakaas (2011), and Kleppe (2012).

Every edition of these four newspapers was studied on a daily basis from 2009 to 2014 (5 years) to identify stories reporting on white-collar cases and the people involved in them. A person was defined as a white-collar criminal if (1) he or she committed an offense in a deliberate and purposeful manner as part of professional activity linked to regular business activities and using nonphysical means, (2) the offense involved large sums of money or large losses for others, and (3) the offender was portrayed in the newspapers as being successful and having high social status and a position of some power and access to organizational resources. In short, our approach to defining white-collar crime is consistent with Sutherland's (1940, 1949) offender-based definition rather than the offense-based definition, since it is about all kinds of financial crime committed by a special kind of offenders.

We focus on offenses committed by people of high social status and respectability in the course of their occupations. All of the offenses involved individuals linked to or working in organizational settings in key positions. A total of 369 white-collar criminals were identified during those 5 years. A person was defined as a white-collar criminal if that individual seemed to satisfy general criteria mentioned above, and if they were sentenced in court to imprisonment. Because our study includes only cases that were of sufficient notoriety or newsworthiness as to garner newspaper coverage, our sample is similar to other studies of high-profile white-collar crime (Brickey, 2006; Steffensmeier et al., 2013).

Verification of facts in newspaper accounts was carried out by obtaining court documents. After registering newspaper accounts as an important indication of a white-collar offender, the contents in newspaper articles were compared to and corrected by court sentences, which typically range from 5 to 50 pages in Norwegian district courts, courts of appeal, and the Supreme Court. Thus, we reduce the effects of countermeasures by firms and individuals to cover up for their wrongdoings (Zavyalova et al., 2012).

We only included cases where someone involved in them was sentenced in court to imprisonment. For this study it was considered sufficient that the person was sentenced in one court, even if the person represented a recent case that still had appeals pending in higher courts. As the case developed, data were updated in our database. A sentence was defined as a jail sentence. Therefore, cases ending with fines only were not included in the sample.

Since our research is based on newspaper articles written by journalists, the reliability and completeness of such a source is a challenge in social research. However, most cases were presented in several newspapers over several days, weeks, or even months, enabling this research to correct erroneous initial facts as more information became available.

We make no distinction between prison and jail in this study. A prison or jail in Norway is a place in which people are physically confined and deprived of a range of personal freedoms. Imprisonment is a legal penalty that is imposed by the state for commission of a crime judged in court. In the United States, the difference between jail and prison is primarily a function of imprisonment length, where the use of prison over jail implies a more serious punishment.

Our operational definition of white-collar crime restricts the sample to those who receive jail time as punishment. This restriction excludes cases of fines as penal response, which is quite common. This sample restriction enables us to only study serious white-collar crime cases. Our intention is not to identify white-collar crime in reference to the law, but mainly with respect to the reporting of these offenses resulting in imprisonment. If the sample would be selected as references by the law, then a number of offenses would be defined in noncriminal statutes. Noncriminal statutes cannot, by their definition, result in jail time, only in civil remedies. Thus, by taking this view, we have essentially omitted most white-collar crime cases of fines from our study, since their severity is of a minor extent. Research articles edited by Gerber and Jensen (2006) suggest that only the most serious white-collar crime offenders end up in prison.

The decision to include only cases that were successfully prosecuted means that the generalizability of our findings does not extend to the broader population of undetected or unprosecuted white-collar cases. Other researchers, such as Steffensmeier et al. (2013), did the same by only including cases that resulted in convictions.

As suggested by Barak (2007), news-making criminology refers to the conscious efforts and activities of criminologists to interpret, influence, or shape the representation of newsworthy items about crime and justice. News-making criminology as a perspective on the theory, practice, and representations of crime and justice is an important approach for understanding white-collar crime. However, Barak's work focused on how the media construct images of crime. In this empirical study, media are used as a source of potentially objective information, where factual information in terms of quantitative numbers is collected from newspaper accounts.

It must again be noted that there are, of course, disadvantages in using newspapers as data sources. According to Burns and Orrick (2002), research suggests that the media present a distorted image of crime by focusing on violent, sensational events that are atypical of crime in society. They argue that the media are neglecting coverage of corporate offenses, and that the media disproportionately focus on conventional crime while neglecting the impact of corporate misbehavior. This line of reasoning does not only acknowledge possible biases in our research, but also can be understood as an argument for our research design, where an important characteristic of our sample is that the white-collar crime cases are prominent in the media.

Nevertheless, some types of corporate crime—probably those that are more typical—may still go unreported compared to other types of corporate crime. For instance, the media may be biased against small corporate offenses preferring larger, more sensational offenses.

Two methodological issues have to be kept in mind because of our decision to use newspapers as sources:

- *Bias because of press coverage.* Financial crime committed by white-collar criminals is only exposed in the press to the extent that they are sensational and possibly revealed and discovered by the press itself. Therefore, no claim is made that the sample is representative of white-collar criminals in general. Rather, there is a bias toward white-collar criminals that, for some reason, are of special interest to journalists and newspapers that cover their story. Therefore, the attribute of news coverage is explicitly added to the list of attributes for white-collar criminals, including items such as position of trust, network, and opportunity.

- *Data errors in press coverage.* Newspaper articles tend to have some errors in them. There may be factual errors, such as offender name, offender age, imprisonment sentence, crime type, and crime year. Furthermore, there may be a disproportionate focus on the sensational aspects of both criminal and crime. Everyone who has ever read about himself or herself in the newspaper will know that there are errors or wrong impressions in the presentation. To minimize this source of error, several newspaper stories of the same case were read and cited based on investigative research. Furthermore, court sentences were obtained in most of the cases to check both factual and story elements concerning both criminal and crime.

Joshi et al. (2010) recognized the limitation of secondary data collection in that secondary data were susceptible to media bias because of unbalanced media attention and reports about different companies across various industries. To address this limitation, they searched a wide range of data sources in terms of news outlets to reduce potential media bias.

It must be noted that journalists in Norway enjoy respectability because of their integrity and seriousness, like journalists in many other countries. Very few newspapers, if any, are engaged in reporting undocumented, sensational stories. In fact, during our research into financial crime by white-collar criminals, we have not found one such newspaper in Norway. Some journalists in the financial press have developed sophisticated skills in digging for criminal cases, where they apply robust and transparent methodologies. Every year in Norway, a prestigious prize, the SKUP Award, is given to the journalist(s) who has conducted an investigation and reported news in a professional way. The prize is awarded by the Norwegian Foundation for a Free and Investigative Press to someone who both found and reported a good story in a respectable and professional way.

The media in some countries might find a very different public vision of the media than in Norway, which enjoys and deserves public trust. For example, in the United States, "it now appears clear that some prominent columnists and commentators placed that trust at risk by accepting substantial fees from Enron" (Rosoff, 2009: 515). Furthermore, Knottnerus et al. (2006) argue that deviance at Enron could be difficult to detect because of special rituals that were an important part of corporate culture. The press, needless to say, depends on public trust.

It is important to keep in mind that our data are about newspaper accounts of white-collar crime, not the distribution of white-collar crime in society, because that is not what is being measured. Using a newspaper sample is different from the population of white-collar crime cases. We argue that a newspaper account is one of the characteristics of white-collar crime, since white-collar crime is committed by high-profile individuals. Therefore, news reports are relevant reflections of knowledge about white-collar crime. We are applying an offender-based rather than an offense-based perspective on crime.

The research technique applied in this study is content analysis of newspaper articles as well as court documents (Riffe and Freitag, 1997). Purpose of content analysis was to identify the likely source of crime detection. Our data come from a content analysis of newspaper articles and court documents. Mainly facts about offender age, prison sentence, and other relevant issues were obtained. But also issues such as leader versus follower in crime, and occupational versus corporate crime, were identified based on content analysis, where interpretations based on several information sources are possible (Krippendorf, 2004; Neuendorf, 2002).

A newspaper sample might suffer from severe selection biases that have to be taken into account when studying research results:

- Jail sentences are longer than those for many other crime cases, since newspaper articles will disproportionately discuss more serious crime cases with longer sentences.
- Selecting crime cases with sentences instead of fines will also produce cases with longer sentences and thus give skewed distribution to the data.
- The average amount involved in each crime case will be higher since newspaper articles generally focus on more serious crime cases.
- Most crime cases were committed by a group, as again, newspaper articles are more likely to discuss these crime cases because conspiracies are more newsworthy than other individual crime cases.
- A significant number of criminals in high management positions will be present in the sample, again, because newspapers are more likely to discuss crime committed by higher-level employees.
- The size in terms of turnover and employees will be at the higher end, and the company will tend to be profitable, since crime against more successful companies is more likely to be newsworthy.

The danger of media as an information source for research into white-collar crime was wisely emphasized by Pontell and Geis (2007: viii):

> We tend to see the media as our colleagues, for in keeping with our critical stance toward the power elite, journalists tantalize us with exposés that

> attack the powerful. In our enthusiasm for the bounty of information that the sensational case produces, we must remind ourselves of what we know about the manufacture of news and the social construction of knowledge for public consumption.

Similarly, Goldstraw-White (2012) warns that journalist research is often biased, aimed at producing a good story rather than a factual report, and tends to highlight particular types of offenders, such as those regarded as famous. However, since being famous or becoming famous is part of our definition, this bias is acceptable for the current research. Goldstraw-White, in her research, applied a small convenience sample of white-collar criminals in prison who were interviewed about their offending behavior.

Newspaper articles are suitable for content analysis, which is the research method applied in the following. This can tell us a lot about how media organizations frame and depict white-collar crime, but it cannot be used as a direct reflection of the real number or nature of white-collar crime in Norway. It has value in its ability to examine the social construction of white-collar criminality in Norway's financial media.

Given our definition of white-collar crime as news in the media, there is no bias in our data. Therefore, the study can be reliably replicated and has sufficient support from outside sources to be valid (Barak, 2007; Briscoe and Murphy, 2012; Knottnerus et al., 2006; Rosoff, 2009; Schnatterly, 2003; Zavyalova et al., 2012).

Characteristics of Sample Criminals

As suggested in the research literature, most white-collar criminals are men. This is confirmed in our sample of 369 persons, which includes only 25 female criminals and 344 male criminals. Less than 7% women can be explained by lack of opportunity (Benson and Simpson, 2009) and other gender-related factors.

Most famous anecdotal cases such as Madoff, Rajaratman, and Schilling are men in their fifties or older. This is confirmed in our sample where the average age is 48 years old when convicted in court. These average numbers are similar to a study by Blickle et al. (2006) of 76 convicted German white-collar criminals. In their responding sample, there were 6 female criminals and 70 male criminals. The mean age of the offenders in Germany was 47 years. Similarly, the sample applied by Langton and Piquero (2007) consisted of 84% men and 16% women in white-collar crime. In their sample, there was a mean age of 40 years.

A study in the Netherlands of 644 prosecuted white-collar criminals between 2008 and 2012 shows that the average age was 42 years. There were

85% men and 15% women. The most common financial crime category was tax fraud (Onna et al., 2014).

The youngest white-collar criminal in Norway was 17 years old and the oldest was 77 years old when convicted. A distinction is made between age upon conviction and age at the time of committing the crime. On average, a person was convicted 5 years after the crime; thus, the average age when committing white-collar crime in Norway and getting caught for it is 43 years old.

All persons in the sample received a jail sentence for white-collar crime. The longest jail sentence is 9 years and the shortest is 26 days, and the mean average is 2.3 years imprisonment. Compared to famous US cases mentioned above, these sentences are quite modest. However, in a Norwegian context these jail sentences are quite substantial and only surpassed by organized crime and murder. Also, when comparing to the sample used by Blickle et al. (2006) of white-collar criminals in Germany, the difference is less pronounced, as the average was 3.9 years imprisonment in Germany in their sample of 76 convicts.

The average jail sentence in Norway is 2.3 years, and 3.9 years in Germany (Blickle et al., 2006). In comparison, white-collar offenders in the United States have faced sentences that far exceed those imposed in previous years. For example, Bernard Ebbers, former CEO of WorldCom, was sentenced to 25 years; Jeffrey Skilling, former CEO of Enron, was sentenced to 24 years and 4 months; and Adelphia founder John Rigas received a sentence of 15 years, along with his son Timothy Rigas, the CFO of the company, who received a 20-year sentence. Podgor (2007) argues that these greatly increased sentences result in part from the application of the US sentencing guidelines structure, which factors in the amount of fraud loss suffered in the computation of time. Although the sentencing guidelines have a degree of flexibility, resulting from a Supreme Court decision in the United States, the culture of mandated guidelines still permeates the structure and, as such, prominently influences the judiciary. Equally influential in such sentencing is the fact that as parole no longer exists in the federal system, the time given to these individuals is likely to closely correlate with the sentence that they will serve.

Despite short jail sentences, white-collar crime cases are taken seriously by the court system as well as the prison service. Also in the public, no excuses are accepted for their crime. When released from prison, very few are able to regain their positions in society: in terms of prestige, network, and financial freedom. When asked what they found the worst consequence to be, whether media attention, duration of imprisonment, family collapse, or financial ruin, answers differ. Many offenders seem to apply techniques based on neutralization theory (Siponen and Vance, 2010).

White-collar crime involves some form of social deviance and represents a breakdown in social order. According to Heath (2008), white-collar criminals tend to apply techniques of neutralization. These techniques are used by offenders to deny the criminality of their actions. Examples of neutralization techniques are (1) denial of responsibility, (2) denial of injury, (3) denial of the victim, (4) condemnation of the condemners, (5) appeal to higher loyalties, (6) everyone else is doing it, and (7) claim to entitlement. The offender may claim an entitlement to act as he did, either because he was subject to a moral obligation or because of some misdeed perpetrated by the victim. These excuses are applied both for occupational crime and for corporate crime at both the rotten apple level and the rotten barrel level, as discussed below.

The average amount involved in the crime was 48 million Norwegian kroner, which is a little more than US$8 million. The average taxable income of each criminal was 384,000 kroner, paying 178,000 kroner in tax, and having 2,805,000 kroner in personal assets. These numbers are according to the Norwegian internal revenue service.

The average size of the company where the criminal had a role was such that annual turnover was 220 million kroner and there were 133 employees. However, the victim of crime was typically another organization: 264 out of 369 criminals victimized another organization, while only 105 criminals victimized their own organization. Tax authority was the most frequent external victim, followed by banks and customers.

Out of 369 convicted, 344 worked in the private sector, while 25 worked in the public sector. Two hundred-nine final convictions were in district courts, 136 in courts of appeal, and 24 in the Supreme Court. Many of the convicts held positions such as chairman of the board, chief executive officer, chief financial officer, investor, entrepreneur, lawyer, and other privileged jobs.

Out of 369 criminals, 97 (26%) were detected and revealed by journalists, 48 (13%) by victims of the crime, 44 (12%) by bankruptcy lawyers, 24 (7%) by tax authorities, 18 (5%) by banks, 18 (5%) by auditors, 5 (1%) by the police, and 4 (1%) by the stock exchange. Remaining criminals were discovered by other sources.

References

Abadinsky, H. (2007). *Organized Crime*, 8th ed. Thomson Wadsworth, Belmont, CA.

Barak, G. (2007). Doing news making criminology from within the academy. *Theoretical Criminology*, 11(2), 191–207.

Benson, M.L., and Simpson, S.S. (2009). *White-Collar Crime: An Opportunity Perspective*, Criminology and Justice Series. Routledge, New York.

Blickle, G., Schlegel, A., Fassbender, P., and Klein, U. (2006). Some personality correlates of business white-collar crime. *Applied Psychology: An International Review*, 55(2), 220–233.

Bookman, Z. (2008). Convergences and omissions in reporting corporate and white collar crime. *DePaul Business and Commercial Law Journal*, 6, 347–392.

Brickey, K.F. (2006). In Enron's wake: Corporate executives on trial. *Journal of Criminal Law and Criminology*, 96, 397–433.

Brightman, H.J. (2009). *Today's White-Collar Crime: Legal, Investigative, and Theoretical Perspectives*. Routledge, Taylor & Francis Group, New York.

Briscoe, F., and Murphy, C. (2012). Sleight of hand? Practice opacity, third-party responses, and the interorganizational diffusion of controversial practices. *Administrative Science Quarterly*, 57(4), 553–584.

Bucy, P.H., Formby, E.P., Raspanti, M.S., and Rooney, K.E. (2008). Why do they do it? The motives, mores, and character of white collar criminals. *St. John's Law Review*, 82, 401–571.

Burns, R.G., and Orrick, L. (2002). Assessing newspaper coverage of corporate violence: The dance hall fire in Gotenborg. *Critical Criminology*, 11, 137–150.

Cheng, H., and Ma, L. (2009). White collar crime and the criminal justice system—Government response to bank fraud and corruption in China. *Journal of Financial Crime*, 16(2), 166–179.

Coburn, N.F. (2006). Corporate investigations. *Journal of Financial Crime*, 13(3), 348–368.

Collins, J.M., and Schmidt, F.L. (1993). Personality, integrity, and white collar crime: A construct validity study. *Personnel Psychology*, 46, 295–311.

Dhami, M.K. (2007). White-collar prisoners' perceptions of audience reaction. *Deviant Behavior*, 28, 57–77.

Dugstad, L. (2010). Ber om politietterforsking (Asks for police investigation). *Dagens Næringsliv* (Norwegian business newspaper), December 28, p. 6.

Eicher, S. (2009). Government for hire. In Eicher, S. (ed.), *Corruption in international business—The challenge of cultural and legal diversity*, Corporate Social Responsibility Series. Gower Applied Business Research, Ashgate Publishing Ltd., Farnham, England.

Füss, R., and Hecker, A. (2008). Profiling white-collar crime: Evidence from German-speaking countries. *Corporate Ownership and Control*, 5(4), 149–161.

Gerber, J., and Jensen, E.L. (2006). *Encyclopedia of White-Collar Crime*. Greenwood, Westport, CT.

Goldstraw-White, J. (2012). *White-Collar Crime: Accounts of Offending Behaviour*. Palgrave Macmillan, London.

Gottfredson, M.R., and Hirschi, T. (1990). *A General Theory of Crime*. Stanford University Press, Stanford, CA.

Haakaas, E. (2011). Fylte konas konto med kundepenger (Filles wife's account with customer money). *Aftenposten* (Norwegian national daily newspaper), September 2, Business section, p. 16.

Haantz, S. (2002). *Women and White Collar Crime*. National White Collar Crime Center. www.nw3c.org

Hansen, L.L. (2009). Corporate financial crime: Social diagnosis and treatment. *Journal of Financial Crime*, 16(1), 28–40.

Heath, J. (2008). Business ethics and moral motivation: A criminological perspective. *Journal of Business Ethics*, 83, 595–614.

Holtfreter, K., Beaver, K.M., Reisig, M.D., and Pratt, T.C. (2010). Low self-control and fraud offending. *Journal of Financial Crime*, 17(3), 295–307.

Huffman, M.L., Cohen, P.N., and Pearlman, J. (2010). Engendering change: Organizational dynamics and workplace gender desegregation. *Administrative Science Quarterly*, 55, 255–277.
Joshi, K.D., Chi, L., Datta, A., and Han, S. (2010). Changing the competitive landscape: Continuous innovation through IT-enabled knowledge capabilities. *Information Systems Research*, 21(3), 472–495.
Kleppe, M.K. (2012). Tromsdal tiltalt for ti luksusbilbedragerier (Tromsdal charged for ten luxury car frauds). *Finansavisen* (Norwegian daily financial newspaper), February 1, pp. 16–17.
Knottnerus, J.D., Ulsperger, J.S., Cummins, S., and Osteen, E. (2006). Exposing Enron: Media representations of ritualized deviance in corporate culture. *Crime Media Culture*, 2(2), 177–195.
KPMG (2009). *KPMG Malaysia fraud survey report 2009*. KPMG, Kuala Lumpur, Malaysia.
Krippendorf, K. (2004). *Content Analysis: An Introduction to Its Methodology*, 2nd ed. Sage, Thousand Oaks, CA.
Langton, L., and Piquero, N.L. (2007). Can general strain theory explain white-collar crime? A preliminary investigation of the relationship between strain and select white-collar offenses. *Journal of Criminal Justice*, 35, 1–15.
Listwan, S.J., Piquero, N.L., and Voorhis, P.V. (2010). Recidivism among a white-collar sample: Does personality matter? *Australian and New Zealand Journal of Criminology*, 43(1), 156–174.
Maddan, S., Hartley, R.D., Walker, J.T., and Miller, J.M. (2012). Sympathy for the devil: An exploration of federal judicial discretion in the processing of white collar offenders. *American Journal of Criminal Justice*, 37, 4–18.
McKay, R., Stevens, C., and Fratzl, J. (2010). A 12-step process of white-collar crime. *International Journal of Business Governance and Ethics*, 5(1), 14–25.
Miri-Lavassani, K., Kumar, V., Movahedi, B., and Kumar, U. (2009). Developing an identity measurement model: A factor analysis approach. *Journal of Financial Crime*, 16(4), 364–386.
Neuendorf, K.A. (2002). *The Content Analysis Guidebook*. Sage, Thousand Oaks, CA.
Onna, J.H.R., Geest, V.R., Huisman, W., and Denkers, J.M. (2014). Criminal trajectories of white-collar offenders. *Journal of Research in Crime and Delinquency*.
Ouimet, G. (2009). Psychology of white-collar criminal: In search of personality. *Psychologie du Travail et des Organisations*, 15(3), 297–320.
Ouimet, G. (2010). Dynamics of narcissistic leadership in organizations. *Journal of Managerial Psychology*, 25(7), 713–726.
Pickett, K.H.S., and Pickett, J.M. (2002). *Financial Crime Investigation and Control*. John Wiley & Sons, New York.
Piquero, N.L., Schoepfer, A., and Langton, L. (2010). Completely out of control or the desire to be in complete control? How low self-control and the desire for control relate to corporate offending. *Crime and Delinquency*, 56(4), 627–647.
Podgor, E.S. (2007). The challenge of white collar sentencing. *Journal of Criminal Law and Criminology*, Spring, 1–10.
Pontell, H.N., and Geis, G. (2007). *International Handbook of White-Collar and Corporate Crime*. Springer, New York.

Price, M., and Norris, D.M. (2009). White-collar crime: Corporate and securities and commodities fraud. *Journal of the American Academy of Psychiatry and the Law*, 37(4), 538–544.

PwC. (2007). *Economic Crime: People, Culture and Controls*, 4th Biennial Global Economic Crime Survey, United States of America. PricewaterhouseCoopers. www.pwc.com/crimesurvey

Ragatz, L.L., Fremouw, W., and Baker, E. (2012). The psychological profile of white-collar offenders: Demographics, criminal thinking, psychopathic traits, and psychopathology. *Criminal Justice and Behavior*, 39(7), 978–997.

Riffe, D., and Freitag, A. (1997). A content analysis of content analyses, twenty-five years of journalism quarterly. *Journalism Mass Communication Quarterly*, 74, 873–882.

Robb, G. (2006). Women and white-collar crime. *British Journal of Criminology*, 46, 1058–1072.

Rosoff, S.M. (2009). The role of the mass media in the Enron fraud. In Pontell, H.N., and Geis, G. (eds.), *International Handbook of White-Collar and Corporate Crime*. Springer, New York.

Schnatterly, K. (2003). Increasing firm value through detection and prevention of white-collar crime. *Strategic Management Journal*, 24(7), 587–614.

Schoepfer, A., Carmichael, S., and Piquero, N.L. (2007). Do perceptions of punishment vary between white-collar and street crimes? *Journal of Criminal Justice*, 35, 151–163.

Simpson, S.S., Alper, M., and Benson, M.L. (2012). Gender and White-Collar Crime in the 21st Century. Paper presented at the American Society of Criminology, Chicago, IL.

Siponen, M., and Vance, A. (2010). Neutralization: New insights into the problem of employee information security policy violations. *MIS Quarterly*, 34(3), 487–502.

Stadler, W.A., and Benson, M.L. (2012). Revisiting the guilty mind: The neutralization of white-collar crime. *Criminal Justice Review*, 37(4), 494–511.

Stadler, W.A., Benson, M.L., and Cullen, F.T. (2013). Revisiting the special sensitivity hypothesis: The prison experience of white-collar inmates. *Justice Quarterly*, iFirst, 1–25.

Steffensmeier, D., Schwartz, J., and Roche, M. (2013). Gender and twenty-first-century corporate crime: Female involvement and the gender gap in Enron-era corporate frauds. *American Sociological Review*, 78(3), 448–476.

Sutherland, E.H. (1940). White-collar criminality. *American Sociological Review*, 5(1), 1–12.

Sutherland, E.H. (1949). *White Collar Crime*. Holt Rinehart and Winston, New York.

Søreide, T. (2006). Business Corruption: Incidence, Mechanisms, and Consequences. Thesis submitted for the degree of dr.oecon at the Norwegian School of Economics and Business Administration, Bergen, Norway.

Wagner, R.E. (2011). Gordon Gekko to the rescue? Insider trading as a tool to combat accounting fraud. *University of Cincinnati Law Review*, 79, 973–993.

Weissmann, A., and Block, J.A. (2010). White-collar defendants and white-collar crimes. *Yale Law Journal*, 116, 286–291.

Zavyalova, A., Pfarrer, M.D., Reger, R.K., and Shapiro, D.L. (2012). Managing the message: The effects of firm actions and industry spillovers on media coverage following wrongdoing. *Academy of Management Journal*, 55(5), 1079–1101.

Empirical Study of Criminals

2

In this chapter, statistical analysis of the sample of convicted white-collar criminals is presented. The sample consists of criminals who were convicted to prison in Norway over a 5-year period from 2009 to 2014. Some of the analyses are based on the updated sample of 369 white-collar criminals, while some other analyses were carried out at an earlier stage with a slightly smaller sample.

Occupational versus Corporate Crime

Scholars have attempted to differentiate white-collar crime into two types: occupational and corporate. Largely individuals or small groups in connection with their jobs commit occupational crime. This includes embezzlement from an employer, theft of merchandise, income tax evasion, and manipulation of sales, fraud, and violations in the sale of securities (Bookman, 2008). Occupational crime is sometimes labeled elite crime. Hansen (2009) argues that the problem with occupational crime is that it is committed within the confines of positions of trust and in organizations that prohibit surveillance and accountability. Heath (2008) found that bigger and more severe occupational crime tends to be committed by individuals who are farther up the chain of command in the firm.

Corporate crime, on the other hand, is enacted by collectivities or aggregates of discrete individuals. If a corporate official violates the law in acting for the corporation it is also considered a corporate crime. But, if he or she gains personal benefit in the commission of a crime against the corporation, it is regarded as occupational crime. A corporation cannot be jailed, and therefore the majority of penalties to control individual violators are not available for corporations and corporate crime (Bookman, 2008).

According to Hansen (2009), individuals or groups commit occupational or elite crime for their own purposes or enrichment, rather than for the enrichment of the organization on the whole, in spite of supposed corporate loyalty.

White-collar crime occurs typically at higher levels in business. It is crime committed by a corporate manager, a high-ranking technical specialist, a procurement manager, an official representative of a corporation, or the owner of a corporation. Included in this term are both the possibility that the white-collar offender acted self-servingly to further private interests or the interests of a group of persons in a corporation, which is typically labeled occupational crime, and the possibility that the person may have acted on behalf of the corporation with the intention of protecting or enhancing the interests of the corporation (Blickle et al., 2006).

Corporate crime occurs when, for example, fraud is being committed on behalf of an organization; that is, the crime is being committed to benefit the business. Other crimes would be classified as against an organization, e.g., occupational fraud. Perri and Brody (2011) argue that corporate crime is rationalized as a behavior acceptable to overcome financial difficulties or to make a profit for the business, while occupational crime is rationalized in other ways: I am borrowing the money and will pay it back, or the company owes me money that I never received, but deserve.

Fleet and Fleet (2006) argue that corporate crime is committed by higher-ranking officers:

> Corporate crime refers to those crimes committed by members of an organization to benefit the organization. White-collar crime refers to those crimes committed by higher-ranking members of an organization to benefit themselves. Occupational or employee crime refers to those crimes committed by members of an organization (generally lower ranking) that are intended to benefit the perpetrators to the detriment of the organization.

In legal terms, a corporation is an unnatural person (Robson, 2010: 109):

> Corporate personality functions between an insentient, inanimate object and a direct manifestation of the acts and intentions of its managers. Nowhere is this duality more problematic than in the application of traditional concepts of criminal law to business organizations. The question of whether business organizations can be criminally liable—and if so, the parameters of such liability—has long been the subject of scholarly debate. Whatever the merits of such debate, however, pragmatic considerations have led courts and legislatures to expand the panoply of corporate crime in order to deter conduct ranging from reprehensible, to undesirable, to merely annoying. In the context of organizational behavior, criminal law is the ultimate deterrent.

Corporations become victims of crime when they suffer a loss as a result of an offense committed by a third party, including employees and managers. Corporations become perpetrators of crime when managers or employees commit financial crime within the context of a legal organization. According to Garoupa (2007), corporations can more easily corrupt enforcers, regulators, and judges than individuals. Corporations are better organized, are wealthier, and benefit from economies of scale in corruption. Corporations are better placed to manipulate politicians and the media. By making use of large grants, generous campaign contributions, and influential lobbying organizations, corporations may advance law changes and legal reforms that benefit their illegal activities.

Occupational crime is typically motivated by greed, where white-collar criminals seek to enrich themselves personally. Similarly, firms engage in corporate crime to improve their financial performance. Employees break the law in ways that enhance the profits of the firm, but which may generate very little or no personal benefit for themselves when committing corporate crime (Heath, 2008: 600):

> There is an important difference, for instance, between the crimes committed at Enron by Andrew Fastow, who secretly enriched himself at the expense of the firm, and those committed by Kenneth Lay and Jeffrey Skilling, who for the most part acted in ways that enriched the firm, and themselves only indirectly (via high stock price).

While legal corporations may commit business crime, illegal organizations are in the business of committing crime. Garoupa (2007) emphasized the following differences between organized crime and business crime: (1) organized crime is carried out by illegal firms (with no legal status), the criminal market being their primary market and legitimate markets their secondary markets, and (2) corporate crime is carried out by legal firms (with legal status), the legitimate market being their primary market and the criminal market their secondary market. Whereas organized crime exists to capitalize on criminal rents and illegal activities, corporations do not exist to violate the law. Organized crime gets into legitimate markets in order to improve its standing on the criminal market, while corporations violate the law so as to improve their standing on legitimate markets.

While occupational crime is associated with bad apples, corporate crime is associated with systems failure. Bad apples theory represents an individualistic approach in criminology, while systems failure theory represents a business approach in criminology (Heath, 2008: 601):

> If the individualistic approach were correct, then one would expect to find a fairly random distribution of white collar crime throughout various sectors of the economy, depending upon where individuals suffering from poor character or excess greed wound up working. Yet, what one finds instead are very high concentrations of criminal activity in particular sectors of the economy. Furthermore, these pockets of crime often persist quite stubbornly over time, despite a complete changeover in the personnel involved.

Information available from newspapers and other open sources included age of offender when convicted in court, age when committing the crime, years in prison according to court sentence, the sum of money (in Norwegian kroner) involved in the crime, personal income of offender in 2009, tax paid in 2009, personal wealth registered in 2009, the number of persons involved in the crime, the business revenue of the organization in which the offender worked, and the number of employees in the organization where the offender worked. These are all listed in Table 2.1.

In Table 2.1, we see that age when convicted was 48 years for occupational criminals and 52 years for corporate criminals. This difference is statistically significant. Thus, corporate criminals who commit crime on behalf of the organization are significantly older than those occupational criminals who commit financial crime to benefit themselves. Similarly, age when committing crime is significantly different for the two groups.

Years in prison are not significantly different, with 1.9 and 2.3 years, respectively, for corporate and occupational criminals.

Financial amount involved in crime is significantly larger in corporate crime, where the average value is 155 million Norwegian kroner (about US$2.5 million).

It is interesting to note that even though the sum of money involved in crime is higher for corporate criminals, they receive a shorter jail sentence. This is contrary to the normal trend, where higher amounts lead to more time in prison. So, even if the magnitude of the financial crime in terms of money was substantially and significantly larger for corporate crime, occupational crime was nevertheless judged more severely in terms of imprisonment.

The next item in Table 2.1 is the personal income of the offender. Although there is no statistically significant difference in monetary terms, the corporate criminal made substantially more than the occupational criminal. While making more money, the corporate criminal also pays much

Table 2.1 Comparison of Characteristics of Occupational Crime versus Corporate Crime

Total 369 Convicted White-Collar Criminals	57 Corporate Criminals	312 Occupational Criminals	*t*-Statistic Difference	Significance of *t*-Statistic
Age convicted	52 years	48 years	2.996	0.003
Age crime	48 years	43 years	3.597	0.000
Years prison	1.9 years	2.3 years	−1.706	0.089
Crime amount	155 m NOK	28 m NOK	5.992	0.000
Personal income	491,000 NOK	365,000 NOK	1.263	0.207
Personal tax	252,000 NOK	164,000 NOK	1.775	0.077
Personal wealth	4.4 m NOK	2.5 m NOK	0.989	0.323
Involved persons	3.0 persons	3.4 persons	−1.286	0.199
Business revenue	442 m NOK	179 m NOK	4.267	0.000
Business employees	288 persons	104 persons	3.575	0.000

more money in tax to the government. Corporate criminals have more assets in terms of person wealth.

The number of persons involved in the financial crime is not significantly different between the two groups. While 3.4 persons on average were involved in occupational crime, the average for corporate crime is 3.0 persons. This result may seem counterintuitive, as crime on behalf of the corporation would seem to need more involvement of others than is necessary for occupational crime.

Corporate criminals operate in significantly larger organizations. Their organizations have a turnover of 442 million in revenue and 288 employees. Where occupational criminals operate, there is a turnover of 179 million in revenue and 104 employees.

Based on a sample of 369 convicted white-collar criminals in Norway, where 312 individuals were occupational criminals and 57 were corporate criminals, we thus found some interesting differences between the two groups. In statistical terms, significant differences were found in terms of age, crime amount, and organizational size. Corporate criminals are involved in more severe crime when measured in the sum of money involved in crime, and they work in larger organizations.

Another interesting aspect is the number of corporate criminals versus occupational criminals in the sample. There were 57 corporate and 312 occupational criminals, i.e., six times as many occupational criminals caught in Norway. This is in line with a survey in Norway where we had chief financial officers as respondents. Almost all responses in his survey implied that the respondents were thinking of occupational crime rather than corporate crime when responding to the following open-ended question: How will you proceed on suspicion of white-collar crime in your company? Only a few responses could be interpreted as being concerned with corporate crime, for example, where respondents would only discuss their suspicions with colleagues they trusted and where they would undertake controls and investigate before contacting outside experts.

Criminal Leaders versus Criminal Followers

White-collar criminals can either take on the role of leader or adopt the role of follower. Bucy et al. (2008) argue that white-collar crime refers to nonviolent, business-related violations of state or federal criminal statues, and they make a distinction between leaders and followers in white-collar crime.

Bucy et al. (2008) found that motives for leaders differ from follower motives. Compared to the view that leaders engage in white-collar crime because of greed, followers are nonassertive, weak people who trail behind someone else, even into criminal schemes. Followers may be convinced of the rightness of their cause, and they believe that no harm can come to them because they are following a leader whom they trust or fear. Followers tend to be naive and unaware of what is really happening, or they are simply taken in by the personal charisma of the leader and are intensely loyal to that person.

Charisma is defined as a certain quality of an individual by which he or she is considered extraordinary and treated as endowed with superhuman or exceptional powers or qualities. Charismatic authority arises from the charisma or gift of grace of the leader. It is up to the followers to recognize this characteristic in leaders and to act accordingly (Aguilera and Vadera, 2008).

However, leadership in general, and the application of different styles of leadership in particular, are not primarily a one-way process, but often the result of dynamics in which the behavior of followers might influence the style as well as the intensity of the leaders' behavior. Accordingly, followers may play a much more active part in such relationships contrary to what is suggested above.

In our sample of 369 white-collar criminals, 234 persons could be identified as leaders in crime, while 135 persons could be identified as followers. A typical leader-follower case in our sample is the CEO who told his CFO to make expenditures for corruption part of the regular accounting. Another example is the woman (follower) who impersonated a rich widow to withdraw money from a bank, after having been told how to do so by an insider in the bank (leader).

Leaders and followers are compared in Table 2.2. Leaders and followers are about the same age. They receive significantly different jail sentences: the average for leaders is 2.7 years and the average for followers is 1.6 years.

Another significant difference in the table is the number of persons involved in the crime. While there are 4.4 persons involved when there are followers, only 2.8 persons are involved when there is a leader.

Table 2.2 Comparison of Characteristics of Criminal Leaders versus Criminal Followers

Total 369 Convicted White-Collar Criminals	234 Criminal Leaders	135 Criminal Followers	*t*-Statistic Difference	Significance of *t*-Statistic
Age convicted	48 years	49 years	−0.503	0.615
Age crime	43 years	44 years	−0.677	0.499
Years prison	2.7 years	1.6 years	5.441	0.000
Crime amount	43 m NOK	56 m NOK	−0.751	0.453
Personal income	404,000 NOK	349,000 NOK	0.732	0.464
Personal tax	198,000 NOK	144,000 NOK	1.433	0.153
Personal wealth	3.5 m NOK	1.6 m NOK	1.312	0.190
Involved persons	2.8 persons	4.4 persons	−6.477	0.000
Business revenue	226 m NOK	208 m NOK	0.377	0.706
Business employees	123 persons	149 persons	−0.672	0.502

So far, we have discussed occupational versus corporate crime, and leaders versus followers in crime. In Figure 2.1 we combine these two classifications to create a matrix. For example, a leader in occupational crime does it to enrich himself or herself together with potential followers. A leader in corporate crime does it to enrich the organization. Maybe the company is in danger of bankruptcy, and the criminal as a leader sees no other way than financial crime to rescue the business enterprise. Similarly, followers can participate in occupational as well as corporate crime.

Figure 2.2 shows the distribution of white-collar criminals in the four categories. There are a total of 57 corporate criminals and 312 occupational criminals, and there are a total of 234 criminal leaders and 135 criminal followers. Most offenders are found within occupational crime where the

Role / Actor	Leader	Follower
Occupational	Occupational crime as leader	Occupational crime as follower
Corporate	Corporate crime as leader	Corporate crime as follower

Figure 2.1 Categories of white-collar crime depending on role and actor.

Role / Actor	Leader	Follower
Occupational	198	114
Corporate	36	21

Figure 2.2 Criminals in each category of white-collar crime depending on role and actor.

Table 2.3 Leaders versus Followers in Corporate versus Occupational Crime

Total 369 White-Collar Criminals	36 Corporate Leaders	21 Corporate Followers	198 Occupational Leaders	114 Occupational Followers
Age convicted	53 years	51 years	47 years	48 years
Age crime	49 years	46 years	42 years	43 years
Years prison	2.3 years*	1.1 years*	2.7 years*	1.7 years*
Crime amount	125 m NOK	205 m NOK	29 m NOK	28 m NOK
Personal income	570,000 NOK	357,000 NOK	374,000 NOK	348,000 NOK
Personal tax	314,000 NOK	147,000 NOK	176,000 NOK	144,000 NOK
Personal wealth	6.5 m NOK	0.7 m NOK	2.9 m NOK	1.8 m NOK
Involved persons	2.6 persons*	3.6 persons*	2.8 persons*	4.6 persons*
Business revenue	276 m NOK*	728 m NOK*	217 m NOK*	112 m NOK*
Business employees	138 persons*	545 persons*	120 persons	76 persons

* Significant statistical differences between groups of corporate criminals and groups of occupational criminals.

white-collar criminal assumes the leader role (198 criminals). There are few convicts in the category of corporate crime followers (21 criminals).

The four groups of criminals are listed in Table 2.3. Among corporate criminals, leaders in crime receive a significantly more severe sentence than followers in crime, i.e., 2.3 and 1.1 years, respectively, even though the sum of money involved in crime is larger for corporate crime followers. There are fewer executives involved for each leader in crime than there are executives involved for each follower in crime. Leaders in corporate crime work in significantly smaller organizations when compared to crime where there are followers. Other differences for leaders versus followers are also interesting, albeit not statistically significant. For example, the follower has a lower income than the leader, and is also less wealthy.

For occupational criminals in the last two columns in the table, there are again significant differences between leaders and followers in terms of imprisonment. Leaders go on average in prison for 2.7 years, while followers go for only 1.7 years. When there is one or more followers in crime, the number of individuals involved in crime is 4.6 persons on average, while the number is only 2.8 persons for each leader in crime. Finally, business revenue in organizations where there is a leader in crime is significantly higher than for a typical follower in occupational crime.

Followers receive a shorter jail sentence than leaders. These differences are significant: 2.3 versus 1.1 years (respectively) for corporate crime, and 2.7 versus 1.7 years for occupational crime.

The present study has shown that white-collar crime is a serious and prevalent problem, in organizations and in society at large. Regarding the criminals, the distinction made between leaders and followers, in terms of agency, is, however, blurred—the present study clearly shows that followers may plan, initiate, and perform criminal acts on their own, indicating that followers may not be as passive, unaware, or naive as suggested by Bucy et al. (2008). On the contrary, it is quite conceivable that some followers may reinforce or even activate destructive and criminal behaviors in their leaders.

According to Padilla et al. (2007), there are two types of destructive followers: conformers and colluders. Conformers go along with destructive leaders out of fear, whereas colluders enthusiastically engage in destructive behaviors. Although both groups are motivated by self-interest, their concerns differ (Higgins, 1997). Conformers try to minimize any consequences of not behaving as expected, while colluders seek personal gratification via their relationship with a destructive leader. Conformers are motivated by basic needs that are unmet, negative self-evaluation, and psychological immaturity. Colluders, on the other hand, are ambitious, selfish, and share the values of the destructive leader (Padilla et al., 2007; Padilla, 2013). They cooperate in secret to achieve a fraudulent, illegal, or deceitful goal. As such, criminal leadership may, in part, be explained by follower behavior, thereby limiting the extent of influence of leaders' individual characteristics and hence responsibility.

Leaders in crime, both corporate leaders and occupational leaders, receive a significantly longer jail sentence when convicted in court than corporate and occupational followers in crime. To date, followers seem to have been studied less frequently than leaders, despite the fact that their role in the criminal process is clearly essential. The result of the present chapter is that a new and interesting perspective on the notion of leader-follower exchange dynamics may be gained. The present study indicates that there are also leader-follower exchange dynamics of a sinister kind, where criminal leaders may form alliances with colluders in order to achieve goals that more greatly concern personal need satisfaction, and the colluders are rewarded for helping them in these endeavors. Although (owing to the design of the present study) we have not established a relationship between the criminal leaders and their followers in all cases, this study clearly indicates that there is a strong need to focus more on both criminal followership and criminal leadership, as well as on potential criminal leader-follower exchange dynamics in future studies.

The aim of this section was to provide a sample of white-collar criminal leaders and followers and to examine differences between the two groups. The sample consists of 369 white-collar criminals in total, comprising 234 leaders and 135 followers. A comparison of average values as well as variations in white-collar characteristics of the leaders and followers reveals significant differences between the two groups, regarding the number of persons involved in the crime and years imprisonment. Leaders committing corporate crime (as opposed to occupational crime) receive a jail sentence that is twice times as long as followers do. The present study clearly indicates that, contrary to statements that claim followers are passive and naive, they may plan and commit criminal acts independently.

Rotten Apples versus Barrel Offenders

Ashforth et al. (2008) argue that it is comforting to assume that one bad apple or renegade faction within an organization is essentially responsible for the crime that is all too prevalent. However, organizations are important to our understanding of crime, because they influence the actions of their members. Therefore, both micro and macro views are important in order to understand crime.

It is certainly an interesting issue whether to view white-collar misconduct and crime as acts of individuals perceived as rotten apples or as an indication of systems failure in the company, the industry, or the society as a whole. The perspective of occupational crime is favoring the individualistic model of deviance, which is a human failure model of misconduct and crime. This rotten apple view of white-collar crime is a comfortable perspective to adopt for business organizations, as it allows them to look no further than suspect individuals. It is only when other forms of group (O'Connor, 2005) or systemic (Punch, 2003) corruption and other kinds of crime erupt upon a business enterprise that a more critical look is taken of white-collar criminality. Furthermore, when serious misconduct occurs and is repeated, there seems to be a tendency to consider crime as a result of bad practice, lack of resources, or mismanagement, rather than acts of criminals.

The rotten apple metaphor has been extended to include the group-level view of cultural deviance in organizations (O'Connor, 2005). Furthermore, Punch (2003) has pushed the notion of rotten orchards to highlight deviance at the systemic level. Punch (2003: 172) notes: "The metaphor of 'rotten orchards' indicate(s) that it is sometimes not the apple, or even the barrel, that is rotten but the *system* (or significant parts of the system)."

When the system is rotten, we can talk about systemic crime or systems crime (Punch, 2003: 172):

> ... in some way encouraged, and perhaps even protected, by certain elements in the system.... "Systems" refers both to the formal system—the police organization, the criminal justice system and the broader socio-political context—and to the informal system of deals, inducements, collusion and understandings among deviant officers as to how the corruption is to be organized, conducted and rationalized.

Out of 369 identified white-collar criminals, 140 emerged as individual rotten apples, while 229 emerged as members of rotten apple barrels (as listed in Table 2.4).

Table 2.4 Comparison of Characteristics of Rotten Apple versus Rotten Barrel Persons

Total 369 White-Collar Criminals in Jail	140 Rotten Apple Persons	229 Rotten Barrel Persons	*t*-Statistic for Difference	Significance of *t*-Statistic
Age convicted	49 years	48 years	0.635	0.526
Age crime	44 years	43 years	1.066	0.287
Years prison	2.4 years	2.2 years	0.980	0.328
Crime amount	25 m NOK	62 m NOK	−2.232	0.026
Personal income	387,000 NOK	383,000 NOK	0.050	0.960
Personal tax	174,000 NOK	181,000 NOK	−0.180	0.857
Personal wealth	2.4 m NOK	3.0 m NOK	−0.431	0.667
Involved persons	2.4 persons*	4.0 persons*	−6.188	0.000
Business revenue	273 m NOK	187 m NOK	1.840	0.067
Business employees	167 persons	112 persons	1.415	0.158

* Significant statistical differences between groups of corporate criminals and groups of occupational criminals.

In Table 2.4 we see that age upon conviction was 49 years for rotten apples and 48 years for members of rotten barrels, and this difference is statistically not significant. Similarly, the difference in age when the crime was committed was not significant either. Rotten apples received a jail sentence of 2.4 years on average, while rotten barrel members received only 2.2 years. This difference is statistically not significant.

The shorter jail sentence for barrel members is particularly interesting when comparing crime amount, when the crime amount is substantially (although not significantly) larger for barrel members. So, even though the crime amount is larger, the jail sentence is shorter (rotten apple criminals on average abused 25 million Norwegian kroner, while rotten barrel criminals on average abused 62 million Norwegian kroner).

Apple and barrel criminals have the same registered personal income, and pay the same amount of tax. Barrel criminals have little more assets than apple criminals.

As might be expected, a greater number of persons are involved in barrel crime: 4.0 versus 2.4. This difference is statistically significant. Barrel crime is characterized by an organization where crime is no surprise.

Apple criminals work in larger organizations than barrel criminals. This means that organizations that are themselves bad and prone to commit crime are on average smaller than organizations where individual offenders operate.

The matrix in Figure 2.3 of leader versus follower, rotten apple versus rotten barrel offender, and occupational versus corporate crime provides a useful framework with which to study white-collar crime. The concepts of leader versus follower, and occupational versus corporate crime, were explained earlier.

Level	Actor \ Role	Leader	Follower
Occupational	Rotten apple	Occupational apple leader	Occupational apple follower
	Rotten barrel	Occupational barrel leader	Occupational barrel follower
Corporate	Rotten apple	Corporate apple leader	Corporate apple follower
	Rotten barrel	Corporate barrel leader	Corporate barrel follower

Figure 2.3 Categories of white-collar crime depending on role, actor, and level.

Based on our sample of 369 convicted white-collar criminals in Norway, where 140 individuals were rotten apple criminals and 229 rotten barrel criminals, we find some interesting differences in the size of the groups, as illustrated in Figure 2.4.

Most of the criminals are occupational criminals, acting in isolation as rotten apples and as leaders (105 criminals). The second biggest group consists of occupational leaders in rotten barrels (93 criminals). Surprisingly few corporate criminals can be classified as rotten apples (6 and 2 criminals), as almost all of them are rotten barrel members (30 and 19 criminals). The distribution in these eight categories is interesting, as it indicates where law enforcement could have the greatest impact.

The varying number of criminals in each category does not justify an analysis of variance (ANOVA). Having only 6 and 2 criminals, respectively,

Level	Actor \ Role	Leader	Follower
Occupational	Rotten apple	105	27
	Rotten barrel	93	87
Corporate	Rotten apple	6	2
	Rotten barrel	30	19

Figure 2.4 Occurrences of white-collar criminals depending on role, actor, and level.

versus as many as 105 criminals in another category, makes it not possible to perform another statistical analysis. Therefore, significant versus nonsignificant differences between eight groups in the figure are not computed here.

A contingent approach to crime response has been discussed thus far as being dependent on whether it is occupational or corporate crime and whether it constitutes leader or follower crime. A third situational factor is whether rotten apple or rotten barrel is suspected, as illustrated in the figure.

When a rotten apple commits occupational crime, it is interesting to study whether the rotten apple as a leader is more harshly judged than a follower is judged. As a follower, the rotten apple may have acted according to obedience pressure. Baird and Zelin (2009) conducted such a study, where they utilized written scenarios to examine whether persons committing fraud in situations involving obedience pressure are judged less harshly by others than persons committing fraud of their own volition. Participants in their study were also asked how likely they would be, in the same circumstances, to commit the same fraudulent acts—higher expectations were predicted for participants receiving the scenarios involving obedience pressure. In their study, they found empirical support for the hypothesis that followers from obedience pressure are less harshly judged.

Agency theory can be applied to discuss our findings. Agency theory describes the relationship between two parties using the metaphor of a contract. It specifically addresses which issues affect the relationship (Benson and Simpson, 2009). Agency theory is explained later in this book as part the organizational dimension.

In the case of corporate crime, the organization is the principal, while the criminal is the agent. In the case of leaders in crime, the leader is the principal, while the follower is the agent. Both principal and agent can be the main player in crime. Problems arise when the two are not quite alike, if they differ in some way (Chrisman et al., 2007). The main reasons for the inability are the principal's lack of information about the agent's work, lack of effective checks and balances, and ineffective enforcement and punishment for criminal executives (Li and Ouyang, 2007). However, crime can just as well be committed by the principal rather than the agent, as exemplified in the leader-follower case. For example, the CFO as an agent provides a board member with inside information, on which the principal acts illegally.

Detection of White-Collar Crime

Our research is concerned with the following question: Who detects white-collar criminals? Our empirical results are listed in Table 2.5, where we find journalists to occupy the top position, followed by crime victims, bankruptcy lawyers, tax authorities, banks, and the police.

Table 2.5 Detection of White-Collar Crime

Rank	Crime Detection Source	Criminals	Fraction
1	Journalists investigating tips from readers	97	26%
2	Crime victims suffering financial loss	48	13%
3	Internal controls of transactions in organization	44	12%
4	Bankruptcy lawyers identifying misconduct	39	11%
5	Tax authorities carrying out controls	24	7%
6	Commercial banks controlling accounts	18	5%
7	Accounting auditors controlling clients	18	5%
8	Police investigations into financial crime	5	1%
9	Stock exchange controls of transactions	4	1%
10	Other detection sources	72	19%
	Total	369	100%

A comparison of the white-collar crime cases detected by journalists, alongside those detected by others, is presented in Table 2.6. There are some interesting differences that are statistically significant. First, the sum of money involved in crime is significantly larger in cases detected by journalists. The average amount for journalist-detected criminals is 110 million Norwegian kroner (approximately US$18 million).

Strangely enough, criminals detected by journalists are registered with lower income, less tax, and fewer assets than white-collar criminals detected by others. Not so strange, however, is that the number of persons involved in criminal activity is larger in cases detected by journalists. Probably is it easier for external detection when more criminals are involved in the offense.

Some of the characteristics are not different. For example, criminals detected by journalists have the same age as criminals detected by others.

Table 2.6 Comparison of Journalist- and Nonjournalist-Detected White-Collar Criminals

Total 369 White-Collar Criminals	97 Detected by Journalists	272 Detected by Others	*t*-Statistic Difference	Significance of *t*-Statistic
Age convicted	48 years	48 years	–0.512	0.609
Age at time of crime	43 years	44 years	–0.893	0.372
Years in prison	2.5 years	2.2 years	1.659	0.098
Crime amount	110 m NOK	26 m NOK	4.783	0.000
Personal income	260,000 NOK	429,000 NOK	–2.058	0.040
Personal tax	113,000 NOK	201,000 NOK	–2.185	0.030
Personal wealth	1.6 m NOK	3.2 m NOK	–1.050	0.294
Involved persons	5.0 persons	2.8 persons	8.186	0.000
Business revenue	234 m NOK	214 m NOK	0.381	0.704
Business employees	136 persons	132 persons	0.094	0.925

Table 2.7 Financial Crime Categories by Detection Sources

Crime Category	Total Detected in Each Crime Category	Journalist Detection in Each Category	Journalist Detection Fraction
Fraud	160	52	33%
Theft	17	2	12%
Manipulation	127	28	22%
Corruption	65	13	20%
Total	369	97	26%

Criminals detected by journalists are associated with organizations of about the same size as criminals detected by others.

When we compare financial crime categories committed by white-collar criminals, in terms of detection, results indicate that journalists tend to detect fraud to a great extent, but less of the other categories, as shown in Table 2.7.

Since a substantial fraction of white-collar criminals are detected by journalists, and very few are detected by traditional law enforcement agencies, there might be lessons to be learned from media working procedures. Journalists review information and information sources in established and developing networks of individuals located in key areas of the economy. Journalists study accounting reports and other information, and receive documents from their network of sources. They interview lawyers, competitors, the police, and authorities. They set a case aside for weeks and months until new information emerges. In the meantime, they keep the information top secret, until publication for the first time.

Investigative journalists tend to develop hypotheses about phenomena and causality. They are very different from reporting journalists who only relate what they have heard or seen. Investigative journalists develop an idea via a study of potential offenders and their victims. They apply systematic analysis and treat their sources with care and professional concern.

In most criminal areas, it is expected that a combination of victim and police are the main sources of criminal detection. After crime victims suffer an injury or a loss, they tend to report the incident to the police, who investigate and hopefully find the offender(s). In cases of financial crime by white-collar criminals, it is often quite different. A victim is frequently not aware of the injury or loss. For example, accounting fraud resulting in tax evasion is not a harm or damage perceived by tax authorities.

A number of angles can be explored in the process of white-collar crime detection within news media. On the one hand, we have the news media (newspapers and online media) that have specialized and focused on financial information of all sorts, and report on this regularly. For them, the sources of information can be traditional through tips, company reports, stock exchange information, and press conferences, as well as other sources. For regular news media spread out over the country, the situation can be quite different. The detection of white-collar crime can come as a tip-off from a whistle-blower or as official information if the police or an economic crime prosecutor performs a search locally. Whistle-blowers in many cases alert journalists to serious crime and are sometimes the true detectors, not the journalists or media (Bjørkelo and Matthiesen, 2011; Johnson, 2005; Rothwell and Baldwin, 2006, 2007; Stansberry and Victor, 2009; Vadera et al., 2009; Varelius, 2009).

Additionally, the way the news is treated in the news media is dependent on many variables that occur at the same time: Do they have the right journalists in place at the time? Do they have an interest in the matter? Do they know anything or anyone related to this? There will also be a resource balance that takes place. The resource perspective in leading media houses is concerned with knowledge management (Joshi et al., 2010; Ko and Dennis, 2011; Lacy et al., 2009; Laise et al., 2005).

Not many news media outside of the larger ones will have the possibility of setting aside journalists to work on an investigative white-collar crime for months. In the cases where they have done this, some experience among editors seems to be that there is an uncertainty as to whether this was worthwhile relative to the size and complexity of the case. For a common, nonspecialist news media, there will always be the balance of resources against the newsworthiness of the matter at hand. If a major white-collar crime story had emerged in Norway in the weeks after the July 22 terrorist attacks in 2011, reasonable doubt can be raised if the matter would have caught much attention in the general public press.

General news media have a constant incoming flow of news on hand, and there is a constant daily priority of what is important and what should be published. For all news items there are some general rules of journalism that come into play: Is it important for many people? Is it really news? Is it possible to get reliable information on this? Is it possible to approach the right people with the right questions? Can both parties in a conflict be approached? And in addition to these questions, there will be a question as to whether the news organization at this point in time has the resources to deal with it. If the journalist knowledgeable of economic matters is on holiday, doubt can be raised if the news media organization will come back to the same matter later. That will depend on the development and the newsworthiness of the case at the second point in time. If the news organization is the first to report on the crime and it is regarded as "hot," it will probably do whatever possible to handle the matter at hand, knowing that other media, and especially online media, can report on the same matter and as such "steal" the story. There is always an internal pride in a news organization when it can report on a matter of significant interest, and be cited by other news organizations.

The organizational culture also has an influence on white-collar crime detection among journalists (Hofstede et al., 1990; Schein, 1990; Veiga et al.,

2000). If you have journalists that are driven by their own interest to win investigative journalist prizes (SKUP in Norway), there is a higher possibility for such stories to emerge in publication. But that will differ greatly among the news organizations. Øvrebø (2004) showed in a study of the Norwegian newspaper *Dagsavisen*, after a change of editor in chief in 2001, that the news profile and priorities of the newspaper changed according to the principles laid down by the new editor when she took up her position. It can be argued that personal preferences of an editor can have influence on the priorities of news in the newspaper, and that this will relate to all types of editorial material, whether it is general news, sports, culture, or financial news.

For a general news organization, white-collar crime is not a big story in itself unless it has repercussions on well-known persons locally or if something happens to the organization where the crime has taken place. Nationally it can be a big story if the person is a well-known profile, or if the crime in itself is of an unusual nature. If a main employer locally has to file for bankruptcy because of a white-collar crime, then the story is more than just another white-collar crime case since it has wider consequences that turn the world upside down for ordinary people in this local area. Then the white-collar crime will take the form of another typical important news story and be followed and treated as such, and the white-collar crime element will be mixed with other elements and consequential stories, building on the starting point as a white-collar crime. Campbell (1997) studied the journalistic process of environmental news in Scotland, and addressed the information sources that are used in the news process. The study showed the preference for human sources as opposed to library-based information and discussed the influence of pragmatic constraints like time and space on the production of news. It can be argued that this process is likewise in the news gathering process for white-collar crime.

The argument of white-collar crime detection among journalists seems to be related to the story's importance in itself, and as such, it will be treated as just another crime or news story and have the same internal process. For smaller news organizations without journalistic specialization in financial matters, the white-collar crime story will be treated according to the news prioritizing structure of that particular organization. For larger news organizations that typically have separate sections for financial and economic news, the story will be treated within the prioritizing of that particular section. And if the story is big enough in total, it will be moved from the particular section for finance into the general news of the organization. The higher the profile of persons involved, the more likely it is that it will have a more centralized coverage, i.e., be moved into what is often the first section of the newspaper or the prioritized areas of a website's front page.

As shown in Table 2.8, 4 of the 10 categories made up 62% of the total crime detecting sources, and out of these the first 2—journalists investigating

Table 2.8 Characteristics of Stimulus in Detection of White-Collar Crime

Rank	Crime Detection Source	Signal Intensity	Signal Alertness	Pattern Recognition	Personal Experience	Total Score
1	Journalists	High	High	Low	Medium	9
2	Crime victims	High	Low	High	Low	8
3	Internal control	Low	Medium	High	Medium	8
4	Bankruptcy lawyers	Low	Low	High	Medium	7
5	Tax authorities	Low	Low	Low	Low	4
6	Commercial bank	Low	High	Low	Low	6
7	Accounting auditors	Low	Medium	Medium	Low	6
8	Police investigations	Low	Medium	High	High	9
9	Stock exchange	Low	Low	Medium	Low	5
10	Other sources					

tips from readers and crime victims suffering loss—made up 39%. It can be argued that these two categories are more susceptible to journalistic interest than the others, simply because it is easier to construct news stories based on these journalistic angles. Themes like manipulation and corruption are much more difficult to make into a story that is interesting for the readers simply because it is more complex and difficult to describe these matters in layman terms. A tip from readers that is given to a news medium is most of the time accompanied by a subjective story from the person giving the tip that in turn gives the journalist clues to work on and discuss internally to assign the right news priority and angle. This is also supported by the breakdown in Table 2.7 showing that fraud is the category having the highest percentage of journalistic detection.

White-collar crime detection and follow-up seems to be related to a number of simultaneous journalistic procedures and cultural elements. For specialized publications in the financial information area, the white-collar crime news arena is closer at hand and the organization will typically be able to go deeper into the matter. If white-collar crime is detected by general or local news organizations, the procedure involved will more often take the form of a general news story with the resource balance that follows from that. It can also be shown that white-collar crime is more often detected by journalists if it is based on a tip from readers or if it is reported as fraud. Underlying all this are the internal news preferences and editorial guidance that are part of the policies of the news medium.

Finally, the most obvious reason for the high detection fraction by journalists is the fact that one of the criteria for our sample is newspaper coverage of the case. Naturally, this will lead to a bias toward journalist detection.

Auditing Role in Crime Detection

The role of auditing in the detection of white-collar crime is an interesting topic, as it is not obvious that auditors are able to detect crime. This might have to do with the responsibilities of auditing functions, as well as procedures and practices followed by auditors in their work (Warhuus, 2011). For example, Beasley (2003) is concerned with the fact that auditors seem to struggle with reducing occurrences of material misstatements due to fraud, even in the light of new standards for auditing. The focus of new standards remains on fraudulent activities that lead to intentional material misstatements due to fraud, and it expands the guidance and procedures to be performed in every audit. The expanded guidance might hopefully lead to improvements of auditor detection of material misstatements due to fraud, by strengthening the auditor's responses to identified high fraud risks.

One of the surprising results of this research is the lack of crime detection by auditors: only 18 (5%) of the 369 criminals in our sample were detected by auditors. Moyes and Baker (2003) asked external, internal, and governmental auditors to evaluate the effectiveness of various standard audit procedures in detecting fraud. Although external and internal auditors differed in the types of audit procedures they recommended, the authors conclude that "the audit procedures judged more effective in detecting fraud were those which provided evidence about the existence of internal controls and those which evaluated the strength of internal controls," and that "strategic use of standard audit procedures may help auditors fulfill their responsibilities under SAS No. 99" (Moyes and Baker, 2003: 199). Furthermore, "the results of this study indicate that fraud detection might be improved through the strategic use of standard audit procedures earlier in the audit examination.... If these audit procedures were applied during the preliminary stages of the audit, they would be more likely to indicate the potential existence of fraud, in which case the auditor would have more time to revise the audit plan and conduct other necessary investigations" (Moyes and Baker, 2003: 216).

Similarly, Albrecht et al. (2001) reviewed fraud detection aspects of current auditing standards and the empirical and other research that has been conducted on fraud detection. They concluded that "even though the red flag approach to detecting fraud has been endorsed by policy makers and written about widely by researchers, there is little empirical evidence that shows the red flag approach is an effective way to detect fraud, especially for fraud that has yet to be discovered" (Albrecht et al., 2001: 4). Their research review on the subject reveals that one of the major conclusions drawn from previous studies included the fact that only 18–20% of frauds appear to be detected by internal and external auditors, and further that only about half of the perpetrators of frauds detected are duly prosecuted. The article also calls for further fraud detection research. These detection rates are loosely corroborated by Silverstone and Sheetz (2003), who estimate that approximately 12% of initial fraud detection is through external audit, and approximately 19% arises from internal audit. (Both of these estimations apply to the American context.)

An article dealing with the responsibilities for prevention and detection of white-collar crime refers to a study undertaken to map how members of the accounting profession viewed the changing role of the external auditor following the introduction of SAS No. 82 (Farrell and Healy, 2000: 25):

> Most of those answering the questionnaire disagreed that they should be responsible for searching for fraud.... Clearly, this notion concerning the auditor's responsibility is not widely held by the public at large.... The general public and Congress certainly sided against the CPAs and was the reason for this legislation.

As to the question of whether the certified public accountants (CPAs) should act as police or detectives when performing the audit, the response was a resounding no (Farrell and Healy, 2000: 25):

> This may also indicate that changes brought about with the implementation of the SAS No. 82 requiring a *policing component* clearly require added responsibility and may necessitate additional training and changes to job description requirements. Again, although the general public may believe policing is within the auditors' duties, even SAS No. 82 does not require this.

Similarly, an investigation into fraud prevention and detection in the United States uncovered that the majority of CPAs that responded to the study believed the external auditor's responsibility for fraud detection extends only to assessing the probability of fraud and planning the audit accordingly. They ranked internal auditors as the group most effective in detecting fraud, followed by fraud examiners and client management (Johnson and Rudesill, 2001).

Jones (2000: 12–13) presents a slightly more balanced view on auditor role in crime detection:

> A persistent debate has dogged relationships between auditors and managers. This debate revolves around the precise roles and duties of each party in relation to fraud and corruption, and particularly who should take responsibility for investigation. Current legal and professional precedents leave little doubt that management bears the main responsibility for ensuring that reasonable measures are taken to prevent fraud and corruption. In any event it is common practice for managers to request assistance and advice from auditors upon suspicion or discovery of fraud. The final responsibility must lie with managers unless the auditor has given specific assurance regarding particular controls or the absence of error or fraud.

In a study in Norway by Warhuus (2011) she found that 11% of her cases of white-collar crime were detected by auditing functions; this is higher than the 4% (according to our sample) reported above, and also significantly higher than the results presented by Albrecht et al. (2001), Moyes and Baker (2003), and Silverstone and Sheetz (2003). The figures of 4 and 11% in Norway indicate that Norwegian auditing has an even less pronounced role in detection of white-collar crime than the measurements performed in the United States, for example.

Iver and Samociuk (2006) argue that fraud risks need to be recorded, monitored, and reported. Such recording includes the nature of each risk, likelihood and consequences, current and suggested controls, and the owner of the risk for follow-up action.

Within the extant accounting and auditing research, a great deal of attention is devoted to how the external auditor is a primary figure in detecting irregularities and corruption, and government and standard setters also stress the importance of the responsibilities of the auditing community in this respect (Olsen, 2007; Telberg, 2004). However, there seems to be limited faith and responsibility in the auditing function among some for this specific purpose: Only in very few cases does auditing in some form seem to be responsible for the detection, unraveling, and exposure of the offense (Ellingsen and Sky, 2005). This opinion is backed up by the work of Drage and Olstad (2008), who analyzed the role of the auditing function in relation to both preventing and detecting white-collar crime. Although their study included a look at the perceived preventative power of the auditing function as well as actual detection of criminal offenses, their findings were consistent with the above-mentioned hypothesis: many of their interviewees were skeptical regarding the auditing function having a central role in the detection of white-collar crime.

Olsen (2007) reminds us that the auditing standards that external auditors must act in compliance with also require them to uncover irregularities should they be present. However, the primary concern of the external auditor is to reduce the auditing risk (i.e., the risk that the financial statements may still contain material misstatements even after the auditor has given a positive auditor report), not the risk of irregularities. In spite of external auditors rarely being credited for the detection of financial crime, Olsen (2007) still believes that the auditing function contributes significantly to the prevention of such crime by reducing temptations and opportunities, thus corroborating the findings of Drage and Olstad (2008) on prevention.

Rendal and Westerby (2010) examined Norwegian auditors' expectations regarding their own abilities in detecting and preventing irregularities and compared these with the expectations other users of financial information have on this same issue. Their findings indicate certain gaps in terms of how the auditor is expected to perform. Auditors themselves answer that they sometimes do not act in accordance with laws and regulations, and both auditors and users of financial information feel that the auditing function should include more than what is required today through standards and regulations, for example, pertaining to companies' internal guidelines. They also uncover unrealistic expectations regarding the extent to which the auditing function is capable of uncovering irregularities. They conclude that, to a certain extent, auditors are too reserved and aloof when it comes to their responsibilities in the prevention and detection of irregularities, and call for improvements.

Crime Signal Detection Theory

Signal detection theory may shed some light into why some actors discover and disclose more white-collar crime than others. Signal detection theory holds that the detection of a stimulus depends on both the intensity of the stimulus and the physical and psychological state of the individual. A detector's ability or likelihood to detect some stimulus is affected by the intensity of the stimulus (e.g., how loud a whistle-blowing is) and the detector's physical and psychological state (e.g., how alert the person is). Perceptual sensitivity depends upon the perceptual ability of the observer to detect a signal or target or to discriminate signal from nonsignal events (Szalma and Hancock, 2013).

Furthermore, detecting persons may have varying ability to discern between information-bearing recognition (called pattern) and random patterns that distract from information (called noise).

Under signal detection theory, some researchers found that people more frequently and incorrectly identify negative task-related words as having been presented originally as positive words, even when they were not present. Liu et al. (2010) found that people have lax decision criteria for negative words. In a different study, Huff and Bodner (2013) applied the signal detection approach to determine if changes in correct and false recognition following item-specific versus relational encoding were driven by a decrease in the encoding of memory information or by an increase in monitoring the test.

According to the theory, there are a number of determinants of how a person will detect a signal. In addition to signal intensity, signal alertness, and pattern recognition, there are other factors, such as personal competence (including knowledge, skills, and attitude), experience, and expectations. These factors determine the threshold level. Low signal intensity, low signal alertness, and limited pattern recognition, combined with low competence, lack of experience, and lack of expectations, will lead to a high threshold level, meaning that the individual will not detect white-collar crime.

Signal detection theory implies that persons make decisions under conditions of uncertainty. The theory assumes that the decision maker is not a passive receiver of information, but an active decision maker who makes difficult perceptual judgments under conditions of uncertainty. Whether a stimulus is present or absent, whether a stimulus is perceived or not perceived, whether a perceived stimulus is ignored or not ignored, will influence the decision in terms of detecting or not detecting white-collar crime.

Signal detection theory characterizes the activity of an individual's discrimination as well as psychological factors that bias his or her judgment. The theory is concerned with the individual's discriminative capacity, or sensitivity that is independent of the judgmental bias or decision criterion the individual may have had when the discrimination was made.

In Table 2.8, an attempt is made to describe signal detection features of observers who have noticed and discover white-collar crime. Signal intensity, signal alertness, pattern recognition and personal experience are derived from signal detection theory as characteristics of detection ability.

We argue that signal intensity for tips to journalists normally is high, as whistle-blowers tend to be upset and want to get attention. Furthermore, we suggest that signal alertness is high among journalists, as they are dependent on tips in their daily work to cover news stories. The issue of pattern recognition is not obvious for journalists, since they often present fragments on a publishing basis, rather than a complete and consistent story of events. Personal experience will vary among journalists who may or may not have been writing about white-collar crime before, depending on the extent of specialization among journalists in the newspaper.

The idea of Table 2.8 is to apply four characteristics of signal detection theory to detection of white-collar crime. At this stage, the items and values represent exploratory research that needs further study to be trustworthy. Both selection of characteristics and judgment along these characteristics for each crime detection source need multiple raters to enable interrater reliability to be computed.

However, it is an interesting personal experiment. For example, the police in Norway are a passive receiver of signals. Norwegian police are not undercover in financial markets and have no informants in business corporations. Therefore, police opportunity to receive signals is very limited.

Based on a sample of 369 convicted white-collar criminals in Norway from 2009 to 2014, where 97 offenders were detected by journalists and 272 were detected by others, we found some interesting differences between the two groups. In statistical terms, significant differences can be found in terms of the sum of money involved in crime and personal finances as registered by the internal revenue service.

There seems to be a lot to learn from investigative media and their journalists. Rather than formal procedures often applied on a routine basis by auditors and internal controllers, information sources in terms of persons in networks seem to be a more fruitful approach to detection of white-collar crime.

References

Aguilera, R.V., and Vadera, A.K. (2008). The dark side of authority: Antecedents, mechanisms, and outcomes of organizational corruption. *Journal of Business Ethics*, 77, 431–449.

Albrecht, C.C., Albrecht, W.S., and Dunn, J.G. (2001). Can auditors detect fraud: A review of the research evidence. *Journal of Forensic Accounting*, II, 1–12.

Ashforth, B.E., Gioia, D.A., Robinson, S.L., and Trevino, L.K. (2008). Re-reviewing organizational corruption. *Academy of Management Review*, 33(3), 670–684.

Baird, J.E., and Zelin, R.C. (2009). An examination of the impact of obedience pressure on perceptions of fraudulent acts and the likelihood of committing occupational fraud. *Journal of Forensic Studies in Accounting and Business*, 1(1), 1–14.

Beasley, M.S. (2003). SAS No. 99: A new look at auditor detection of fraud. *Journal of Forensic Accounting*, IV, 1–20.

Benson, M.L., and Simpson, S.S. (2009). *White-Collar Crime: An Opportunity Perspective*, Criminology and Justice Series. Routledge, New York.

Bjørkelo, B., and Matthiesen, S.B. (2011). Preventing and dealing with retaliation against whistleblowers. In Lewis, D., and Vandekerckhove, W. (eds.), *Whistleblowing and Democratic Values*. International Whistleblowing Research Network.

Blickle, G., Schlegel, A., Fassbender, P., and Klein, U. (2006). Some personality correlates of business white-collar crime. *Applied Psychology: An International Review*, 55(2), 220–233. Presented at the 2nd International Whistleblowing Research Conference (2011 at Middlesex, London). http://papers.ssrn.com/sol3/papers.cfmabstract_id=1998293

Bookman, Z. (2008). Convergences and omissions in reporting corporate and white collar crime. *DePaul Business and Commercial Law Journal*, 6, 347–392.

Bucy, P.H., Formby, E.P., Raspanti, M.S., and Rooney, K.E. (2008). Why do they do it? The motives, mores, and character of white collar criminals. *St. John's Law Review*, 82, 401–571.

Campbell, F. (1997). Journalistic construction of news: Information gathering. *New Library World*, 98(2), 60–64.

Chrisman, J.J., Chua, J.H., Kellermanns, F.W., and Chang, E.P.C. (2007). Are family managers agents or stewards? An exploratory study in privately held family firms. *Journal of Business Research*, 60(10), 1030–1038.

Drage, K., and Olstad, T. (2008). *Ekstern revisor og økonomisk kriminalitet—En analyse av revisors ansvar og brukernes forventninger* (External Auditor and Financial Crime—An Analysis of Auditor Responsibility and User Expectations). BI Norwegian School of Management, Oslo.

Ellingsen, D., and Sky, V. (2005). *Virksomheter som ofre for økonomisk kriminalitet* (Companies as Victims of Economic Crime), Vol. 2005/14, *Rapporter*. SSB (Census Bureau of Norway), Oslo.

Farrell, B.R., and Healy, P. (2000). White collar crime: A profile of the perpetrator and an evaluation of the responsibilities for its prevention and detection. *Journal of Forensic Accounting*, I, 17–34.

Fleet, D.D. van, and Fleet, E.W. van. (2006). Internal terrorists: The terrorists inside organizations. *Journal of Managerial Psychology*, 21(8), 763–774.

Garoupa, N. (2007). Optimal law enforcement and criminal organization. *Journal of Economic Behavior and Organization*, 63, 461–474.

Hansen, L.L. (2009). Corporate financial crime: Social diagnosis and treatment. *Journal of Financial Crime*, 16(1), 28–40.

Heath, J. (2008). Business ethics and moral motivation: A criminological perspective. *Journal of Business Ethics*, 83, 595–614.

Higgins, E.T. (1997). Beyond pleasure and pain. *American Psychologist*, 52, 1280–1300.

Hofstede, G., Neuijen, B., Ohayv, D.D., and Sanders, G. (1990). Measuring organizational cultures: A qualitative and quantitative study across twenty cases. *Administrative Science Quarterly*, 35(2), 286–316.

Huff, M.J., and Bodner, G.E. (2013). When does memory monitoring succeed versus fail? Comparing item-specific and relational encoding in the DRM paradigm. *Journal of Experimental Psychology: Learning, Memory, and Cognition*, 39(4), 1246–1256.

Iver, N., and Samociuk, M. (2006). *Fraud and Corruption: Prevention and Detection*. Gower Publishing, Farnham, Surrey, UK.

Johnson, G.G., and Rudesill, C.L. (2001). An investigation into fraud prevention and detection of small businesses in the United States: Responsibilities of auditors, managers, and business owners. *Accounting Forum*, 25(1), 56.

Johnson, R.A. (2005). Whistleblowing and the police. *Rutgers University Journal of Law and Urban Policy*, 1(3), 74–83.

Jones, E. (2000). Remaking the firm: How KM is changing legal practice. *Knowledge Management Magazine*. http://www.kmmag.com/

Joshi, K.D., Chi, L., Datta, A., and Han, S. (2010). Changing the competitive landscape: Continuous innovation through IT-enabled knowledge capabilities. *Information Systems Research*, 21(3), 472–495.

Ko, D.G., and Dennis, A.R. (2011). Profiting from knowledge management: The impact of time and experience. *Information Systems Research*, 22(1), 134–152.

Lacy, P., Arnott, J., and Lowitt, E. (2009). The challenge of integrating sustainability into talent and organization strategies: Investing in the knowledge, skills and attitudes to achieve high performance. *Corporate Governance*, 9(4), 484–494.

Laise, D., Migliarese, P., and Verteremo, S. (2005). Knowledge organization design: A diagnostic tool. *Human Systems Management*, 24, 121–131.

Liu, D., Ray, G., and Whinston, A.B. (2010). The interaction between knowledge codification and knowledge-sharing networks. *Information Systems Research*, 21(4), 892–906.

Moyes, G.D., and Baker, C.R. (2003). Auditor's beliefs about the fraud detection effectiveness of standard audit procedures. *Journal of Forensic Accounting*, IV, 199–216.

O'Connor, T.R. (2005). Police deviance and ethics. In part of web cited MegaLinks in Criminal Justice. http://faculty.ncwc.edu/toconnor/205/205lect11.htm (retrieved February 19, 2009).

Olsen, A.B. (2007). *Økonomisk kriminalitet: Avdekking, gransking og forebygging* (Financial Crime: Detection, Investigation and Prevention). Universitetsforlaget, Oslo.

Øvrebø, T. (2004). Nyhetsproduksjon—Kjønn og makt. En studie av endring i Dagsavisen 2000–2003 (News production—Sex and power. A study of change in Dagsavisen [Norwegian daily newspaper] 2000–2003). Hovedoppgave i Medievitenskap (Master thesis in media science), Universitetet i Oslo (University of Oslo).

Padilla, A. (2013). *Leadership: Leaders, Followers, and Environments.* Wiley, Hoboken, NJ.

Padilla, A., Hogan, R., and Kaiser, R.B. (2007). The toxic triangle: Destructive leaders, susceptible followers, and conducive environments. *Leadership Quarterly,* 18, 176–194.

Perri, F.S., and Brody, R.G. (2011). The Sallie Rohrbach story: Lessons for auditors and fraud examiners. *Journal of Financial Crime,* 18(1), 93–104.

Punch, M. (2003). Rotten orchards: "Pestilence," police misconduct and system failure. *Policing and Society,* 13(2), 171–196.

Rendal, S., and Westerby, T. (2010). *Hvilke forventninger har revisor i forhold til brukere av finansiell informasjon når det gjelder revisors plikter til forebygging og avdekking av misligheter?* (What Expectations Does the Auditor Have in Relation to Users of Financial Information Concerning Auditor Responsibility for Prevention and Detection of Misconduct?) S. Rendal, Oslo.

Robson, R.A. (2010). Crime and punishment: Rehabilitating retribution as a justification for organizational criminal liability. *American Business Law Journal,* 47(1), 109–144.

Rothwell, G.R., and Baldwin, J.N. (2006). Ethical climates and contextual predictors of whistle-blowing. *Review of Public Personnel Administration,* 26(3), 216–244.

Rothwell, G.R., and Baldwin, J.N. (2007). Whistle-blowing and the code of silence in police agencies. *Crime and Delinquency,* 53(4), 605–632.

Schein, E.H. (1990). Organizational culture. *American Psychologist,* 45(2), 109–119.

Silverstone, H., and Sheetz, M. (2003). *Forensic accounting and fraud investigation for non-experts.* Wiley, Hoboken, NJ.

Stansbury, J.M., and Victor, B. (2009). Whistle-blowing among young employees: A life-course perspective. *Journal of Business Ethics,* 85, 281–299.

Szalma, J.L., and Hancock, P.A. (2013). A signal improvement to signal detection analysis: Fuzzy SDT on the ROCs. *Journal of Experimental Psychology: Human Perception and Performance,* 39(6), 1741–1762.

Telberg, R. (2004). A joint effort to fight corporate fraud. *Journal of Accountancy,* 197(4), 53–56.

Vadera, A.K., Aguilera, R.V., and Caza, B.B. (2009). Making sense of whistle-blowing's antecedents: Learning from research on identity and ethics programs. *Business Ethics Quarterly,* 19(4), 553–586.

Varelius, J. (2009). Is whistle-blowing compatible with employee loyalty? *Journal of Business Ethics,* 85, 263–275.

Veiga, J., Lubatkin, M., Calori, R., and Very, P. (2000). Measuring organizational culture clashes: A two-nation post-hoc analysis of a cultural compatibility index. *Human Relations,* 53(4), 539–557.

Warhuus, C. (2011). Present Principle: The Role of Auditing in Detection of White-Collar Crime. Master of Science thesis, BI Norwegian Business School, Oslo, Norway.

General Theory of Crime

3

In Gottfredson and Hirschi's (1990) classic book on the general theory of crime, there is a significant chapter on theories about white-collar crime. They talk about pressure crime and something others refer to as general strain theory. They also discuss occupational theories, meaning the fact that they have jobs allows them to commit a crime, as opposed to those who steal because they are without work. It becomes an issue of socioeconomics.

The general theory of crime is often referred to as the self-control theory of crime. It is a criminological theory about the lack of individual self-control as the main factor behind criminal behavior (Gottfredson and Hirschi, 1990). Although individuals with low self-control are not expected to commit crime at every opportunity, research has shown that low self-control is almost always a significant correlate of criminal and analogous behaviors (Piquero et al., 2010).

General strain theory is about pressure to commit crime, as defined by Agnew (2012). Langton and Piquero (2007) examined how general strain theory can explain white-collar crime. Using data from convicted white-collar offenders, they found that the theory can be useful for predicting a select group of white-collar offenses, but might not be generalizable to individuals committing corporate-type crime.

According to Gottfredson and Hirschi (1990), low self-control develops early in a child's life, generally by age 8, as a result of poor parental socialization, and so remains relatively stable throughout an individual's life. Although low self-control is conceived as a single-dimensional trait, it actually comprises six components: impulsivity, risk taking, preference for physical activity, quick temperedness, preference for simple tasks, and concern with the here and now (shortsightedness). These six components come together to form the underlying trait of low self-control.

A number of theories on white-collar crime are presented in the following chapters. Theories help us understand and predict, explain and analyze phenomena such as crime.

Theorizing White-Collar Crime

In recent years, most published research work on white-collar crime seems to be struggling to define what is and what is not included in the concept. This chapter represents an initiative to debate and clarify the concept, so that future research might have an easier avenue to follow when studying a sample. White-collar criminals commit all kinds of financial crime, but their situation has particular characteristics. In this book, white-collar crime is defined by economical, organizational, and behavioral dimensions. These three dimensions combined suggest an avenue toward a general theory of white-collar crime. To illustrate the organizational dimension, a sample of convicted white-collar criminals at different organizational levels in Norway is analyzed in terms of their age, prison sentence, crime amount, and personal income.

There is a continuing debate on what to include and what to exclude when the concept of white-collar crime is introduced and applied (Alalehto and Larsson, 2009; Benson and Simpson, 2009; Blickle et al., 2006; Bookman, 2008; Brightman, 2009; Bucy et al., 2008; Comey, 2009; Dhami, 2007; Dodge, 2009; Füss and Hecker, 2008; Goldstraw-White, 2012; Heath, 2008; Holtfreter et al., 2008, 2010; Kempa, 2010; Langton and Piquero, 2007; Listwan et al., 2010; Maddan et al., 2012; McGurrin et al., 2013; McKay et al., 2010; Onna et al., 2014; Ouimet, 2009, 2010; Piquero, 2012; Piquero et al., 2008; Podgor, 2007; Price and Norris, 2009; Ragatz et al., 2012; Robb, 2006; Schoepfer and Piquero, 2006; Schoepfer et al., 2007; Simpson et al., 2012; Stadler and Benson, 2012; Stadler et al., 2013; Steffensmeier et al., 2013; Weissmann and Block, 2010).

However, it seems that all agree that white-collar crime has to do with financial crime, where economic profit is the purpose. The profit perspective rather than the harm perspective so often found in other kinds of crime makes financial crime a distinct class of offense. It seems that most agree that white-collar offense is crime against property for personal or organizational gain, which is committed by nonphysical means and by concealment or deception. It is deceitful, it is intentional, it breaches trust, and it involves losses.

The debate struggles with what a white-collar criminal is and is not. The offender and the situation—rather than the offense—make the term *white-collar crime* challenging. Over the years since Sutherland (1940, 1949) introduced the term, it seems that scholars want to include more and more into the concept, thereby eventually making it less and less useful.

Certainly, there is a need to update the term, but not by including everything and everyone. For example, information technology in general and the Internet in particular were not known to Sutherland. It has been argued that the Internet opens up for new kinds of white-collar criminals. But it is important to recognize that information technology is just like any other tool known to fraudsters in the past. You could fake your identity on paper, and you can fake your identity on the Internet. Both can be checked and monitored. Although personal computers and the Internet allow individuals from all social classes to buy and sell stocks or engage in similar activities that were once the bastion of the financial elite (Brightman, 2009), this is not a sufficient argument to include virtually any nonviolent act committed for financial gain, regardless of one's social status, into the term *white-collar* crime.

Theorizing white-collar crime is occurring both at the individual micro-level and at the organizational and society macro-level, a typical micro-level question is why individuals break the law. A host of theoretical perspectives attempt to identify the factors that differentiate criminals from noncriminals. The focus on individuals rests on practical considerations. Individuals can be easily surveyed or interviewed or registered in other ways. Macro-level analysis examines how characteristics of organizations, cities, or nations are related to rates of crime. Macro-level theories seek to explain why certain characteristics, but not others, account for the distribution of crime. Empirical research attempts to establish which of these characteristics are predictors of (that is, explain statistical variation in) crime rates (Pratt and Cullen, 2005).

Over the years, three major characteristics have been attributed to white-collar crime:

1. *Economics*: Nonviolent acts are committed for financial gain (Brightman, 2009). It is for the benefit of the enterprise or the individual(s). It is a rational choice where advantages and disadvantages are judged by the offender, and expected utility of the action clearly outweighs the expected disadvantages resulting from the action (Blickle et al., 2006; Bucy et al., 2008). It has to do with transactions where ownership to assets changes illegally. While some economic transactions are one-sided, such as fraud, other transactions are two-sided, such as corruption. Supply and demand for illegal services and goods are a matter of economics, where the market price is determined by elasticity.
2. *Organization*: Offenders take advantage of positions of professional authority and power as well as opportunity structures (Kempa, 2010). Benson and Simpson (2009) argue that many white-collar offenses manifest the following three properties: (a) the offender has legitimate access to the location in which the crime is committed, (b) the offender is spatially separated from the victim, and (c) the offender's actions have a superficial appearance of legitimacy.
3. *Behavior*: Criminal behavior by members of the privileged socioeconomic class (Podgor, 2007) who are using their power and influence (Alalehto and Larsson, 2009). Offenders are charismatic, have a need to control, have a tendency to bully subordinates, fear losing their status and position, exhibit narcissistic tendencies (Arnulf and Gottschalk, 2013; Ouimet, 2009, 2010), lack integrity and social conscience (Price and Norris, 2009), have no guilt feelings (Stadler and Benson, 2012), and do not perceive themselves as criminals (Dhami, 2007).

This chapter sets out to suggest a general theory of white-collar crime consisting of these three perspectives: economic dimension, organizational dimension, and behavioral dimension. These dimensions do all find support in a number of specific theories that explain small pieces of the puzzle. The cause of white-collar crime in this book is here traced to economical, organizational, and behavioral situations. This is the sequence, where it often starts with economic motivation and opportunity (Huisman and Erp, 2013), linked to an organizational platform and availability, and in a setting of people where the individual with behavioral traits commits crime.

To illustrate the organizational dimension of white-collar crime theory, which makes the general theory most distinct, this chapter presents an empirical study of convicted white-collar criminals. Offenders are classified into three different organizational levels: top executives and business professionals, middle managers and business advisors, and functional managers and personal investors. The purpose is to illustrate the increasing magnitude of white-collar crime incidents at higher organizational levels.

Definitions of Theory

Just like the concept of white-collar crime is continuously debated, so is the concept of theory. Two decades ago, there was an important debate about what theory is and is not, where the main contributors were DiMaggio (1995), Sutton and Staw (1995), and Weick (1995).

Sutton and Staw (1995: 378) define theory in the following way:

> Theory is about the connections among phenomena, a story about why acts, events, structure, and thoughts occur. Theory emphasizes the nature of causal relationships, identifying what comes first as well as the timing of such events. Strong theory, in our view, probes underlying processes so as to understand the systematic reasons for a particular occurrence or nonoccurrence. It often burrows deeply into microprocesses, laterally into neighboring concepts, or in an upward direction, tying itself to broader social phenomena. It usually is laced with a set of convincing and logically interconnected arguments. It can have implications that we have not seen with our naked (or theoretically unassisted) eye. It may have implications that run counter to our common sense.

Theory acts as an educational device that creates insights into criminal phenomena (Colquitt and Zapata-Phelan, 2007):

> A theory might be a prediction or explanation, a set of interrelated constructs, definitions, and propositions that present a systematic view of phenomena by specifying relations among variables, with the purpose of explaining natural phenomena. The systematic view might be an argument, a discussion, or

a rationale, and it helps to explain or predict phenomena that occur in the world. Some define theory in terms of relationships between independent and dependent variables, where theory is a collection of assertions, both verbal and symbolic, that identifies what variables are important and for what reasons, and that specifies how they are interrelated and why. It identifies the conditions under which variables should be related or not related. Other scholars have defined theory in terms of narratives and accounts.

Corley and Gioia (2011: 12) provide a shorter definition of theory:

Theory is a statement of concepts and their interrelationships that shows how and/or why a phenomenon occurs.

Various disciplines such as criminology, sociology, psychology, strategy, marketing, and management have developed a number of theories with the aim of explaining how and why individuals involve themselves in crime, and how they get involved in crime. Some of the theories are individualistic and look at risk factors in personality traits and family conditions (Listwan et al., 2010). Other theories emphasize ideology and culture, which represent the environment in terms of economy, society, and structures.

The sociological theory of white-collar crime, for example, postulates that managers who commit economic offenses live in a social setting, i.e., culture, in which a very high value is placed on material success and individual wealth. Both economic theory and sociological theory are of the opinion that strong striving for wealth and enjoyment in some way contributes to economic crime committed by managers (Blickle et al., 2006).

It is difficult to overstate the importance of theory to preventive understanding of white-collar crime. Theory allows analysts to understand and predict outcomes on a basis of probability (Colquitt and Zapata-Phelan, 2007). Theory also allows analysts to describe and explain a process or sequence of events. Theory prevents analysts from being bewildered by the complexity of the real world by providing a linguistic tool for organizing a coherent understanding of the real world.

Theory acts as an educational tool, which can be used to develop insights into criminal phenomena such as financial crime in general and white-collar crime in particular. A theory is an undocumented explanation of a phenomenon or relationship. The opposite of theory is not practice. The opposite of theory is empirical findings. Both theory and empirical study are concerned with practice. While theory presents thoughts about practice, empirical study presents facts about practice.

In this book, theories of white-collar crime are classified into categories of economic theory, organizational theory, and behavioral theory. There are, of course, alternative classifications that can be thought of. A classification scheme should satisfy the following criteria: (1) cover all kinds of theories, (2) be at the same level, and (3) have as little overlap as possible. It can be argued that the current classification into three categories satisfies these requirements. In addition, the classification satisfies requirements from theory building, as the dimensions are interrelated concepts that show how and why white-collar crime occurs. Simply stated, the economic dimension enables financial crime, taking place in the organizational dimension, and by people acting in the behavioral dimension. This will be illustrated by the white-collar crime triangle.

Economical Dimension of Crime

White-collar crime is profit-driven crime based on economic opportunities and threats. As argued by Naylor (2003), transfers of property occur by free-market exchange or fraud, and those transfers involve redistribution of wealth and distribution of income. Fraud is generally defined as the procurement of a private asset or means of advantage through deception or through the neglect of care for the interests of an asset required by duty. In particular, fraud includes heterogeneous forms such as misappropriation, balance manipulation, insolvency, and capital investment abuse (Füss and Hecker, 2008). Opportunity is a flexible characteristic of financial crime and varies depending on the type of criminals involved (Michel, 2008). An opportunity is attractive as a means of responding to desires (Bucy et al., 2008).

Threats can come from loss-making business and special market structure and forces. Economic power available to certain corporations in concentrated industries, but not to others, may generate criminal conduct. The threat of losing what has already been made by bankruptcy can cause executives to rescue and save the company by illegal means. An entrepreneur who has spent all his time building the enterprise might be unable to let it disappear. The intention is to protect economic interests of the corporation (Blickle et al., 2006). Threats can come from a monopoly, where potential competitors have the choice either to commit crime or to join the monopoly (Chang et al., 2005). A financial gain is needed for survival in all markets (Brightman, 2009).

Transaction costs reduce the profitability of white-collar crime. Transaction costs include costs of conflict and misunderstandings that lead to delays, breakdowns, and other malfunctions. They can include such things as the costs of incentives and of ensuring coordination. The costs of each transaction are part of the risks involved in criminal operations. Betrayal of the group by informers leading to disruption of operations, seizure of profit, and possible arrest of group members is the predominant transaction cost in crime cases (Wright, 2006).

The economic model of rational self-interest considers incentives and probability of detection (Welsh et al., 2014). Rational choice argues that it is indeed rational to be a criminal provided that two conditions are satisfied: the potential profit is great and the punishment is small. Persons who do not commit crime decide that completing the act successfully is too risky or not worth the benefits. The rational choice model finds support in an empirical study by Bucy et al. (2008), who identified a number of motives for white-collar crime. According to their study, greed is the most common reason for white-collar criminal acts. Money and other forms of financial gain were found to be a frequent motivator. Criminals pursue desired goals, weigh up likely consequences, and make selections from various options. When criminal opportunity is attractive as a means of responding to desires, rational actors will choose it. Goldstraw-White (2012) defines greed as socially constructed needs and desires that can never be completely satisfied. Because participating in crime is a rational choice, crime rates will be lower where levels of punishment are more certain or more severe (Pratt and Cullen, 2005).

Aguilera and Vadera (2008: 434) describe a criminal opportunity as "the presence of a favorable combination of circumstances that renders a possible course of action relevant." Opportunity arises when individuals or groups can engage in illegal and unethical behavior and expect, with reasonable confidence, to avoid detection and punishment. Opportunity to commit crime may include macro- and micro-level factors. Macro-level factors encompass the characteristics of the industries in which the business is embedded, such as market structure; business sets of an industry, that is, companies whose actions are visible to each other; and variations in the regulatory environment (Aguilera and Vadera, 2008).

Organizational Dimension of Crime

Agency theory has long been applied to crime, where normally the agent, rather than the principal, is in danger of committing crime. Problems arise in the relationship because of diverging preferences and conflicting values, asymmetry in knowledge about activities, and different attitudes toward risk. Agency theory describes the relationship between the two parties using the concept of work-based interactions. The agent carries out work on behalf of the principal in an organizational arrangement. Principal-agent theory holds that owners (principals) have different interests from administrators (agents), such that principals must always suspect agents of making decisions that benefit themselves, to the cost of the principals. For example, CEOs may always be suspected of cheating the owners, and purchasing managers may always be suspected of cheating CEOs (Chrisman et al., 2007).

In general, agency models view corruption and other kinds of financial crime as a consequence of the principal's inability to effectively prevent the agent from abusing its power for his or her personal gain (Li and Ouyang, 2007). However, crime can just as well be committed by the principal rather than the agent. For example, the CFO as an agent provides a board member with inside information, on which the principal acts illegally.

An organization is a system of coordinated actions among individuals and groups with boundaries and goals (Puranam et al., 2014). An organization can be a hierarchy, a matrix, a network, or another kind of relationship between people in a professional work environment. Dysfunctional network theory suggests that corporate crime emerges as a consequence of the dysfunction of value networks. A value network is the context within which a firm identifies and responds to customers' needs, solves problems, procures input, reacts to competitors, and strives for profit. Within this context, the firm may opt for deviant behavior, in line with its competitors in the industry.

Dion (2009) argues that organizational culture makes it possible to adopt organizational purposes or objectives, which are basically deviant in comparison with social norms yet in line with the competition. Deviant purposes can be chosen when business corporations are trapped by doubtful, immoral, or disloyal means that are used by competitors. They could also be trapped by the business milieu as a social institution. Furthermore, they could be trapped by their own sector-based morality, which is oriented toward profit maximization.

Yet another interesting theory to illustrate the organizational dimension is institutional theory of moral collapse. Shadnam and Lawrence (2011: 379) applied institutional theory to explain moral decline and potential crime in organizations:

> Our theory of moral collapse has two main elements. First, we argue that morality in organizations is embedded in nested systems of individuals, organizations and moral communities in which ideology and regulation flow "down" from moral communities through organizations to individuals, and moral ideas and influence flow "upward" from individuals through organizations to moral communities. Second, we argue that moral collapse is associated with breakdowns in these flows, and explore conditions under which such breakdowns are likely to occur.

Dodge (2009: 15) argued that it is tough rivalry that makes people in an organization commit crime:

> The competitive environment generates pressures on the organization to violate the law in order to attain goals.

Behavioral Dimension of Crime

Most theories of white-collar crime can be found along the behavioral dimension. Numerous suggestions have been presented to explain individuals such as Madoff and Schilling. In fact, many otherwise serious researchers have given famous white-collar criminals all kinds of psychiatric and psychological diagnoses of abnormal personality traits. Although none of the researchers have ever met these criminals, they present all kinds of behavioral and motivational assumptions. There is indeed a need to be cautious to avoid losing credibility in the research community.

Along the behavioral dimension we find strain theory (Langton and Piquero, 2007), deterrence theory (Comey, 2009; Holtfreter et al., 2008), self-control theory (Holtfreter et al., 2010; Piquero et al., 2010), obedience theory (Baird and Zelin, 2009), fear of falling (Piquero, 2012), negative life events (Engdahl, 2014); slippery slope (Welsh et al., 2014), and the American dream (Schoepfer and Piquero, 2006)—just to name a few.

Much attention in recent years has been paid to neutralization theory, where white-collar criminals think they have done nothing wrong. They deny responsibility, injury, and victim. They condemn the condemners. Offenders claim appeal to higher loyalties and normality of action. They claim entitlement, and they argue the case of legal mistake. They find their own mistakes acceptable. They argue a dilemma arose, whereby they made a reasonable trade-off before committing the act (Siponen and Vance, 2010).

Much attention has also been paid to strain theory, ever since Gottfredson and Hirschi (1990) in their classic book on the general theory of crime wrote about pressure crime. Agnew (2012) identified three categories of strain: failure to achieve positively valued goals, the removal of positively valued stimuli, and the presentation of negative stimuli. Strain theory posits that each type of strain ultimately leads to deviance for slightly different reasons. All three types tend to increase the likelihood that an individual will experience negative emotions in proportion to the magnitude, duration, and closeness of the stress. Strain is defined as an event or condition that is disliked by individuals. The theory argues that structural strain weakens the ability of normative standards to regulate behavior (Pratt and Cullen, 2005).

Research by Ragatz et al. (2012) is an example of work that explores psychological traits among white-collar offenders. Their research results suggest that white-collar offenders have lower scores on lifestyle criminality, but higher scores on some measures of psychopathology and psychopathic traits than non-white-collar-offenders. Similarly, McKay et al. (2010) examined the psychopathology of the white-collar criminal acting as a corporate leader. They looked at the impact of a leader's behavior on other employees and the organizational culture developed during his or her reign. Narcissistic behavior is suggested often to be observed among white-collar offenders (Arnulf and Gottschalk, 2013; Ouimet, 2009, 2010).

Some theorists believe that crime can be reduced through the use of deterrents. Crime prevention (the goal of deterrence) is based on the assumption that criminals or potential criminals will think carefully before committing a crime if the likelihood of getting caught and the fear of swift and severe punishment are present. According to Comey (2009), deterrence works best when punishment is swift and certain.

Self-control theory can be used in two different directions. First, the theory proposes that individuals commit crime because of low self-control. The theory contends that individuals who lack self-control are more likely to engage in problematic behavior—such as criminal behavior—over their life course because of its time-stable nature (Gottfredson and Hirschi, 1990). Second, the desire to control and the general wish to be in control of everything and everybody might be a characteristic of some white-collar criminals, meaning that low self-control can lead to heavy control of others. Desire for control is the general wish to be in control over everyday life events. Desire for control is similar to low self-control in terms of behavioral manifestations and influence on the decision-making power (Piquero et al., 2010).

Slippery slope means that a person slides over time from legal to illegal activities. Arjoon (2008: 78) explains slippery slope in the following way:

> As common sense experience tells us, it is the small infractions that can lead to the larger ones. An organization that overlooks the small infractions of its employees creates a culture of acceptance that may lead to its own demise. This phenomenon is captured by the metaphor of the slippery slope. Many unethical acts occur without the conscience awareness of the person who engaged in the misconduct. Specifically, unethical behavior is most likely to follow the path of a slippery slope, defined as a gradual decline in which no one event makes one aware that he or she is acting unethically. The majority of unethical behaviors are unintentional and ordinary, thus affecting everyone and providing support for unethical behavior when people unconsciously lower the bar over time through small changes in their ethical behavior.

Welsh et al. (2014) argue that many recent scandals can be described as resulting from a slippery slope in which a series of small infractions gradually increase over time. Committing small indiscretions over time may gradually lead people to complete larger unethical acts that they otherwise would have judged to be impermissible.

Benson and Simpson (2009: 145) found that white-collar criminals seldom think of injury or victims:

> Many white-collar offenses fail to match this common-sense stereotype because the offenders do not set out intentionally to harm any specific individual. Rather,

the consequences of their illegal acts fall upon impersonal organizations or a diffuse and unseen mass of people.

Organizational Level of Criminals

In general terms, this proposed theory suggests that white-collar crime has to do with money, structure, and deviance. Especially the structure in terms of an organizational setting distinguishes white-collar criminals from other kinds of financial criminals. As so well argued by Benson and Simpson (2009), it is the opportunity of crime in a legal environment that makes white-collar criminals so special. It is the position in the organizational setting that enables criminal behavior.

To illustrate this point, a sample of 369 white-collar criminals will be introduced. The sample consists of individuals who were convicted to jail sentences from 2009 to 2014 in Norway. Individuals at level 1 were most influential and include board members, chief executives, and professional investors. Level 2 individuals were medium influential, including lawyers, brokers, accounting executives, and purchasing managers. Level 3 individuals were least influential, and this group included accountants and other administrative staff as well as small business owners. Offenders at level 1 are closest to the classical picture of ideal white-collar criminals, who had a heroic status and belonged to the elite (Heath, 2008), having received official recognition for contributions and fame prior to their being exposed and convicted as white-collar criminals (Arnulf and Gottschalk, 2013).

Table 3.1 lists 104 heroic individuals at level 1, 176 powerful individuals at level 2, and 89 influential individuals at level 3. An issue here is whether level 3 should be excluded, because they are the ones that least satisfy general criteria for selection of white-collar criminals according to the organizational

Table 3.1 Characteristics of White-Collar Criminals at Three Organizational Levels

White-Collar Criminals Convicted to Jail Sentence in Norway, 2009–2014	Number of Persons in the Sample	Average Age When Convicted	Number of Years in Prison	Sum of Money in Crime	Personal Income Reported
Level 1 Heroic individuals	104	52	2.7	74	611,000
Level 2 Powerful individuals	176	48	2.1	41	346,000
Level 3 Influential individuals	89	44	2.1	31	195,000
Total/average	369	48	2.3	48	382,000

dimension. Before making such a decision, it is interesting to note differences between groups. The average age of high-level white-collar criminals when convicted is 52 years, they receive a jail sentence of 2.7 years, the money amount involved in the crime is 74 million Norwegian kroner (approximately US$12 million), and the personal income registered at the state revenue service is 611,000 Norwegian kroner (about US$100,000).

Table 3.1 illustrates a decline in offender age, prison sentence, crime money, and personal income from top-level criminals via middle-level criminals to low-level criminals. Opposite, the most powerful top-level white-collar criminals are older, commit crime for more money, receive a longer jail sentence, and have a higher personal income. This is in line with research by Heath (2008), who found that the bigger and more severe occupational crime tends to be committed by individuals who are further up the chain of command in the firm.

Statistically, there is in Norway a strong and significant relationship between crime amount and prison sentence, as illustrated in Table 3.1. Some readers may find imprisonment variation modest, and some may find the prison sentences modest. However, average numbers are not comparable to sentences in the United States of individuals such as Madoff and Schilling, who have to set a world record in life age expectancy to be able to serve in prison according to their sentences. The most severe sentence in Norway so far is 9 years in prison for a white-collar criminal. Blickle et al. (2006) found in a sample of 76 convicted German white-collar criminals that the average sentence was 3.9 years. The average age of the Germans was 47 years, while the average age of 644 prosecuted white-collar criminals in the Netherlands was 42 years (Onna et al., 2014). As listed in Table 3.1, the average sentence in Norway was 2.3 years, and the average age of convicted Norwegians was 48 years, which is comparable to Germany and the Netherlands.

Table 3.2 lists results of statistical analysis of variance (ANOVA) to identify significant differences between groups. There is indeed a significant difference in age, where high-level white-collar criminals are significantly older than low-level criminals. Also, the registered income for high-level criminals is significant, as they make much more money than low-level criminals.

There are no significant differences in sum of money in crime, although level 3 criminals commit crime for a substantially higher money amount than level 2 criminals. Differences in prison sentence are not significant, although

Table 3.2 Significance of Differences between Criminals at Three Organizational Levels

White-Collar Criminals Convicted to Jail Sentence in Norway, 2009–2014	Average Age When Convicted	Number of Years in Prison	Sum of Money in Crime	Personal Income Reported
Statistical *F*-value	12.917	2.951	2.262	9.432
Statistical significance	0.000	0.054	0.106	0.000

level 1 criminals are convicted to substantially longer imprisonment. It is interesting to note that level 1 criminals receive a substantially longer jail sentence, and the reason can probably be found in the higher crime amount, as mentioned above. Top-level white-collar criminals commit crime for the highest amount and receive the longest prison sentences, but these differences are not significant, as listed in Table 3.2.

Benson and Simpson's (2009) three properties that many white-collar offenses manifest come together in the levels applied above, where top-level criminals have legitimate access to the main location, are totally in charge of transactions, and are successful in concealment based on key resources used to hide the crime.

This is crime of the most powerful based on conspiracy (Benson and Simpson, 2009: 86):

> The object of the conspiracy is to conceal and coordinate activities so as to illegally benefit the members of the conspiracy without ever revealing that anything illegal has taken place.

Top-level offenders are here labeled heroic white-collar criminals. Leaders as heroic and charismatic figures—sometimes also celebrities—have been central to leadership thinking for many decades. However, omnipotent, self-centered leaders are prone to destructive leadership behaviors and bad decision making (Arnulf and Gottschalk, 2013).

An interesting organization where white-collar crime occurs is the pyramid, where the Ponzi scheme is a special kind (Nolasco et al., 2013). While a pyramid generally depends on multiple actors, a Ponzi scheme can be perpetrated by one individual acting alone. As long as the pyramid grows at the bottom, there will always be money for those at the top. The offender's actions have a superficial appearance of legitimacy as an investment fund or other kind of organizational arrangement (Wells, 2010). In the database of 369 convicts in Norway, there were 5 criminals in three cases convicted of Ponzi fraud.

The issue of whether or not to exclude level 3 criminals is relevant for our theory, as the theory suggests that all dimensions of economics, organization, and behavior should be visible to justify classification of an offense into the group of white-collar crime. Since our theory suggests a consistent and somewhat restrictive classification, the decision would be to exclude level 3 criminals from further study.

Challenging a General Theory

Most classic research work on white-collar crime from the previous century has been ignored in this chapter. Research is an art of accumulation, where previous research is supposed to be absorbed in recent research. The only two exceptions are, of course, Sutherland (1940, 1949), who coined the term *white-collar crime*, and Gottfredson and Hirschi (1990), with their general theory of crime. The term *white-collar crime* has survived for almost a century and has been subject to much research, making an updated general theory of white-collar crime a necessity and requirement to strengthen future research. Too much struggle has occurred in numerous recent articles to apply the concept of white-collar crime. Reviewers may argue that the sample is not of white-collar crime, while authors say it is.

Of course, three suggestions here—economical, organizational, and behavioral dimensions of such a theory—will not survive for long. The contribution of this chapter lies more in an initiative, rather than a conclusion. It is an initiative to take a step back to reflect on the concept, rather than determine in specific terms and cases what is or is not white-collar crime.

The purpose is to present a systematic view of the phenomenon of white-collar crime. It can be illustrated as the white-collar crime triangle in Figure 3.1. White-collar crime is (1) based on an opportunity for illegal profit, (2) carried out in the arena of an organization, (3) where the decision of criminal acts is causing deviant behavior.

The systematic view is an argument to explain phenomena of white-collar crime. If the profit is both available and desirable, if the arena is both accessible and secret, and if deviant behavior is both acceptable and defendable, then white-collar crime is likely to occur. The theory represents both the conditions under which crime occurs and the sequence of factors. A decision of deviant behavior is based on availability and desirability of profit that is secretly accessible in a legally perceived organizational setting.

The more well-known fraud triangle of opportunity, pressure, and rationalization (Baird and Zelin, 2009) is implicit in the white-collar crime triangle. Opportunity can be found in desirable profit in the accessible arena, while pressure and rationalization lead to the decision to commit crime. Pressure

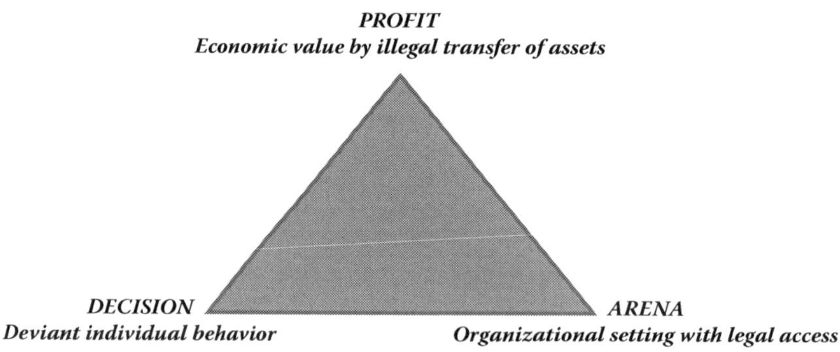

Figure 3.1 The white-collar crime triangle.

and rationalization are criteria in decision making. Pressures can also be found in the organization as well as in its competitive environment (Dodge, 2009).

Despite McGurrin et al.'s (2013) finding that few educational criminology programs include white-collar crime, research on white-collar crime is currently growing. There is research on how white-collar criminals are sentenced differently and possibly milder (Maddan et al., 2012; Schoepfer et al., 2007; Stadler et al., 2013), gender gap (Robb, 2006; Simpson et al., 2012; Steffensmeier et al., 2013), occupational versus corporate crime (Bookman, 2008; Heath, 2008; Perri and Brody, 2011), criminal leaders versus criminal followers (Bucy et al., 2008; McKay et al., 2010), criminal profiles (Onna et al., 2014), white-collar defense in court (Weissmann and Block, 2010), and many other interesting perspectives. Such specific perspectives will of course challenge a general theory of white-collar crime.

The white-collar crime triangle covers both offense-based and offender-based perspectives. The offense is economic in nature, and it occurs in an organizational setting. The offender makes a decision to commit the crime. It is based on a criminal opportunity with the following five characteristics (Huisman and Erp, 2013): the effort required to carry out the offense, the perceived risks of detection, the rewards to be gained from the offense, the situational conditions that may encourage criminal action, and the excuse and neutralizations of the offense.

Pratt and Cullen (2005) distinguished between micro-level and macro-level perspectives on crime. Issues of strain, self-control, and other behavioral indicators belong to the individual explanations of crime at the micro-level. Issues of organizational setting, inequality, and availability of illegal profits belong to the people explanations of crime at the macro-level. Thus, our proposed theory covers both micro- and macro-level predictors of crime.

White-collar crime involves some form of social deviance and represents a breakdown in social order (Heath, 2008). Many scholars emphasize the nonphysical and nonviolent act committed for financial gain as a key characteristic of white-collar crime (Bookman, 2008; Brightman, 2009). While it is included as a characteristic in the proposed general theory here, it is relevant to notice that Perri (2013) documents that even white-collar criminals may resort to violence, including murder, to cover up their crime.

Hansen (2009) suggests that a distinction can be made between economic crime, business crime, and elite crime. Freewheeling predators that are not attached to organizations commit some white-collar crimes, but individuals employed by, and in, legitimate organizations probably commit the bulk of such crimes. Individuals or groups commit occupational or elite crime for their own purposes or enrichment, rather than for the enrichment of the organization on a whole, in spite of supposed corporate loyalty. The origins of elite crime can be explored and then summarized by examining several criminology theories that offer explanations regarding why this type of crime is so prevalent among seemingly respectable individuals.

Maybe future research on a general theory of white-collar crime should focus on theorizing rather than theory. As argued by Weick and cited in Michailova et al. (2014), theory cannot be improved until we improve the theorizing process, and we cannot improve the theorizing process until we describe it more explicitly. Theorizing involves a mixture of observing something, penetrating something, and finding something out, where there is not necessarily a linear process at all. The activities that make up theorizing—observing, choosing something interesting, formulating the central concept, building the theory, and completing the tentative theory—can happen in a very different order or in no order at all. Observing white-collar criminals is not easy; it will always be in retrospect a story told by newspapers, police, prosecutors, defendants, defense lawyers, witnesses, victims, and court documents. Penetrating the crime is difficult, but penetrating the criminal as an inmate in prison might be easier. Some white-collar inmates may be reluctant to be interviewed, while others would like their story to be told. For those of us who have had the opportunity to interview white-collar inmates, we observe interesting individuals who have the ability to present themselves and their actions in fascinating ways.

Compared to research on members of Hells Angels in organized crime and research on pedophiles who have groomed children on the Internet, research on white-collar criminals is in so many respects different. A white-collar criminal is simply one of us. Maybe that is why Sutherland's (1940, 1949) analysis of white-collar criminality serves as the catalyst for an area of research that continues and grows today. What Podgor (2007) found to be the most interesting aspect of Sutherland's work is that a scholar needed to proclaim that crime of the upper socioeconomic class was in fact crime that should be prosecuted. It is apparent that prior to the coining of the term *white-collar crime*, wealth and power allowed some persons to escape criminal liability.

Michailova et al. (2014) argue that theorizing is inherently personal. It is even argued that there is no theory that is not a fragment carefully prepared of some autobiography, and that all scholarship is self-revelatory. Michailova et al. (2014) suggest that since it is impossible to make sense of a situation without a personal identity, it is important for theorists to decide and declare who they are. Without going too far in this direction, I, as the author of this chapter, am certainly willing to testify that I have never committed white-collar crime, that I have observed white-collar crime as a business executive, that I have interviewed and done statistical research on a large sample of convicted white-collar criminals as a professor, and that I have done empirical research on other convicted criminals as well. My background has led me to the belief that people with wealth and power who commit crime against other people's property should be punished just as severely as drug barons and murderers. This is not the case in Norway today, where drug barons and murderers are sentenced to 10 years on average, while white-collar criminals are sentenced to only 2 years on average. Let me add that pedophiles that destroy lives of young children also only get 2 years. Maybe white-collar criminals and offending pedophiles should receive 10 years on average, while drug barons should only be sentenced to 2 years in prison, as long as we don't want the prison population to grow as a whole. This is not in support of deterrence theory, but about relative seriousness of criminal actions as perceived by society. It is just a thought to tell who I am.

In recent years, most published research work on white-collar crime seems to have struggled to define what is and what is not included in the concept. This chapter represents an initiative to debate and clarify the concept, so that future research will have an easier avenue to follow when developing a sample. Specifically, to identify financial crime as white-collar offense, there has to be an economical dimension, an organizational dimension, and a behavioral dimension.

It is the organizational dimension that probably will create most debate, as a computer hacker sitting in his home alone to commit bank fraud is not considered a white-collar criminal. Neither is a fake bank on the Internet white-collar crime, as criminal activities are not hidden in legal activities. Some will find the organizational requirement too restrictive.

For example, Bookman (2008) avoids the organizational dimension by defining white-collar crime as an illegal act committed by nonphysical means and by concealment, to obtain money or property, to avoid payment or loss of money or property, or to obtain business or personal advantage. The organizational dimension requires that white-collar crime is committed in a setting of legal and organized work, where people relate to each other in a professional environment. However, to stress at the end of this chapter, it is important to emphasize that the term *organization* itself can be many things, as long as it can be portrayed as (1) a multiagent system with (2) identifiable boundaries and (3) system-level goals (purpose) toward which (4) the constituent agent's efforts are expected to make a contribution (Puranam et al., 2014).

References

Agnew, R. (2012). Reflection on "A revised strain theory of delinquency." *Social Forces*, 91(1), 33–38.

Aguilera, R.V., and Vadera, A.K. (2008). The dark side of authority: Antecedents, mechanisms, and outcomes of organizational corruption. *Journal of Business Ethics*, 77, 431–449.

Alalehto, T., and Larsson, D. (2009). The roots of modern white-collar crime: Does the modern form of white-collar crime have its foundation in the transition from a society dominated by agriculture to one dominated by industry? *Critical Criminology*, 17, 183–193.

Arjoon, S. (2008). Slippery when wet: The real risk in business. *Journal of Markets and Morality*, 11(1), 77–91.

Arnulf, J.K., and Gottschalk, P. (2013). Heroic leaders as white-collar criminals: An empirical study. *Journal of Investigative Psychology and Offender Profiling*, 10, 96–113.

Baird, J.E., and Zelin, R.C. (2009). An examination of the impact of obedience pressure on perceptions of fraudulent acts and the likelihood of committing occupational fraud. *Journal of Forensic Studies in Accounting and Business*, 1(1), 1–14.

Benson, M.L., and Simpson, S.S. (2009). *White-Collar Crime: An Opportunity Perspective, Criminology and Justice Series*. Routledge, New York.

Blickle, G., Schlegel, A., Fassbender, P., and Klein, U. (2006). Some personality correlates of business white-collar crime. *Applied Psychology: An International Review*, 55(2), 220–233.

Bookman, Z. (2008). Convergences and omissions in reporting corporate and white collar crime. *DePaul Business and Commercial Law Journal*, 6, 347–392.

Brightman, H.J. (2009). *Today's White-Collar Crime: Legal, Investigative, and Theoretical Perspectives*. Routledge, Taylor & Francis Group, New York.

Bucy, P.H., Formby, E.P., Raspanti, M.S., and Rooney, K.E. (2008). Why do they do it? The motives, mores, and character of white collar criminals. *St. John's Law Review*, 82, 401–571.

Chang, J.J., Lu, H.C., and Chen, M. (2005). Organized crime or individual crime? Endogeneous size of a criminal organization and the optimal law enforcement. *Economic Inquiry*, 43(3), 661–675.

Chrisman, J.J., Chua, J.H., Kellermanns, F.W., and Chang, E.P.C. (2007). Are family managers agents or stewards? An exploratory study in privately held family firms. *Journal of Business Research*, 60(10), 1030–1038.

Colquitt, J.A., and Zapata-Phelan, C.P. (2007). Trends in theory building and theory testing: A five-decade study of the *Academy of Management Journal*. *Academy of Management Journal*, 50(6), 1281–1303.

Comey, J.B. (2009). Go directly to jail: White collar sentencing after the Sarbanes-Oxley Act. *Harvard Law Review*, 122, 1728–1749.

Corley, K.G., and Gioia, D.A. (2011). Building theory about theory building: What constitutes a theoretical contribution? *Academy of Management Review*, 36(1), 12–32.

Dhami, M.K. (2007). White-collar prisoners' perceptions of audience reaction. *Deviant Behavior*, 28, 57–77.

DiMaggio, P.J. (1995). Comments on 'what theory is not.' *Administrative Science Quarterly*, 40, 391–397.

Dion, M. (2009). Corporate crime and the dysfunction of value networks. *Journal of Financial Crime*, 16(4), 436–445.

Dodge, M. (2009). *Women and White-Collar Crime*. Prentice Hall, Upper Saddle River, NJ.

Engdahl, O. (2014). White-collar crime and first-time adult-onset offending: Explorations in the concept of negative life events as turning points. *International Journal of Law, Crime and Justice*. DOI: 10.1016/j.ijlcj.2014.06.001.

Füss, R., and Hecker, A. (2008). Profiling white-collar crime: Evidence from German-speaking countries. *Corporate Ownership and Control*, 5(4), 149–161.

Goldstraw-White, J. (2012). *White-Collar Crime: Accounts of Offending Behaviour*. Palgrave Macmillan, London.

Gottfredson, M.R., and Hirschi, T. (1990). *A general theory of crime*. Stanford University Press, Stanford, CA.

Hansen, L.L. (2009). Corporate financial crime: Social diagnosis and treatment. *Journal of Financial Crime*, 16(1), 28–40.

Heath, J. (2008). Business ethics and moral motivation: A criminological perspective. *Journal of Business Ethics*, 83, 595–614.

Holtfreter, K., Slyke, S.V., Bratton, J., and Gertz, M. (2008). Public perceptions of white-collar crime and punishment. *Journal of Criminal Justice*, 36, 50–60.

Holtfreter, K., Beaver, K.M., Relsig, M.D., and Pratt, T.C. (2010). Low self-control and fraud offending, *Journal of Financial Crime*, 17(3), 295–307.

Huisman, W., and Erp, J. (2013). Opportunities for environmental crime. *British Journal of Criminology*, 53, 1178–1200.

Kempa, M. (2010). Combating white-collar crime in Canada: Serving victim needs and market integrity. *Journal of Financial Crime*, 17(2), 251–264.

Langton, L., and Piquero, N.L. (2007). Can general strain theory explain white-collar crime? A preliminary investigation of the relationship between strain and select white-collar offenses. *Journal of Criminal Justice*, 35, 1–15.

Li, S., and Ouyang, M. (2007). A dynamic model to explain the bribery behavior of firms. *International Journal of Management*, 24(3), 605–618.

Listwan, S.J., Piquero, N.L., and Voorhis, P.V. (2010). Recidivism among a white-collar sample: Does personality matter? *Australian and New Zealand Journal of Criminology*, 43(1), 156–174.

Maddan, S., Hartley, R.D., Walker, J.T., and Miller, J.M. (2012). Sympathy for the devil: An exploration of federal judicial discretion in the processing of white collar offenders. *American Journal of Criminal Justice*, 37, 4–18.

McGurrin, D., Jarrell, M., Jahn, A., and Cochrane, B. (2013). White collar crime representation in the criminological literature revisited, 2001–2010. *Western Criminology Review*, 14(2), 3–19.

McKay, R., Stevens, C., and Fratzl, J. (2010). A 12-step process of white-collar crime. *International Journal of Business Governance and Ethics*, 5(1), 14–25.

Michailova, S., Piekkari, R., Plakoyiannaki, E., Ritvala, T., Mihailova, I., and Salmi, A. (2014). Breaking the silence about exiting fieldwork: A relational approach and its implications for theorizing. *Academy of Management Review*, 39(2), 138–161.

Michel, P. (2008). Financial crimes: The constant challenge of seeking effective prevention solutions. *Journal of Financial Crime*, 15(4), 383–397.

Naylor, R.T. (2003). Towards a general theory of profit-driven crimes. *British Journal of Criminology*, 43, 81–101.

Nolasco, C.A.R.I., Vaughn, M.S., and Carmen, R.V. (2013). Revisiting the choice model of Ponzi and pyramid schemes: Analysis of case law. *Crime, Law and Social Change*, 60, 375–400.

Onna, J.H.R., Geest, V.R., Huisman, W., and Denkers, J.M. (2014). Criminal trajectories of white-collar offenders. *Journal of Research in Crime and Delinquency.*
Ouimet, G. (2009). Psychology of white-collar criminal: In search of personality. *Psychologie du Travail et des Organisations*, 15(3), 297–320.
Ouimet, G. (2010). Dynamics of narcissistic leadership in organizations. *Journal of Managerial Psychology*, 25(7), 713–726.
Perri, F.S. (2013). Visionaries or false prophets. *Journal of Contemporary Criminal Justice*, 29(3), 331–350.
Perri, F.S., and Brody, R.G. (2011). The Sallie Rohrbach story: Lessons for auditors and fraud examiners. *Journal of Financial Crime*, 18(1), 93–104.
Piquero, N.L. (2012). The only thing we have to fear is fear itself: Investigating the relationship between fear of falling and white collar crime. *Crime and Delinquency*, 58(3), 362–379.
Piquero, N.L., Carmichael, S., and Piquero, A.R. (2008). Assessing the perceived seriousness of white collar and street crimes. *Crime and Delinquency*, 54(2), 291–312.
Piquero, N.L., Schoepfer, A., and Langton, L. (2010). Completely out of control or the desire to be in complete control? How low self-control and the desire for control relate to corporate offending. *Crime and Delinquency*, 56(4), 627–647.
Podgor, E.S. (2007). The challenge of white collar sentencing. *Journal of Criminal Law and Criminology*, Spring, 1–10.
Pratt, T.C., and Cullen, F.T. (2005). Assessing macro-level predictors and theories of crime: A meta-analysis. *Crime and Justice*, 32, 373–450.
Price, M., and Norris, D.M. (2009). White-collar crime: Corporate and securities and commodities fraud. *Journal of the American Academy of Psychiatry and the Law*, 37(4), 538–544.
Puranam, P., Alexy, O., and Reitzig, M. (2014). What's "new" about new forms of organizing? *Academy of Management Review*, 39(2), 162–180.
Ragatz, L.L., Fremouw, W., and Baker, E. (2012). The psychological profile of white-collar offenders: Demographics, criminal thinking, psychopathic traits, and psychopathology. *Criminal Justice and Behavior*, 39(7), 978–997.
Robb, G. (2006). Women and white-collar crime. *British Journal of Criminology*, 46, 1058–1072.
Schoepfer, A., Carmichael, S., and Piquero, N.L. (2007). Do perceptions of punishment vary between white-collar and street crimes? *Journal of Criminal Justice*, 35, 151–163.
Schoepfer, A., and Piquero, N.L. (2006). Exploring white-collar crime and the American dream: A partial test of institutional anomie theory. *Journal of Criminal Justice*, 34, 227–235.
Shadnam, M., and Lawrence, T.B. (2011). Understanding widespread misconduct in organizations: An institutional theory of moral collapse. *Business Ethics Quarterly*, 21(3), 379–407.
Simpson, S.S., Alper, M., and Benson, M.L. (2012). Gender and White-Collar Crime in the 21st Century. Presented at the American Society of Criminology, Chicago.
Siponen, M., and Vance, A. (2010). Neutralization: New insights into the problem of employee information security policy violations. *MIS Quarterly*, 34(3), 487–502.

Stadler, W.A., and Benson, M.L. (2012). Revisiting the guilty mind: The neutralization of white-collar crime. *Criminal Justice Review*, 37(4), 494–511.
Stadler, W.A., Benson, M.L., and Cullen, F.T. (2013). Revisiting the special sensitivity hypothesis: The prison experience of white-collar inmates. *Justice Quarterly*, 30(6), 1090–1114.
Steffensmeier, D., Schwartz, J., and Roche, M. (2013). Gender and twenty-first-century corporate crime: Female involvement and the gender gap in Enron-era corporate frauds. *American Sociological Review*, 78(3), 448–476.
Sutherland, E.H. (1940). White-collar criminality. *American Sociological Review*, 5(1), 1–12.
Sutherland, E.H. (1949). *White Collar Crime*. Holt Rinehart and Winston, New York.
Sutton, R.I., and Staw, B.M. (1995). What theory is not. *Administrative Science Quarterly*, 40, 371–384.
Weick, K.E. (1995). What theory is not, theorizing is. *Administrative Science Quarterly*, 40, 385–390.
Weissmann, A., and Block, J.A. (2010). White-collar defendants and white-collar crimes. *Yale Law Journal*, 116, 286–291.
Wells, J.T. (2010). Ponzis and pyramids: What CPAs need to know. *CPA Journal*, 80(2), 6–10.
Welsh, D.T., Oronez, L.D., Snyder, D.G., and Christian, M.S. (2014). The slippery slope: How small ethical transgressions pave the way for Larger future transgressions. *Journal of Applied Psychology*. http://dx.doi.org/10.1037/a0036950.
Wright, A. (2006). *Organised Crime*. Willan Publishing, Devon, UK.

Private Investigations 4

Fraud investigations into individuals and organizations by private investigators have increased in intensity. No amount of legislation can protect against dishonesty (Coburn, 2006). When an organization wants to investigate facts, causes, and responsibilities for an incident, the investigation can be carried out by financial crime specialists and fraud examiners. Fraud examination has elements of intelligence, investigation, and analysis, like we know it from police work. Characteristics of inquiries where the term *fraud examination* is used include fact finding, causality study, change proposals, and suspect identification.

Fraud examination as intelligence emphasizes the systematic and goal-oriented collection of information that is transformed and analyzed according to a rigid procedure to detect suspects' capacity, dispositions, and intentions. The purpose is to improve both prevention and detection of crime. Risk-based techniques can be applied to survey environments and persons in order to collect information on their moves. Intelligence can also be defined as the result of information collection about possible offenses and potential suspects to make conclusions about threats, point out problems, and identify criminal activity with an intention to follow the case.

Fraud examination as investigation is the systematic and goal-oriented collection of information to confirm or disconfirm that an action is crime and that the actor is a criminal. Investigation is to prepare evidence for court proceedings. An investigation occurs only when something wrong has happened, while intelligence occurs when something wrong might happen.

Fraud examination as analysis is the process of breaking down a complex material or subject into smaller pieces to improve understanding and insight into the case. Analysis is to create meaning based on data by manipulating, interpreting, and reorganizing the structure of collected evidence. To analyze is to ask questions such as what, where, how, who, when, and why. What happened? How did it happen? Why did it happen? Elements of know-what, know-how, and know-why are created through analysis.

While fraud examination has elements of intelligence, investigation, and analysis as we know it from police work, it is something different. For intelligence, something might happen. For investigation, something has happened. For analysis, evidence is to be produced. In fraud examinations, something might happen or something has happened. Fraud examiners do not know when they start their work.

Wikipedia applies the following definition of *private investigator*:

> A private investigator (often abbreviated to PI and informally called a private eye), a private detective or inquiry agent, is a person who can be hired by individuals or groups to undertake investigatory law services. Private detectives/investigators often work for attorneys in civil cases. A handful of very skilled private detectives/investigators work with defense attorneys on capital punishment and criminal defense cases. Many work for insurance companies to investigate suspicious claims. Before the advent of no-fault divorce, many private investigators were hired to search out evidence of adultery or other conduct within marriage to establish grounds for a divorce. Despite the lack of legal necessity for such evidence in many jurisdictions, according to press reports collecting evidence of adultery or other "bad behavior" by spouses and partners is still one of the most profitable activities investigators undertake, as the stakes being fought over now are child custody, alimony, or marital property disputes.
>
> Private investigators can also be used to perform due diligence for an investor who may be considering investing money with an investment group, fund manager or other high-risk business or investment venture. This could serve to help the prospective investor avoid being the victim of a fraud or Ponzi scheme. By hiring a licensed and experienced investigator, they could unearth information that the investment is risky and or that the investor has suspicious red flags in his or her background. This is called investigative due diligence, and is becoming much more prevalent in the 21st century with the public reports of large-scale Ponzi schemes and fraudulent investment vehicles such as Madoff, Stanford, Petters, Rothstein and the hundreds of others reported by the SEC and other law-enforcement agencies.

Wells (2003) argues that becoming a fraud examiner—a kind of a financial detective—is not for everyone. Detectives—either in law enforcement or in the private sector—typically have distinct personality traits. They need to be as good with people as they are with numbers, and they need to be inclined to be aggressive rather than shy and retiring.

Financial Crime Specialists

The Association of Certified Financial Crime Specialists (ACFCS) was created to respond to a growing need for documented, verifiable, and certifiable knowledge and skill in the financial crime field and to meet the career development needs of the diverse and growing number of specialists in the private and public sectors who work in this field (CFCS, 2013).

ACFCS is a member organization that provides training, news, analysis, and networking to a worldwide membership of professionals in the financial crime field. ACFCS awards the Certified Financial Crime Specialist (CFCS) certification to persons who meet certain qualifications and pass a rigorous examination offered at 700 authorized testing centers worldwide. It is a credential that tests competence and skill across the financial crime spectrum, including money laundering, corruption, tax evasion, compliance, investigations, and other fields.

A private investigation is conducted by a variety of private sector financial crime specialists who can be investigators, forensic accountants, or lawyers, all of whom may be supported by investigative analysts, who the government usually calls intelligence analysts.

ACFCS stresses the importance of the following topics for financial crime specialists:

1. Challenge of financial crime
2. Financial crime overview, commonalities, and convergence
3. Money laundering
4. Understanding and preventing fraud
5. Global anticorruption compliance and enforcement
6. Tax evasion and enforcement
7. Asset recovery
8. Financial crime investigations
9. Interpreting financial documents
10. Money and commodities flow
11. Compliance programs and controls
12. Data security and privacy
13. Ethical responsibility and best practices
14. International agreements and standards

In the UK, it is expected that companies contribute to detection of law violations in terms of self-reports. For a self-report to be taken into account as a public interest factor tending against prosecution, it must form part of a genuinely proactive approach adopted by the corporate management team. Prosecutors will consider whether it has provided sufficient information, including making witnesses available and disclosing the details of any internal investigation, about the operation of the corporate body in its entirety. This is according to the UK serious fraud office (SFO) guidance on corporate prosecutions.

According to the UK serious fraud office guidance on corporate prosecutions:

1. Initial contact, and all subsequent communication, must be made through the SFO's Intelligence Unit. The Intelligence Unit is the only business area within the SFO authorized to handle self-reports.

2. Hard-copy reports setting out the nature and scope of any internal investigation must be provided to the SFO's Intelligence Unit as part of the self-reporting process.
3. All supporting evidence including, but not limited to, emails, banking evidence, and witness accounts must be provided to the SFO's Intelligence Unit as part of the self-reporting process.
4. Further supporting evidence may be provided during the course of any ongoing internal investigation.

ACFCS (www.acfcs.org) offers the CFCS certification exam from its headquarters in Miami, Florida. This is the CFCS examination outline:

- Understanding financial crime: Financial crime commonalities, money laundering controls and investigation, ethical responsibility and best practices.
- Investigating financial crime: Financial crime investigation, fraud detection and investigation, money and commodities flow.
- Enforcement actions and mechanisms: Tax evasion and enforcement, asset recovery.
- Compliance: Programs and controls, global anticorruption compliance and enforcement, international regulations and standards, data security and privacy.

The University of New Haven and the Association of Certified Financial Crime Specialists (ACFCS.org) announced in 2013 that the Department of Criminal Justice at the University of New Haven was the first to offer a course leading to ACFCS certification. Students enrolled in the course on investigating financial crimes were to learn the legal, ethical, and practical aptitudes necessary to become financial crime specialists. The course was to use the 340-page *CFCS Certification Examination Study Manual* and online the on-demand preparation course from ACFCS as its educational materials (www.newhaven.edu).

Certified Fraud Examiners

The Association of Certified Fraud Examiners (ACFE) was created for similar reasons as the ACFCS. Becoming a certified fraud examiner requires documented academic and professional qualifications. Formal education in the fraud examination field is new and limited (Wells, 2003). The ACFE website (www.acfe.com) addresses the needs of ACFE members and also provides free resources to the general public (Anders, 2006). Certified fraud examiners have ample career opportunities, since the CFE certification was created in response to the demand for expertise in fraud prevention and detection (Morgan and Nix, 2003).

Perhaps Debbie Cutler was born to be a fraud examiner (Wells, 2003: 77):

> "When I was young, my family referred to me as Perry Mason," she said. "I was a very inquisitive child who wouldn't give up until I got the answers." It was happenstance that led her to combine her natural talents with her accounting degree. "I'd spent 10 years in public accounting performing traditional audit work," Cutler said. "One day a partner invited me to help investigate an accounting malpractice case that included fraud allegations against a U.S. senator. I jumped at the chance, and as it turned out, I loved the work."

Like in other countries, investigators in the United States have a variety of backgrounds. It is not only lawyers, accountants, and business consultants who are investigators. Sociologists and criminologists may also undertake tasks relating to the investigation. Examples are mentioned by Kennedy (2013), who writes about forensic sociology and criminology. Investigation by sociologists and criminologists might be concerned about people who have neglected responsibility, people who have abused their positions, or organizations where training and guidelines have been missing.

Thus, fraud examiners encompass a wide array of professions, including auditors, accountants, fraud investigators, loss prevention specialists, attorneys, educators, sociologists, and criminologists. While fraud examiners in the United States can work independently, many are also members of the ACFE. Fraud examiners provide a broad range of services to businesses and governmental agencies as either employees or independent consultants (ACFE, 2008). A fraud examiner may assist in a fraud investigation by procuring evidence, taking statements, and writing reports (Machen and Richards, 2004).

When hiring a fraud examiner, a company should seek an evaluation that is both disinterested and reliable (Machen and Richards, 2004: 68):

> These objectives, however, can occasionally conflict. Where employees within the organization conduct the fraud investigation, the results of such an investigation may be considered suspect because they are obtained by parties who are or at least appear to be biased. Thus, while the company may prefer to use examiners with historical knowledge and details about the company, personnel, and accounting systems, their retention may raise issues of credibility. On the other hand, while the investigation of a fraud examiner who has no prior connection with the company may be unbiased, the resulting evaluation may also exhibit the examiner's inexperience with the particular organization and its business practices.

In balancing the twin goals of disinterestedness and reliability, Machen and Richards (2004) suggest that a company should consider the purpose of the investigation. Where the results are to be used in-house or where the company is simply establishing a fraud prevention system, there is less concern regarding credibility. Thus, a fraud examiner who has knowledge of the business may be a wiser choice in that instance because of such examiner's familiarity with the company. In contrast, where information from the fraud investigation may be subject to scrutiny by those outside the company, the appearance of disinterestedness becomes more critical and the company should consider hiring an independent fraud examiner.

Within the broad category of fraud examiners are forensic accountants who specialize in a unique brand of accounting that departs from the traditional methods employed in the accounting field (Machen and Richards, 2004).

Similar to the situation in the UK, where companies are expected to contribute to detection of law violations in terms of self-reports, companies in the United States are expected to make disclosures. Prosecutors in the United States consider whether the company made a voluntary and timely disclosure as well as the company's willingness to provide relevant information and evidence and identify relevant actors inside and outside the company, including senior executives. This is according to a resource guide to the US Foreign Corrupt Practices Act.

In its report to the nations on occupational fraud and abuse, ACFE (2014) analyzed more than a thousand cases of occupational fraud. The majority of cases reported (61%) were referred to law enforcement for criminal prosecution. The median loss for cases referred to prosecution was $200,000, while cases that were not referred had a median loss of $75,000.

The Association of Certified Fraud Examiners is not a US-only organization. The CFE designation is an international designation and the ACFE has reported approximately 40% of its membership is outside of the United States. These are all fraud fighters. Rumors tell that there are at least 16 CFEs in Norway. Some of these individuals work at the large accounting firms and may have been involved in fraud examination reports presented later in this book.

Markopolos in the Madoff Case

Harry Markopolos was a portfolio manager for an equity derivatives asset management firm in Boston when he was asked to conduct a fraud examination of Bernard Madoff's money-making methods in 2000. He discovered Madoff was running a Ponzi fraud scheme (Carozza, 2009).

The fraud examination was caused by an event in 1999. Frank Casey, a marketing senior vice president for the Boston firm, returned from New York with marketing materials for a high-performing, derivatives-based hedge fund managed by Madoff. In early 2000, Markopolos was asked by firm partners to reverse-engineer the strategy of Madoff. After he modeled the strategy, Markopolos determined that the returns could only be coming from illegal front running of the Madoff broker and dealer arm's client orders or from fictional returns that were the result of a Ponzi scheme (Carozza, 2009).

When Markopolos was examining the materials that Casey brought with him from New York, he discovered that Madoff's name was never on them (Carozza, 2009):

> That was clue no. 1. I've never seen a product offering where the manager's name wasn't listed up front. The marketing literature describes a derivatives-based strategy with 37 moving parts, but I was very familiar with the math, and the strategy as described shouldn't have been able to earn a positive return after fees. He made some very simple portfolio construction errors in that he foolishly retained single-stock price risk that would have led to a lot more down months than he reported to investors.
>
> If he had designed the product correctly, he could have avoided this single-stock risk, so I knew that Madoff didn't know the first thing about portfolio construction mathematics. Literally, it took five minutes after reading his strategy paragraph to determine that he wasn't really using the described strategy to earn the returns he said he was. Under existing securities law, if you tell clients that you are using Strategy A to invest their money but, in fact, you use an undisclosed Strategy B to really invest their money, you've committed fraud.

Markopolos submitted his evidence to the Securities and Exchange Commission (SEC) for the first time in 2001, and updated it in 2005, 2007, and 2008. In 2008, the stock market crumbled, investors rushed to redeem their investments, and Madoff ran out of cash (Carozza, 2009).

The Federal Bureau of Investigation (FBI) arrested Bernard L. Madoff on a rainy morning in December 2008, based on tips from his two sons. They confiscated dozens of checks, totaling $173 million, that were made out by him to his close friends, key employees, and family members. Madoff was charged with multiple felonies, including securities fraud, investment advisor fraud, mail fraud, and wire fraud. The US District Court judge in New York City released him on a $10 million bond, gave orders to put electronic bracelets on him, and confined him to his Manhattan apartment. It was a disappointment for the prosecutors, who wanted him jailed. However, the prosecutors got their wishes when the judge also ordered Madoff and his immediate family members to not sell or transfer any personal assets. The FBI confiscated the passports of Madoff and his wife, Ruth. A federal judge froze the assets of Madoff Investment Securities (Ragothaman, 2014).

After his high school graduation in 1956, Madoff attended the University of Alabama for a year, where he was a member of a Jewish fraternity. He transferred to Hofstra University in 1957 and graduated with a degree in political science from Hofstra in 1960. Madoff and his wife held several small jobs, in the early years, including installing sprinklers, babysitting, and performing lifeguard duties in Manhattan. He started his investment business in 1968 with a capital of $5,000, which he and his wife had saved during the previous 6 years (Ragothaman, 2014).

Madoff's business grew slowly in the initial yeas. When he got a chance to become a market maker on the National Association of Securities Dealers Automated Quotations (NASDAQ) in 1984, he grabbed the opportunity. His eldest son, Mark, had just finished his MBA at Columbia University and was eager to enter the family business. While Madoff looked after his investment management and advisory business, he put Mark in charge of the market maker end of the business. Madoff Investment Securities directly executed orders from retail brokers. About the same time, Madoff invested in computer equipment and software to automate the order system. Peter Madoff, his brother, spearheaded the computerization project and successfully developed a fast, automated system to handle customer orders. This automated trading system brought fame to the investment firm, which by 2008 was the sixth largest market maker on the NASDAQ (Ragothaman, 2014).

Madoff was esteemed by friends, investors, regulators, and the securities industry. He was perceived as instrumental in NASDAQ's rise as a major competitor to the New York Stock Exchange (NYSE) because he was on the forefront of embracing technology in the securities industry, which allowed him to be one of the first actors to take part in payment for order flow (Nichols, 2011). Madoff targeted thousands of wealthy investors, Jewish charities, celebrities, and retirees. The scam unraveled in 2008 when the economic crisis led to more withdrawals than he could afford to pay.

Madoff Investment Securities was governed by a small, closely knit board of directors. Madoff was the founding chairman and retained that position until his arrest in 2008. Brother Peter Madoff was the managing director. Peter's daughter, Shana Madoff, served as the compliance attorney for the investment firm. In addition, Madoff's two sons, Mark and Andrew, served as the lead officers in the market maker division of the firm. The chief financial officer, Frank DiPascali, was a long-term associate of Madoff. In short, the management of Madoff Investment Securities was dominated by family members and friends (Ragothaman, 2014).

Madoff created false trading reports based on the returns that customers liked to see. He used his firm to conduct an international Ponzi scheme. A Ponzi scheme is a fraudulent investment scheme that pays returns to investors from their own money or money paid by subsequent investors rather than from any actual profit earned (Nolasco et al., 2013). Madoff used a network of feeder funds to access the global financial market and to grow his hedge fund fraud into billions of dollars. Madoff's control of all service providers to his hedge fund business allowed his fraud to continue undetected by regulators (Nichols, 2011).

Bernard Madoff pled guilty to 11 felony charges (securities fraud, investment advisor fraud, mail fraud, money laundering, false statements, and others) in March 2009. He was awarded the maximum possible prison sentence of 150 years in July 2009 and was asked to pay a restitution of $170 billion. Mark Madoff, the oldest son, committed suicide in December 2010. Brother Peter Madoff was sentenced to 10 years in jail for his role in the Madoff fraud in December 2012. Frank DiPascali pled guilty to 10 felony charges and was awaiting sentencing (Ragothaman, 2014).

Madoff's financial crime became a symbol for the greediness and immorality of a financial meltdown he did not necessarily cause. Some victims felt that Madoff was somehow responsible for the economic downturn generally in the United States. Some victims believed that Madoff's fraud proves him to be of unparalleled evil (Ionescu, 2010).

In 2014, five former employees of Bernard L. Madoff Investment Securities were found guilty in Manhattan Federal Court on all counts. They were Daniel Bonventre, Annette Bongiorno, Joann Crupi, Jerome O'Hara, and George Perez, who were all found guilty of 31 counts in connection with their long-time employment at Madoff's. The verdict was announced in March 2014 after a more than 5-month trial (FBI, 2014).

Bonventre was employed at Madoff Securities for 40 years and served as its director of operations. Bongiorno managed hundreds of investment advisory accounts. Crupi handled the receipt of funds sent to Madoff Securities by its clients for investment. O'Hara and Perez were employed as computer programmers. They were responsible for developing and maintaining computer programs that supported the operations. For example, they developed special programs that created books and records to help hide the scope and nature of the business. Names of account holders were changed in the programs, and the programs altered details about the number of shares, execution times, and transaction numbers for trades by employing algorithms that produced false and random results (FBI, 2014).

Madoff's last surviving son, Andrew, who insisted he had nothing to do with his father's massive Ponzi scheme, died at the age of 48 in 2014. Both sons denied knowing about the fraud and were never charged criminally in connection with the scheme. They turned their father in to authorities in December 2008.

Bernard Madoff was an inmate in Butner Medium prison in 2014. According to the Federal Bureau of Prisons (www.bop.gov), Madoff has a release date of November 14, 2139!

Harry Markopolos discovered Madoff's Ponzi scheme in 2000 based on his team's fraud examination, and he submitted evidence to the SEC in the following years. He tried to encourage others to look into this in order to protect investors (Carozza, 2009).

But the starting point in his Boston firm was quite different. There were no fraud suspicions. When Casey in his firm returned from New York with marketing materials from Madoff, his idea was to try to copy it so that their Boston firm could offer this successful product to the firm's customers. It was Markopolos's discovery that turned his work into a fraud examination. He went to the firm's partners and jokingly asked if they really wanted to get into that business. They hastily replied, "No way, if that's what he's doing then we don't want to compete in that space" (Carozza, 2009).

Harry Markopolos (born 1956) was a securities industry executive, an independent forensic accountant, and a financial fraud investigator. Markopolos discovered evidence over 9 years suggesting that Bernard Madoff's wealth management business, Madoff Investment Securities, was actually a massive Ponzi scheme (Nolasco et al., 2013). Madoff was sentenced in 2009 to 150 years in prison. In 2010, Markopolos's book on uncovering the Madoff fraud was published: *No One Would Listen: A True Financial Thriller.*

The Markopolos (2010) book tells the story of how his investigative team uncovered Madoff's scam years before it made the headlines, and how they tried to warn the government, the industry, and the financial press. The book describes Markopolos's pursuit of the criminal. Markopolos presents himself as a whistle-blower. The book became a *New York Times* bestseller.

Fraud examiner Harry Markopolos is a member of the Boston Chapter of the Association of Certified Fraud Examiners (ACFE). He worked in 2014 as a forensic accountant and analyst for attorneys. His educational background includes a bachelor's degree in business administration from Loyola College in Maryland and a master's degree from Boston College.

Person-Oriented Investigation

Traditionally, crime suspicion is handled by talking to people who may have some relevant information. This approach is called person-oriented investigation, where suspects and witnesses are interviewed.

Financial crime investigators take testimony of witnesses. Testimony may explain records and transactions, clarify relationships, identify leads, and establish organizational structures. Records and documents do not speak for themselves and are often created to mislead. Interviewing skills are critical.

Informants usually request anonymity, which may make their information inadmissible, but a source of excellent leads and intelligence.

As argued by H.E. Williams (2006), there are many sides to every question and many questions for every accusation in white-collar crime investigations. The issues in dispute are seldom simple or easily understood, and each questionable issue may be inescapably intertwined with other equally ambiguous issues.

Nevertheless, it remains the duty of the investigator to seek the truth by identifying relevant facts about events (Williams, 2006: 142):

> During any investigation, facts will appear from many sources, but the spoken word remains the most important source of all the forms of evidence available to the investigator.

Thus, few skills are as important to the white-collar crime investigator as having command of the techniques for interview and interrogation. In financial investigations, evidence often develops in small bits and pieces (Williams, H.E., 2006).

Law enforcement agencies have clear powers to interview suspects after appropriate warnings and notices are issued. However, in conducting private investigations, fraud examiners may be required to interview persons with their consent. The purpose of such an interview is to obtain information, not to judge anyone. If witnesses are interviewed, the investigator should have prepared a list of questions. These should be wide enough to be flexible, but should have a structure of questioning that sets out to establish the required evidence (Coburn, 2006).

In person-oriented investigation, the most important rule is to listen and let the interviewee do the talking. The second most important rule, according to Coburn (2006), is to be organized and for the investigator to control the process. The interviewee may be asked to attend a private office at a time and place in an area controlled by the investigative team. Interviewees should be asked if they consent to the conversation being recorded. It should be explained to the interviewee what the investigation is about. This is helpful to both parties because it helps prevent interpretations being placed on information.

Place-Oriented Investigations

Forensic accountants may perform a variety of fieldwork, such as inspecting company facilities to investigate whether goods and equipment are in accordance with company records (Machen and Richards, 2004).

There are almost no limits to the evidence that can be obtained by a well-drafted and properly executed search on relevant sites. The seizure may be financial information, videotapes, transaction records, and many other things.

Archive-Oriented Investigation

Forensic accounting is the application of financial skills and investigative mentality to unresolved issues, conducted within the context of the rules of evidence. As a method, it encompasses financial expertise, fraud knowledge, and a strong knowledge and understanding of business reality and the working of the legal system. Expertise as part of the method represents skillful execution of knowledge and skill to achieve effective investigation results (Taylor et al., 2013). Forensic accountants turn traditional accounting principles on their head by questioning and investigating the accounting methods and financial practices of a company (Machen and Richards, 2004: 68):

> Unlike traditional accountants who assume honesty and integrity in the examination of a corporation's finances, a forensic accountant typically will question figures and numbers until they are validated. For example, while the traditional accountant may examine a company's records to determine whether they are accurate, the forensic accountant will search for badges of fraud in financial statements, balance sheets, and underlying corporate documents. Furthermore, as part of their investigations, forensic accountants may perform a variety of fieldwork from inspecting company facilities to participating in witness interviews. Accordingly, a forensic accountant may be useful not just in assisting an organization create a fraud prevention program, but may also detect and identify instances and responsible parties once the organization has determined that fraud has in fact occurred.

A financial crime specialist needs to interpret and handle financial documents as if they will be used in a legal case. During the investigation it may be hard to know what will be relevant, so all documents must be treated with an assumed degree of relevance. For the financial crime investigator, financial statements are viewed as a source of leads to specific financial transactions that could form the basis of violations of criminal and civil law and regulations. The financial specialist's job is to discover the story behind the numbers. Chain of custody procedures include a documented chronology of the handling of the document or physical evidence. Important chain of custody documentation may include where the item was initially located, who collected it, where it was filed, and documentation of each person who handled it.

Technology-Oriented Investigation

One method of detecting improper activities in corporations where financial crime is suspected is through the use of information technology. Most organizational information is usually created and managed electronically.

Computer forensics allows private investigators to uncover more of the facts, support otherwise unsubstantiated information, confirm or refute allegations, and analyze competing theories in relation to those facts. Computer forensics involves identifying, collecting, analyzing, and protecting large amounts of data and peripheral evidence (Newman, 2009).

Computer forensics is defined as a scientific, systematic inspection of the computer system and its contents for evidence or supportive evidence of a crime or other computer use that is being inspected. It includes the art and science of applying computer systems to aid the inquiry process. Additionally, analytical and investigative techniques are used to examine this evidence and data that are magnetically stored or encoded using the binary number system. The computer might have been the target of some illegal activity, the medium through which the illegal activity is committed, incidental to the commission of the illegal activity, or a combination of the previous three (Newman, 2009).

Data mining is about extracting information from large databases (Srinivasa et al., 2007: 4295):

> Data mining is a process of extracting nontrivial, valid, novel and useful information from large databases. Hence, data mining can be viewed as a kind of search for meaningful patterns or rules from a large search space that is the database.

Forensic ToolKit tells about its products in this way (http://www.accessdata.com/products/digital-forensics/ftk):

> FTK is a court-accepted digital investigations platform built for speed, stability and ease of use. It provides comprehensive processing and indexing up front, so filtering and searching is faster than with any other product. This means you can zero in on the relevant evidence quickly, dramatically increasing your analysis speed. The database-driven, enterprise-class architecture allows you to handle massive data sets, as it provides stability and processing speeds not possible with other tools. Furthermore, because of this architecture, FTK can be upgraded easily to expand distributed processing and incorporate web-based case management and collaborative analysis.

Some caution is needed before getting too excited about data mining, according to Lind et al. (2007):

> Whenever huge masses of personal data are stored at one place, and especially when tied to a system with the intelligence to tailor this data, there is enormous privacy risk. The idea is that strict access control surrounds the data. Will that be the case? We can only hope. We see a risk of abuse from corrupted personnel and from hackers or other intruders. Also, there is a risk that data

> be overly interpreted as true, and that end users be wrongly accused. With the ease in accessing and perhaps performing data mining on huge amounts of personal data, the risk that a police investigation might take the wrong turn is much greater.

Kroll Ontack is a UK firm specializing in data recovery, information management, and computer forensics (http://www.krollontrack.co). Data stored on hard drives, mobile devices, and other damaged electronic media can be recovered. Specialized software can read files from damaged devices. Information management is combining documents, email, and other private investigation material. Computer forensics represents a shift away from paper files to an increased reliance on computers and other electronic devices to enhance efficiency. This shift has created new challenges for companies as they safeguard intellectual property, investigate fraud within their organizations, and protect their reputations from external threats.

Similarity is a concept applied in digital investigations. As humans we are used to applying similarity by visualization. For example, a picture in color is similar—in fact identical—to the same picture in black and white. Information is carried in different colors versus shades of gray. Unfortunately, a computer is blind and cannot see. Similarity is applied by humans in content analysis, where word phrases are analyzed in terms of their meaning, for example, as positive or negative statements.

In digital investigations, Bjelland et al. (2014) define similarity in terms of syntactic versus semantic similarity. Syntactic similarity is from the perspective of a computer, while semantic similarity is from the perspective of a human. Two documents are semantically similar if they communicate the same meaning, while they are semantically identical if they communicate the same information.

In their article, Bjelland et al. (2014) suggest the application of approximate hash-based matching, also known as fuzzy matching, to identify data that might have similarity. Hatch-based algorithms are mathematical computer programs designed to match binary data by comparing sets of data from different files. Content-based matching computes the extent of difference between files.

A similar concept to data mining is process mining in auditing. Process mining aims to extract knowledge from the event logs maintained by a company's systems, such as the enterprise resource planning (ERP) system. Jans et al. (2013) argue that the capabilities of process mining include (1) analysis of the entire population of data and not just a sample, (2) data can be entered independent of the actions of the auditee, (3) process mining allows the auditor to have a way of implementing the audit risk model in terms of walk-throughs of processes and analytic procedures, and (4) identifying social relationships between individuals. The latter capability is important, as crime is always committed by criminals and not by systems. Even when a malfunction in a system is programmed, the programmer is an individual.

Process mining is concerned with business processes, which are defined as a set of business activities that represent the steps required to achieve a business objective. The identification and analysis of processes is central to process mining. Event logs can be studied by forensic accountants. Event log data are captured from operating systems in the organization (Jans et al., 2013).

In a data mining case study by Jans et al. (2010), internal fraud detection is exemplified. As a first step, the business process most worth investigating is selected. A characteristic that can counter high risk is the employment of senior managers with sophisticated IT experience. Second, the stored data are collected, manipulated, and enriched. Manipulation involves organizing the data in the structure and format that is needed for processing. Enrichment is the creation of extra attributes by combining or transforming attributes, e.g., computing ratios and averages. During step 3, the technical data are translated into behavioral data. This translation builds upon domain knowledge and is not just a technical transformation. The core of the methodology, step 4, is to apply descriptive data mining to obtain more insights into the behavioral data. The last step is to have domain experts audit observations.

Process mining diagnoses processes by mining event logs. This way one can expose opportunities to commit fraud in the followed process. A process with high risk of fraud is the procurement process (Jans et al., 2011).

Hypotheses Testing

Theory enables private investigators to create an overview over complexities in the real world by offering a verbal tool to organize a common and consistent understanding of reality (Colquitt and Zapata-Phelan, 2007): a theory might be a prediction or explanation, a set of interrelated constructs, definitions, and propositions that presents a systematic view of phenomena by specifying relations among variables, with the purpose of explaining natural phenomena.

Investigators formulate hypotheses about what might have happened. Hypotheses represent assumptions about occurrences and assumptions about connections and cause-and-effect relationships. A hypothesis is an untested view of reality, a possible explanation of a phenomenon.

Did investigators in case studies presented toward the end of this book formulate and discuss competing hypotheses in their reports? As suggested by Brightman (2009), competing hypotheses represent analysis characterized by thorough examination of alternatives, identification of key bits of data that carry the most diagnostic weight, and painstaking attention to refuting hypotheses.

In the investigation of the Norwegian Football Association conducted by Lynx (2013), presented later in this book, the following alternative hypotheses for crime categories were formulated:

1. Risks of misconduct in terms of abuse of funds in football clubs
2. Risks of criminal behavior by participation in corruption when buying players
3. Risks of criminal behavior by participation in corruption when selling players
4. Risks of embezzlement, kickbacks, and abuse of funds
5. Risks of misleading accounting of costs when buying players
6. Risks of misleading accounting and taxation of income for foreign players
7. Risks of breaching rules when compensating trainers and reporting trainers' compensation

These seven hypotheses are alternatives for evidence collected in the investigation. Significant evidence and arguments include not only the facts known, but also the opinions and points of view from analysts on the case and other experts. This type of evidence may result in further critical questioning about what one might expect to be seeing if, in fact, the evidence or opinion presented is indeed true (Brightman, 2009).

Competing hypotheses are subject to key bits of data that carry the most diagnostic weight. Throughout the duration of step 2, it is important to look beyond the obvious, and attempt to discover what is actually missing (Brightman, 2009).

Investigative Thinking Styles

Financial crime specialists and fraud examiners might be compared to police detectives in their thinking styles and investigative approaches. As argued by Wells (2003), becoming a fraud examiner—a kind of a financial detective—is not for everyone. Detectives—either in law enforcement or in the private sector—typically have distinct personality traits. They are as good with people as they are with numbers and documents, and they are inclined to be curious, creative, and aggressive, rather than shy, isolated, and retiring.

Dean (2005) developed a set of four thinking styles, which later were enhanced by Staines (2013):

- *Thinking style 1: Investigation as method.* Detectives describe this way of thinking as following a method that is driven by a set of basic procedural steps and conceptual processes for legally gathering information and building evidence. The method style is underpinned by a preference for following established rules and procedures, such as standard operating procedures, in order to gather information and build evidence in investigation.

The investigator is trained in procedural steps of investigation and takes an evidence-focused rather than suspect-focused approach (Tong, 2009b). According to Tong (2009b), the science of investigation exists in direct opposition to the conception of the art of investigation, which is related to the risk thinking style. The science of investigation is taught in classrooms and documented in manuals and handbooks, while the art of investigation is stimulated by creativity as well as innovative and untraditional approaches.

Method thinkers are characterized by the desire to avoid confusion, a rigidity of thought, and a reluctance to consider alternative views as long as they are not along the main lines of investigation. They process information extensively and carefully and focus their attention on a few critical hypotheses. They work within existing rules and frameworks. They are checking all the boxes on a checklist. They apply a structured approach to investigative procedures.

- *Thinking style 2: Investigation as challenge.* Detectives describe this way of thinking as a challenge driven by the intensity that is generated by the four key processes of the job, the victim, the criminal, and the crime. The challenge style is underpinned by an intense motivation, and the job is perceived by the challenge thinker as an opportunity to fight crime and make community safe.

  There is also a perceived need to seek justice for the victim. The stimulating nature of whether or not a crime has occurred provides motivation for the challenge thinker, and generally, the more interesting the possible crime, the more challenged and motivated the detective becomes. Because the challenge thinking style often involves deep emotional involvement by the detective, it can lead to extreme feelings of sympathy and antipathy as well as immense satisfaction if the case is successfully solved. Alternatively, failure to solve the case can result in feelings of being a loser and extreme frustration.

  At the extreme, the challenge style can lead to the fragmentation of other aspects of the detective's life in such a way that often the price to be paid for this addiction to the investigative challenge is marriage problems, financial problems, and unstable private personality. The challenge thinker is really a crime fighter, as discussed by Siegel (2009). The challenge thinker is vulnerable to problematic outcomes in life if he or she is not able to mediate personal enthusiasm or passion for the job. Some level of drive and enthusiasm is of course necessary to maintain commitment to the job. However, it is more desirable for detectives to subscribe to the challenge style only to the extent that it keeps them interested and committed to their job, and not to the extent they become overwhelmed and experience burnout. This is also important when considering the possibility of the challenge style acting as a force that can potentially motivate police honesty as well as private investigator honesty in an impatient search for answers (Goldschmidt and Anonymous, 2008).

Goldschmidt and Anonymous (2008) reviewed the circumstances that may lead police officers to act dishonestly. One reason was to see a case won, the suspect convicted and sent to prison, and justice seemingly served. Another reason was to respond to a system they perceive to be overly sympathetic toward offenders, while neglectful of victims, and which ignores common sense and the expected guilt of offenders. These two circumstances are conceptually related to the challenge style, where the detective is motivated by the need to seek justice for the victim and rid the organization or the community of offenders.

- *Thinking style 3: Investigation as skill.* Detectives describe this way of thinking as a skill that requires a set of personal qualities and abilities that revolve around the central skill of relating effectively to a diversity of people at a number of different levels throughout an investigation. A detective who employs the skill style is successful at relating to and building relationships with others in order to ensure successful prosecution of a suspect.

  Relationships are built with witnesses, whistle-blowers, victims, suspects, and managers. In the case of police investigations, relationships are built with people in the criminal justice system, such as magistrates, judges, and juries. In the case of private investigations, relationships are built with the client, various internal and external information sources, as well as others involved in the investigation. In order to relate to the various individuals, the detective is required to master several abilities, such as communication, personal flexibility, investigative focus, and emotional detachment. The skill style is grounded by the notion of information as the lifeblood of an investigation, and the presumption is that most of the important investigative information comes from communicating with others.

  A detective has to be able to share and trade information with individuals who might be useful to the investigation. Sometimes there is a need to turn a blind eye in order to gather important case-related information. It is important to be persistent, yet fair. The detective needs to approach investigative interviewing with an open mind. Sometimes a detective needs to display a certain level of warmth, flexibility, and emotion in order to successfully communicate and retrieve important information. In this regard Tong (2009b) discussed the craft of detective work, which emphasizes the importance of understanding and being able to relate to others. It is important to be able to deal with individuals from a range of backgrounds, and it is also critical when questioning individuals who are suspected of having some form of mental illness, intellectual disability, or personality disorder (Herrington and Roberts, 2012).

- *Thinking style 4: Investigation as risk.* Detectives describe this way of thinking as taking a risk, that must be legally justifiable, in order to be proactive through the use of creativity in discovering and developing information into evidence. By taking proactive risks, the detective aims to create new leads. This proactivity revolves around three investigative processes: creativity (the creation of new/different ideas), discovery (of relevant and important information), and development (of information into knowledge and evidence). The risk style is particularly useful in protracted and complex investigations whereby strict adherence to the method style has been unfruitful.

  The risk thinking style is underpinned by the notion of taking justified risk. Risks taken by detectives must be legally justifiable, logical (make sense as pertaining to the rest of the investigation), and laterally justified (that is, be economically and conceptually practicable). By taking proactive risks, the detective aims to create new leads. This proactivity revolves around three investigative processes: creativity (the creation of new and different ideas), discovery (of relevant and important information), and development (of information into knowledge and evidence).

  Risk thinkers demonstrate creativity in their investigative approaches. Creativity and intuition are perceived as essential qualities of any criminal investigator. Fictional characters such as Sherlock Holmes have worked to further entrench these notions of the "born detective" who is naturally creative and intuitive. Detectives can be creative in their job by generating new ways of performing their work, by coming up with novel procedures and innovative ideas, and by reconfiguring known approaches into new alternatives.

  Detectives emphasizing the risk style tend to be entrepreneurs, who are characterized to see possibilities and openings where others see problems and locked doors, based on their intuition (Tong, 2009a). Generally, an entrepreneur is a person who operates a new unit or venture and assumes some accountability for the inherent risk. It is a person who takes the risks involved to undertake a procedural venture. Entrepreneurship is the practice of starting new investigative steps or revitalizing mature procedures in response to identified opportunities.

These stages are illustrated in Figure 4.1. Sometimes investigation can remind of a production line, where cases are investigated after each other, in a routine fashion (Corsianos, 2003: 305):

> Detective work tends to parallel an assembly line; that is, detectives routinely process one case after the other with little or no difference in officers' investigative approaches and/or attitudes towards cases. But, police decision making and officers' overall treatment of cases are significantly influenced in specific situations. Specific factors such as the time and energy dedicated to solving the crime, the number of officers, technology, budget, and police attitudes towards the accused and officers' perception as to the seriousness of the case affect the investigation.

In the production line, experienced detectives are able to discern good from bad information intuitively and at the same time be creative in their approach to investigation. Historically, investigation has been thought of as an art form resembling thinking style 4, because it is difficult to articulate and exists beyond procedures and protocols taught to recruits and novice detectives. The qualities that make a good investigator go beyond academic degrees, specialized training, or book learning, because all the theory in the world means nothing if the detective cannot read an organization in search of white-collar crime. In this respect, Tong (2009a) highlights the need to capture and articulate the qualities of the artistic and intuitive investigator so that they may be passed on.

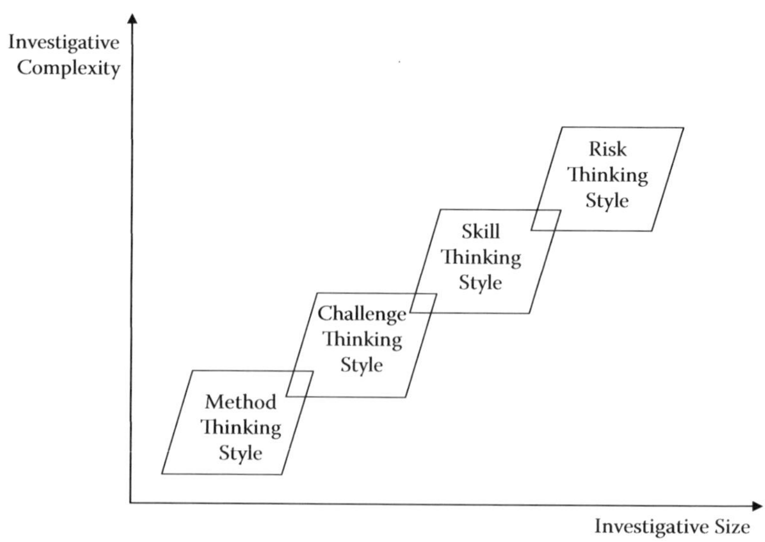

Figure 4.1 Contingent approach to investigative thinking styles.

Thinking styles can be viewed in a hierarchical continuum as illustrated in Figure 4.1.

Investigative complexity and time taken to complete investigation require more advanced thinking styles. This does not necessarily reflect the idea that one thinking style is better than another style. Instead, thinking styles are more or less appropriate depending upon complexity and time for investigation. While a less complex and new investigation might be solved using only the method style, a more complex or a more time-consuming investigation will require the challenge, skill, or risk style, or a combination of these. This represents a contingent approach to investigative thinking styles, where the appropriateness of a thinking style is dependent on the investigative situation.

Investigative instinct is very important in conducting complex fraud examinations. Coburn (2006) argues that investigators tend to ignore other possibilities because there is no evidence, rather than using instinct to lead them to evidence. It is important to think outside the box.

The Case of Kelly Paxton

Kelly Paxton is a certified fraud examiner and licensed private investigator. She was educated at the University of Oregon, University of Southern California, and the Federal Law Enforcement Training Center. Prior to starting Financial CaseWorks she worked as an analyst for the Washington County Sheriff's Office Fraud Identity Theft Enforcement Team. Before joining the team she performed background investigations for the sheriff's office. She also has seven years of experience as a contract special investigator for the Office of Personnel Management and the Department of Homeland Security.

Kelly Paxton was a special agent for the US Customs Office of Investigations from 1993 to 1998. During this time she was assigned to the money laundering and white-collar crime unit. She has prior financial industry experience, which includes a stock broker's license and a commodity broker's license. She has the website www.pinkcollarcrime.com, where she presents herself:

> Everyone knows the saying White Collar Criminal (think Bernie Madoff and Martha Stewart), but when I say Pink Collar Criminal they get a blank look. Most people don't realize it but they probably are neighbors, co-workers, friends or acquaintances with either a Pink Collar Criminal or someone who has been embezzled by a Pink Collar Criminal. A Pink Collar Criminal can be a PTA mom, your dentist's office manager, and yes even someone's grandma. The statistics on Pink Collar Criminals are alarming. According to

the FBI, male embezzlers have increased only 4% since 1990 while Pink Collar Criminals have increased over 40% during that time period.

The term pink-collar crime was coined by Kathleen Daly during the 1980s to describe embezzlement type crimes that typically were committed by females based on limited opportunity. In this context, women were more likely to have committed low level crimes such as check kiting and bookkeeping fraud from positions of less power compared to men who had engaged in acts of white-collar crime.

In 2010 the Association of Certified Fraud Examiners Report to the Nations on Occupational Fraud and Abuse found that men were responsible for stealing larger amounts of money (median = $232,000) compared to women (median = $100,000). A handful of embezzlement studies, though dated, have focused on female offenders and have confirmed trends that women tend to commit embezzlement at a higher rate, but steal less money. Women also invoke different rationalizations for their actions compared to men. The glass ceiling as we know it today represents women making about .81 on the dollar compared to men. However, when they steal they only steal about .43 on the dollar.

Why did I become interested in Pink Collar Crime? When I started working at the Sheriff's Office I became intimately involved in seeing the devastation caused by small business embezzlements. What I did not know was the perp committing these crimes. When I was a federal agent most of my targets were typical White Collar Criminals—in other words men. Now I was seeing women who had violated the trust of their employers. Out of all the cases I worked at the Sheriff's Office there was only one male embezzler we came across. The rest were women. And all kinds of women: old, young and middle aged. Some gambled and some just wanted to keep up with the Joneses. Whatever their motivation, however, they did have two things in common—trust and opportunity.

Paxton works as certified fraud examiner at Financial CaseWorks LLC, a boutique investigative firm located in the Portland, Oregon area. The firm was established to assist in the detection and discovery of fraud-related matters. Embezzlement by trusted employees, background investigations of employees, due diligence on possible business relationships, and civil matters involving litigation support are all types of cases with which Financial CaseWorks LLC can provide assistance.

Financial CaseWorks LLC specializes in the following areas of fraud detection (www.financialcaseworks.com):

- *Embezzlement.* A long-time trusted employee is discovered to have embezzled funds from her employer. What does the employer do upon discovery? Financial CaseWorks LLC works with the victim to immediately start the civil and/or criminal processes. Most victims are reluctant to ask for advice from friends and business associates when this happens. We work with you to put together a strategy to best recover funds. Kelly's background in law enforcement allows her to prepare your case for prosecution. Identifying assets for recovery/restitution, preparing documents for presentation to law enforcement and assisting the victim in putting the records back together are just some of the services we provide to you.

- *Elder Abuse.* What happens when a parent starts to lose control over their finances? Elder financial abuse happens by a family member in approximately 60% of all cases. An example of this is when a family member has a Power of Attorney. Do the other family members start to question the accounting of the parent's finances? We work with you to assist in the documentation of the funds. This type of work is provided to assist in civil and/or criminal proceedings.
- *Asset Tracing.* Do you need to locate assets from a dishonest employee, ex-spouse or vendor who won't pay a judgment? We work with you to identify assets that have been stolen or misappropriated. Through analysis of bank records, interviews of associates, and searching through commercial databases and the Internet, we assist you with locating assets.
- *Fraud Prevention.* We provide fraud-prevention consulting to private and public companies and non-profits. With Kelly's background in law enforcement and financial services, we can show you how to put anti-fraud measures into place. We are also able to do a fraud assessment and help you identify areas of weakness. If you have been a victim of fraud we can assist in making sure your business puts into place the right preventive measures so it won't happen again.
- *Background Investigations.* Do you know who your employees really are or what they were doing at their previous employers? Background investigations are one of the tools an employer has the ability to use to get a better picture of their potential employees.
- *Due Diligence.* Information is knowledge. Having due diligence performed prior to negotiations is even more important with all the information on the Internet these days. Can you afford to not know what a possible vendor/business partner is doing in their business? We work with multiple web sources, commercial databases and interviewing to be able to get a more complete picture of a potential strategic alliance.
- *Litigation Support.* Financial CaseWorks LLC works with your legal team to assist in quantifying economic losses and providing documentation of monies.

References

ACFE. (2008). *2008 Report to the Nation—On Occupational Fraud and Abuse.* Association of Certified Fraud Examiners, Austin, TX.

ACFE. (2014). *Report to the Nations on Occupational Fraud and Abuse, 2014 Global Fraud Study.* Association of Certified Fraud Examiners, Austin, TX.

Anders, S.B. (2006). Website of the month: Association of Certified Fraud Examiners. *CPA Journal*, August, 71.

Bjelland, P.C., Franke, K., and Årnes, A. (2014). Practical use of approximate hash based matching in digital investigations. *Digital Investigation.* http://dx.doi.org/10.1016/j.diin.2014.03.003

Brightman, H.J. (2009). *Today's White-Collar Crime: Legal, Investigative, and Theoretical Perspectives.* Routledge, Taylor & Francis Group, New York.

Carozza, D. (2009). Chasing Madoff. *Fraud Magazine*, May/June. http://www.fraud-magazine.com/article.aspx?id=313

CFCS. (2013). *CFCS Certification Examination Study Manual*, 4th ed. Certified Financial Crime Specialist, Association of Certified Financial Crime Specialists, Miami, FL.

Coburn, N.F. (2006). Corporate investigations. *Journal of Financial Crime*, 13(3), 348–368.

Colquitt, J.A., and Zapata-Phelan, C.P. (2007). Trends in theory building and theory testing: A five-decade study of the *Academy of Management Journal. Academy of Management Journal*, 50(6), 1281–1303.

Corsianos, M. (2003). Discretion in detectives' decision making and 'high profile' cases. *Police Practice and Research*, 4(3), 301–314.

Dean, G. (2005). *The Cognitive Psychology of Police Investigators.* Konferansebidrag, School of Justice Studies, Faculty of Law, Queensland University of Technology, Brisbane, Australia.

FBI. (2014). Five Former Employees of Bernard L. Madoff Investment Securities Found Guilty in Manhattan Federal Court on All Counts. Federal Bureau of Investigation. www.fbi.gov

Goldschmidt, J., and Anonymous. (2008). The necessity of dishonesty: Police deviance, 'making the case' and the public good. *Policing and Society*, 18(2), 113–135.

Herrington, V., and Roberts, K. (2012). Addressing psychological vulnerability in the police suspect interview. *Policing*, 6(2), 177–186.

Ionescu, L. (2010). Madoff's fraudulent financial scheme, his decades-long swindle, and the failure of operational risk management. *Economics, Management, and Financial Markets*, 5(3), 239–244.

Jans, M., Alles, M., and Vasahelyi, M. (2013). The case of process mining in auditing: Sources of value added and areas of application. *International Journal of Accounting Information Systems*, 14(1), 1–20.

Jans, M., Lybaert, N., and Vanhoof, K. (2010). Internal fraud risk reduction: Results of a data mining case study. *International Journal of Accounting Information Systems*, 11, 17–41.

Jans, M., Werf, J.M., Lybaert, N., and Vanhoof, K. (2011). A business process mining application for internal transaction fraud mitigation. *Expert Systems with Applications*, 38(10), 13351–13359.

Kennedy, D.B. (2013). Applications of forensic sociology and criminology to civil litigation. *Journal of Applied Social Science.* Published online before print April 12, 2013, doi: 10.1177/1936724413477752.

Lind, H., Hjelm, J., and Lind, M. (2007). Privacy surviving data retention in Europe? Paper presented at W3C Workshop on Languages for Privacy Policy Negotiation and Semantics-Driven Enforcement. www.w3.org.

Lynx. (2013). *1192-rapporten. Gransking av internasjonale spilleroverganger 2007–2011* (Examination of player transfers). Lynx law firm, Oslo.

Machen, M.J., and Richards, R.E. (2004). The use of fraud examiners in the battle against occupational fraud and abuse. *Journal of Investment Compliance*, Winter, 67–71.

Markopolos, H. (2010). *No One Would Listen: A True Financial Thriller.* John Wiley & Sons, Hoboken, NJ.

Morgan, M., and Nix, W. (2003). CPA perceptions of the marketability, career enhancements and quality of services of certified fraud examiners. *Southern Business and Economic Journal*, 31–50.

Newman, R. (2009). Computer forensics fraud investigations. *Journal of Forensic Studies in Accounting and Business*, Winter, 69–81.

Nichols, C. (2011). Addressing inept SEC enforcement efforts: Lessons from Madoff, the hedge fund industry, and Title IV of the Dodd-Frank Act for U.S., and global financial systems. *Northwestern Journal of International Law and Business*, 31, 637–698.

Nolasco, C.A.R.I., Vaughn, M.S., and Carmen, R.V. (2013). Revisiting the choice model of Ponzi and pyramid schemes: Analysis of case law. *Crime, Law and Social Change*, 60, 375–400.

Ragothaman, S.C. (2014). The Madoff debacle: What are the lessons? *Issues in Accounting Education*, 29(1), 271–285.

Siegel, L. (2009). *Introduction to Criminal Justice.* Wadsworth Cengage Learning, Stamford, CT.

Srinivasa, K.G., Venugopal, K.R., and Patnaik, L.M. (2007). A self-adaptive migration model genetic algorithm for data mining applications. *Information Sciences*, 177, 4295–4313.

Staines, Z. (2013). Managing tacit investigative knowledge: Measuring "investigative thinking styles." *Policing: An International Journal of Police Strategies and Management*, 36(3), 604–619.

Taylor, T.Z., Elison-Bowers, P., Werth, E., Bell, E., Carbajal, J., Lamm, K.B., and Velazquez, E. (2013). A Police Officer's Tacit Knowledge Inventory (POTKI): Establishing construct validity and exploring applications. *Police Practice and Research*, 14(6), 478–490.

Tong, S. (2009a). Introduction: A brief history of crime investigation. In Tong, S., Bryant, R., and Hovath, M. (eds.), *Understanding Criminal Investigation.* Wiley & Sons, Chichester, UK, pp. 1–10.

Tong, S. (2009b). Professionalising investigation. In Tong, S., Bryant, R., and Hovath, M. (eds.), *Understanding Criminal Investigation.* Wiley & Sons, Chichester, UK, pp. 197–216.

Wells, J.T. (2003). The fraud examiners. *Journal of Accountancy*, October, 76–80.

Williams, C.C. (2006). *The Hidden Enterprise Culture: Entrepreneurship in the Underground Economy.* Edward Elgar Publishing, Cheltenham, UK.

Williams, H.E. (2006). *Investigating White-Collar Crime.* Thomas Publisher, Springfield, IL.

Investigation Characteristics

5

When an organization wants to investigate facts, causes, and responsibilities for an event, where there is suspicion of white-collar crime, the investigation can be carried out by fraud examiners. A private investigation can comprise elements of intelligence work, detective work, and analytic work, as we know it from police work. Characteristics that can be attributed to private investigations include a serious and unusual event, an extraordinary examination to find out what happened or why it did not happen, developing explanations, and suggesting actions toward individuals and changes in systems and practices.

Extraordinary Examination

Fraud examination as intelligence is the systematic and goal-oriented collection of data, which are transformed and processed according to a determined approach to uncover suspects' capacities, dispositions, and purpose, so as to improve disclosure and clarification. Risk-based techniques can be applied to get an overview of departments, groups, and individuals, and how they act. Intelligence can also be defined as the result of the collection and assessment of information about potential fraud and potential suspects by default, to evaluate and draw conclusions about the risk situation, point out potential problems, and identify potential criminal activity with the intent to pursue the matter.

Fraud examination as investigation is targeted at collection of information to confirm or disconfirm an action or omission of action, and work to prove both guilt and innocence. Fraud examiners need to prepare evidence and documents so that they appropriately can serve as a basis for managerial assessment of the case. Investigation is about seeking, collecting, and securing evidence that substantiates the merits in its true context, so that the accused's or suspect's guilt as well as innocence is evaluated.

Fraud examination as analysis is the process of breaking down a complex topic or subject to smaller parts to improve understanding and insight. Analysis means to create meaning out of data by processing, interpreting, reorganizing, and seeking a structure from the gathered material. To analyze is to ask questions: what, where, how, who, when, which, and why. What has happened? Where did it happen? How has it happened? Who may have done what? When did it happen? Which sequence of events is most likely? Why did it happen? How can such events be prevented in the future?

Investigation by a private fraud examiner is not the same as investigation by the police, because investigations by the police normally are based on evidence that crime has occurred. In private investigations, there is only an assumption that misconduct or crime might have occurred. The fraud examiner has to find out what has happened and the sequence of events. This examination will clarify whether misconduct or crime has occurred. A police report assumes that something wrong has happened, while a warning means that something may have happened. Therefore, private investigations tend to start earlier than police investigations. Many private investigations that found evidence of white-collar crime have led to police investigations at a later point in time. A classic example in Norway is the fraud examination of the Great Norwegian Spitsbergen Coal Company on the island of Spitsbergen, where fraud examiners from consulting firm PricewaterhouseCoopers (PwC) found evidence of fraud. Then Norwegian police started investigations, and the chief executive officer (CEO) of the company, Mr. Robert Hermansen, was prosecuted in court and sentenced to imprisonment for 2 years.

Private investigation is extraordinary examination and evaluation of incidents. The purpose is to document what happened in a given situation in order to identify and clarify suspicions of financial crime or other kinds of misconduct. Examiners base their research on documents, interviews, and other available sources. The investigation may be conducted by internal experts in the business being reviewed, or by external investigators in roles such as auditors, lawyers, or detectives. Upon investigation it is important to answer the question what has happened or not happened.

The purpose of an investigation is to obtain accurate and reliable information to arrive at the truth or close to the truth about the conditions and events in question. Truth means conformity or compliance with reality. An investigation involves reconstructing an event or chain of events.

Investigation is about obtaining the most reliable, accurate, and relevant information so that the client can make good or even optimal decisions. Investigators will not solve the issue; the entity hiring investigators has to handle the issue after receipt and presentation of the examination report. What investigators think or believe in the case is not important. It is what can be stated and documented that counts. This is completely analogous to police investigators, who hand over to prosecutors and other actors in the judicial process to follow up on evidence and discoveries that have been made.

Investigators are to find out about a situation or an event that is or has been done. There may be a situation domestically or abroad. Investigators are to be independent and not be involved in the relevant event or chain of events. A neutral party who has no connection to negative incidents should conduct the investigation. Professional investigation is characterized by prudence, caution, and due process.

The work of fraud examiners is typically called private investigations, but to examine can also be to scan, to scrutinize, to assess, to review, to monitor, to audit, or to verify. Thus, several words are treated as synonyms in this book, such as *examination*, *investigation*, *assessment*, *review*, *audit*, *study*, *verification*, *evaluation*, *inquiry*, *monitor*, and *scan*. For example, *scrutinize* means to review in detail.

The task for examiners is dependent on the situation and the client. Examples include:

- Clarification of the actual course of events: What was it that actually happened?
- Evaluation and detection of system failure: How has it happened?
- Location of liability and assessment of individuals' behavior: Who did what?
- Help to prevent similar cases from happening in the future: How can such incidents be prevented in the future?

Professional investigations are scientifically based, which means that hypotheses are developed and tested by means of collected evidence, and the procedure is transparent, so that others will arrive at the same conclusion given the same assumptions. The term *examination* does not have a clear legal content, and various forms of private investigations with different objectives are referred to as inquiries. It is very often the professional examiner who has to decide what should be acceptable procedures for an examination.

Need for Investigation

Recent years have seen an increasing use of investigation in terms of the assessment of financial irregularities. This inquiry form—which primarily takes place in public and private companies—aims to uncover failing internal controls and any financial irregularities such as corruption, embezzlement, tax evasion, and other forms of economic crime. Such investigations are sometimes conducted as part of the ordinary or extraordinary audit, or as separate studies conducted by private law firms, accounting firms, consulting firms, or other kinds of professional service firms. The investigation examines internal affairs of a business or relationships between entities. The results of an investigation are presented in an examination report. An examination report's purpose is to help shed light and insight into a complex matter, which is controversial in some ways.

Most businesses experience from time to time incidents and negative events. Normally such incidents are handled by internally checking what might have happened, then trying to establish the facts, before measures are taken to correct the situation. In some cases, however, organizations find that there is a need to hire third parties to carry out inquiries, for example, because special expertise is required or complete independence has to be secured. The client gets in contact with external resources that are known and recommended. A mandate for the examination is developed, which describes what events the client wants to get examined, what questions the client wants to get answered, what reviews the client wants to be made, and what hypotheses the client wants to get tested. The mandate defines a time limit applicable to the conduct of the mission. In addition, a budget is agreed upon between client and examiner, especially when there is an external fraud examiner hired by a client organization.

Private investigations are often undertaken as part of an adaptation of a subject matter that is unclear, controversial, and emotional. The investigation is to contribute to the clarification by identifying facts, events, incidents, and causes. The investigation should not take a position on the offense. Investigators should not judge the actions in a criminal law perspective. That is up to courts in society to decide. Investigators, however, can judge the actions reprehensible, that they are violations of rules or procedures, and that they are ethically unacceptable.

Generally, fraud examinations are used to improve corporate governance, provide decision support for the board and management, meet the need for knowledge and understanding of misconduct and deviant behaviors, and become proactive rather than reactive. However, an investigation can also be triggered by the need to calm the situation, to keep something hidden, to ensure credibility, and possibly to achieve later sentence reduction.

Examination Characteristics

The purpose of private investigations is to clarify facts, analyze events, identify reasons for incidents, evaluate whether there is a systems failure, and if required, propose measures and consider the responsibility of individuals. In fraud examinations, the focus of examiners is on potential financial crime. One or multiple examiners are appointed to collect and go through an often large stack of documentation. The reason for an investigation is often suspicions that form the basis for hypotheses of fraud. Hypotheses typically imply that business owners, directors, managers, or employees are responsible for unacceptable circumstances. To clarify the situation, an extraordinary examination is often a suitable solution.

Not everyone who is studying or examining something is in the business of investigations. Investigation is characterized by the fact that it is an extraordinary measure, where people other than the usual staff will investigate suspicions of misconduct and crime. Investigation is a form of inquiry that government agencies and private legal entities implement in extraordinary situations. An independent investigation team is often appointed, unlike existing commissions, committees, departments, and project groups within the organization. Therefore, private and public units that are in the business of private investigations on a full-time basis within their own entities do not really count as fraud examiners in this context. Only when there is an extraordinary task in the form of a mission, to be performed by and with external experts, which are inserted into and engaged in one errand to clarify internal circumstances, can we talk about an investigation.

In line with this definition, bankruptcy lawyers and auditors are not private investigators. There is a trustee common task to check all matters, including fraud and financial crime, which may have harmed remaining assets in the bankrupt enterprise. A trustee can conduct special kinds of inspections and additional inspections, but we still do not include these inquiries as fraud examinations, since the tasks are common in the role of trustee. Upon bankruptcy a trustee is appointed, also in all cases where basically no suspicions about financial crime exist. Included in the trustee standard tasks is the pursuit of economic crime. Investigation, on the other hand, is characterized by being something unusual and extraordinary, as a special and limited mission, which normally never occurs or takes place in the organization. Fraud examiners are an unusual sight in an organization, creating all kinds of conspiracy theories of what might be going on. For business bankruptcies of a certain magnitude, inquiries into possible misconduct and crime always take place.

Work procedures and information retrieval in private investigations are very similar to bankruptcy inquiries by trustees. At the core of every investigation the job is to collect, verify, and analyze information, including documents, computer files, and interviews. The purpose is to find facts about incidents and possible causes, to check if there has been systems failure, and to evaluate whether wrongdoing by individuals has occurred. While a private investigator is paid by the client, a trustee is paid by remaining assets in the bankrupt enterprise.

Investigation may be a mere examination of facts or inquiry into possible unacceptable circumstances by looking at causal relationships, which may have led to the facts. Misconduct can represent violation of the law, and thus criminal offenses, or it may be violation of ethical rules or other internal guidelines. Investigation may focus on the identification of irregularities committed by individuals, or investigation may focus on the identification of systems failures in organizations.

While police investigators complete their work when suspects are prosecuted in court, private investigators are in the business of providing advice for crime prevention in the future. Clients would like to know how similar negative incidents and events can be avoided in the future. Crime prevention can be defined as any intervention intended to block or reduce the likelihood of the occurrence of a criminal act at a given location or the onset of criminal behavior within an individual. To prevent means to keep something from happening or existing. Crime prevention is any action designed to reduce the actual level or crime. It is an intervention in mechanisms that cause criminal events, in a way that seeks to reduce the probability of an occurrence. Crime prevention is the anticipation, recognition, and appraisal of a crime risk and the initiative of some action to remove it.

Private investigations are often undertaken as part of a preparation of a subject matter that may be controversial and emotional. An organization can, for example, be experiencing internal conflicts with accusations between internal actors, which makes it desirable that persons from outside, unrelated to the subject matter, do investigate the matter. If board members of senior executives are part of the conflict, it is indeed appropriate to ask outside experts to look into the case.

Fraud examination is a term typically used when the investigation team shall clarify the facts and causes of an event, or a series of events that are studied together. Second, it is used when the investigation team shall make a judgment as to whether or not facts point in a direction of guilt or innocence by persons or institutions. It is a judgment, not a verdict, which is to be produced by fraud examiners. Third, the investigation team shall make statements about the need for systemic changes in terms of regulations, controls, routines, and organizational structure.

A fourth characteristic that is often present in private investigations is that the examiner or examination team or committee is independent. The mandate from the client defines the mission of importance in terms of what should be investigated. The client defines what is to be investigated, while examiners have the freedom to define how it is to be investigated. Procedure and method selection ensures independence, and thus the credibility of examination conclusions. The client decides who should investigate and what must be investigated. The client does not decide how it should be investigated. Examiners cannot be instructed by the client during investigation, in terms of either procedure, premises, or conclusions. But of course, the client may set certain limits and some restrictions for examiners.

The main tool for the client is to define an investigation mandate for examiners. The mandate tells examiners what to do and who should do it. In the mandate, the client has the freedom to define a perspective, to limit investigation to certain parts of the organization, and to define the scope in general. Furthermore, the client effectively defines the scope by offering a financial budget. If there is little money, then the investigation will be very limited. If there is sufficient funding, then the investigation can become comprehensive.

If the examiner disagrees with the mandate, there is the choice of negotiating the contents of the mandate or withdrawing from the assignment. An examiner has to protect his or her own reputation by avoiding examination projects where the client orders and pays for a certain conclusion. It is not a good idea for a professional examiner to blame the mandate or the client when a private investigation results in nothing or in a limited or misleading conclusion.

If the client disagrees with investigators' approach, the client may neither instruct nor stop investigators in their work. However, the client may terminate the contract, if there is a contractual reason for terminating the assignment.

Examiners have an independent position in relation to the client as principal and the principal's command authority. Independence is also needed in relation to all parties involved in the investigation. If there is a lawyer who conducts the investigation, it is important that the client understands that the investigation does not form part of any lawyer's ongoing legal quest for the client. Thus, the regular attorney-client privilege does not apply. The privilege ensures that a client may provide information to his or her attorney, in confidence, with the knowledge that such information is protected, and neither the client nor the attorney may be forced to disclose the information that has been shared to his or her judicial adversaries (Kopon and Sungaila, 2012). Since the lawyer acts as an examiner, and not as an attorney, the attorney-client privilege is not present in private investigations. The same applies to an auditor who undertakes an investigation mission.

A lawyer is a person doing legal work for clients. However, a lawyer is a knowledge worker, who combines legal insights with client problems to find a good or even optimal solution to problems (Gottschalk, 2014). Therefore, some lawyers take the role of fraud examiner as well.

One of the tasks of internal auditors is to conduct reviews and inspections. For them, an investigation is an independent and extraordinary inquiry that aims to identify the facts in order to answer a defined and limited mandate. The investigation may include recommendations and will form the basis for judgments and decisions. An investigation into suspicions of fraud is also a comparison of the facts with the legal framework.

So far, we have discussed four characteristics of private investigations. A fifth characteristic is that the investigation is completed when examiners hand over their report to the client. The report is, legally speaking, an expression of opinion and is no decision that changes the legal positions for persons or institutions.

A sixth characteristic is that entities other than the examination group are responsible for monitoring and following up the investigation report.

Issues of systems changes or reporting to the police are normally handled by the client, not the investigators.

There are several more characteristics or features of private investigations:

- *Justifiability.* A private investigator must act within the framework of general requirements of soundness. The way an investigation is conducted needs to be justifiable and acceptable. For example, all involved parties have to be given access to relevant information in order to safeguard their interests. Moreover, similar cases are treated alike.
- *Care.* Unlike the police investigation, the private fraud examiner must be careful in exercising discretion and in drawing conclusions. This is particularly true in relation to issues concerning responsibility and guilt. The private investigator's main objective is to identify facts and subject matters through descriptions and reviews. The investigator will not normally consider criminal liability.
- *Rule of law.* The rule of law means that citizens should have security for their rights. The rule of law applies with regard to the content of decisions made (formal rule of law) as well as to the actual process that takes place before and after decisions are made (procedural rule of law). The rule of law includes the right to privacy, requirement for a fair trial, presumption of innocence, and protection against self-incrimination.

In comparison to police investigations of financial crime, fraud examiners often face a greater extent of multitude of accusations, assumptions and theories. Private investigations are mutually very different. Therefore, a contingent approach to examination is needed, where the situation determines what measures and means are appropriate for examiners. A diagnostic assessment of the situation determines the contingent approach to inquiry. Situational investigation is about selecting relevant methods and procedures that are appropriate for the situation.

Sometimes investigations are carried out in combination with other activities. There might be an element of investigation in other missions, such as business checks (due diligence), alert signal handling (whistle-blowing), and in cases where fact finding is included.

Examples of situational investigations include:

- Provision of documentation and discussion of the existence of possible misconduct at the senior level, based on criticism of top management
- Implementation of company procedures or management control where there may be an element of fraud examination
- Investigation of cases received through whistle-blowing channels or other matters that require collecting facts or factual statements

- Clarification of whether there is a rule violation
- Development of measures to help prevent similar adverse conditions in the future

Investigation is characterized by professions such as accountants, lawyers, economists, former police detectives, and engineers conducting research. The typical investigation commission in Norway has a budget of US$200,000. Some investigation missions are small and performed for US$20,000 or 30,000. The investigation of Statoil-Hydro in 2007 had fraud examination costs of US$30 million, the investigation of Yara in 2011 had costs of US$10 million, while the investigation of Troms Kraft in 2013 had costs of US$6 million. Chairman Inge K. Hansen in Troms Kraft refused to pay an additional bill of US$2 million from fraud examiner Leiv Nergaard, as the agreed limit was US$6 million (Grande, 2013).

A skilled investigator can be characterized by credibility and respect. The investigator conducts interviews in a good way for getting the most relevant information. The investigator can assemble facts and see the whole picture. The investigator can find reasons why the incident occurred. The investigator thus develops knowledge of what happened (know-what), knowledge of how it happened (know-how), and knowledge of why it happened (know-why). The investigator must also be willing and able to understand others' arguments, perspectives, and legal positions.

Independence for the examiner is not just an issue in relation to the client and people who get in touch with the investigation. For example, a lawyer in a law firm cannot take on a fraud examination assignment if another lawyer in the same firm already has other roles in relation to the client or people who get in touch with the investigation. A colleague in the law firm may already have taken the role as advisor and defense attorney for one of the executives who are suspected of misconduct and possible white-collar crime. Is the CEO suspected of misconduct and an attorney in a law firm has agreed to take the case? If so, then another lawyer in the same firm cannot undertake to investigate fraud, where the CEO might have been involved. When a lawyer undertakes to defend a white-collar person for suspected economic crime, then the attorney is sometimes called a white-collar crime lawyer. Role mixture must not only be avoided in law firms. The same applies to other professional service firms, such as audit firms and consultancies (Gottschalk, 2014).

Police Investigations

Private investigation may be limited public investigation, since the police have a monopoly on investigating crime that violates laws in society. Criminal law says that an investigation is to be initiated and carried out by the police. The term *police* refers to public authority, where the police have the authority to use physical force against citizens. Officials in the police force have the authority to decide that an investigation is to be undertaken, and police officers are leading and carrying out the investigation. The term *investigation* refers mainly to the purpose of determining whether there has been a criminal offense and clarifying the terms of punishment available.

Private investigators are not police officers, and they have to take into account that the police have priority, and that police work should not be hindered but supported. Private examiners can come in and prevent undesirable and unwanted events, and assist businesses that do not know whether a crime has occurred before they report it to the police.

The police are sometimes worried that private investigators can ruin a public investigation in that evidence will be destroyed, explanations coordinated, and witnesses exhausted before police officers start their work. The criminal procedure act can be a barrier for private investigation assignments.

There are three main differences between private and public investigations. One difference is that coercion may be used in police investigations. Another difference is that the conclusion of a police investigation has legal effects in the form of dismissal, preparation of witnesses, or indictment. A third difference is that while police investigations are regulated by criminal procedure acts, police acts, and other laws and regulations, private investigations are not officially regulated at all. Thus, while the police have more powers, they also have rules and regulations to follow in their investigations.

If the police initiate an investigation, there is a reason to be cautious in private examination simultaneously. When the police investigate, the distinct investigative steps are determined by the provisions of the criminal law and prosecution. This legislation gives prosecutors and police authority to use coercive measures in investigation work. The rules also entail restrictions on the right to apply coercive measures in police work, so that the legal rights of the suspects are protected. The person being investigated has, regardless of the status of the case, certain rights. For example, someone who has been arrested by the police and will not be released within 24 hours is entitled to appoint a defense counsel at public expense according to the criminal procedure act.

Coercive measures are, for example, arrest, seizure, and communication control. Here the police are a power organ in the community, which does not rely on the voluntary participation of suspects. Other public authorities also have special powers. For example, tax authorities can seek a place and order cooperation. Businesses have an obligation of participation.

A civil, nonjudicial investigation by an auditor, an attorney, or a consultant in other areas of expertise is not regulated as police work is. Civilian investigators do not have access to the use of the same coercive means and methods that the police have. Some aspects of a private investigation and the consequences of investigation are of such a nature that certain principles of investigation should be followed, for example, that a person is innocent until proven guilty, and that an examiner will at least work as much to prove innocence as to prove guilt.

Some have called for laws and regulations for private investigation. We return to this topic later in the book. Private investigations are of concern as long as there are no formal accountability structures for their work. Private investigations are also of concern because they involve privatization of police work and police investigations into possible criminal actions. We do not want a private police force in society next to the public police force.

However, it can be argued that private investigations have a number of other purposes besides possible criminal offenses. A private investigation is usually undertaken to study a subject matter that may be controversial and emotional. A properly conducted investigation may give an organization greater insight into a subject matter that is often complex and controversial in some form or another. In addition, an investigation can help identify improvements in the organization, such as adjustments of internal practices, procedures, and organizational structure. For example, the opportunity structure for chief executives and board members to commit financial crime can be improved, so that they have less opportunity to commit white-collar crime.

A private investigation may seem less threatening and less dangerous for the company to implement, and could be seen as positive by the environment and stakeholders. Being under investigation by the police, however, has an unfortunate symbolic effect for the organization, which may affect the company's reputation.

A private examination should never be a substitute for police work, but a supplement. Private investigators can provide useful assistance in areas that are not included as part of the police investigation. In addition, examiners can give aggrieved persons useful aid when meeting resourceful counterparts, a task that only to very little extent is addressed by the police.

Still, the question remains whether private investigations represent a privatization of a public task. It may be argued that private investigations often have a broader mandate and a different mandate than police investigations. Fraud examiners often have a mandate that goes far beyond that of considering possible violations of laws. It may further be argued that private investigators never perform a complete analysis and evaluation of whether criminal and imprisonment offenses are committed.

An examiner's collection of information is based on the consent of those who are in possession of the information. Private investigators can neither compel someone to explain and make a statement, nor obtain documents against someone's will. An examiner must act within the framework of the general requirement of soundness. Unlike police detectives, private examiners must be careful by exercising discretion and by drawing substantiated conclusions. This is particularly true in relation to issues concerning responsibility and guilt.

An examiner's main objective is to identify facts and subject matters through descriptions and reviews. A police officer's main objective is to evaluate whether someone has broken the law. An examiner's main contribution is often organizational and managerial improvements in the client organization. A police officer's main contribution is often either to get a case dismissed and release suspected individuals or to get a case prosecuted in court and to convince the judge to sentence the white-collar criminal to prison.

Police investigations are described in penal codes of criminal law, which says something about what the purpose is of an investigation. The purpose of an investigation is to obtain information necessary to decide the question of prosecution, to serve as preparation for the court's handling of the question of guilt, to potentially suggest the reaction such as imprisonment, and to prevent and stop crime. If a particular person is suspected, the investigation will seek to clarify both facts in favor of innocence and facts in favor of guilt. The investigation shall be completed as quickly as possible and so that nobody is unnecessarily exposed to suspicion or disadvantage. The fact finding that the investigation involves shall be accomplished within the legal framework. The focus of a police investigation is to determine whether a criminal offense has been or is being committed, which represents a violation of the law.

In the United States, police investigators specializing in financial crime on a national level are sometimes called FBI special agents. The Federal Bureau of Investigation has special agents responsible for conducting investigations into white-collar crime. To become an FBI special agent, one has to be between 23 and 37 years of age and possess a 4-year degree from a college or university. *Special agent* is usually the title for a detective or investigator who conducts criminal investigations and has arrest authority. An agent, on the other hand, is a federal law enforcement officer with arrest authority, but who does not conduct criminal investigations or who may conduct investigations but does not have arrest authority. Special agents are distinctively able to do both.

The FBI has defined the following areas for investigations into white-collar crime: antitrust, bankruptcy fraud, corporate fraud, financial institution fraud and failures, health care fraud, insurance fraud, mass marketing fraud, money laundering, mortgage fraud, piracy and intellectual property theft, securities and commodities fraud, and more white-collar frauds.

Investigation Science

Detection and investigation of economic crime in the private and public sector is much about using law enforcement thinking at work. Investigative thinking styles among police detectives are based on police science. Police science has neither nationally nor internationally found its shape, but as a science discipline, police science has established itself through a series of theoretical and empirical studies in recent years. It is an occupational science that is developing (Jaschke et al., 2007), where especially German police researchers' Polizeiwissenschaft is in the driver's seat (Kersten and Burchard, 2013). Police science is located at the intersection of police development as a profession and basic disciplines such as law, criminology, sociology, political science, economics, business, and organization.

Police work against economic crime and police investigation of white-collar crime have the value shop as its dominant value configuration. The value shop creation logic is problem solving by the change from an existing to a more desired state. The following phases are repeated in the value shop:

- Problem finding and acquisition: Activities associated with the recording, reviewing, and formulating of the problem to be solved and choosing the overall approach to solving the problem.
- Problem solving: Activities associated with generating and evaluating alternative solutions.
- Choice: Activities associated with choosing among alternative problem solutions.
- Execution: Activities associated with communicating, organizing, and implementing the chosen solution.
- Control and evaluation: Activities associated with measuring and evaluating to what extent implementation has solved the initial statement.

Value creation logic determines priorities and resource allocation. The value that might be created by working on and solving a problem determines how each problem is perceived and understood. A value organization makes strategic decisions about the role of the organization as it relates to the specter of problems with which is confronted. Performance goals are important at this stage, where goal setting is part of the strategy process, while goal achievement is part of the management process.

The same value creation logic applies to fraud examinations. It is the iterative rather than the sequential that characterize inquiries. Generally, private investigation science or science of private investigations is a new occupational discipline founded on the same basic disciplines mentioned above for police work. In addition, private investigations are located at the intersection of a number of occupational disciplines such as auditing, finance, law, and management. Fraud examination is a specialist field, a science, and a distinct craft.

Objectives of investigation science are to develop the knowledge that investigators need to perform their mission. Investigation science tries to explain phenomena and develop knowledge about examination reality so that an examiner's methods and results can be subject to constant improvements. At the same time, investigation science should contribute to critical reflection on an examiner's role and activities in the community.

Investigation science involves an analytical, knowledge-based, and problem-oriented approach to investigation work. Investigation science is research-based knowledge of an examiner's work procedures and challenges in society. Both empirical studies and theoretical perspectives are needed to strengthen the research-based knowledge. Knowledge-driven investigation involves systematic and methodical gathering of relevant information and knowledge that is analyzed with the purpose to make informed strategic and operational decisions about conclusions and possible actions that the client may choose to take.

Given all synonyms applied in this book, investigation science might as well be labeled examination science, assessment science, review science, audit science, verification science, evaluation science, inquiry science, monitoring science, and scanning science. In combination, terms such as *fraud investigation*, *forensic investigation*, *corruption inquiry*, and *financial crime inquiry* are all expressions for basically the same kind of work.

There are many challenges associated with private investigations: no rules in this area, no clear parties in a case, unclear who will be affected, overly complex framework, and the combination of inquisition and judgment. It is the same examiners who detect and provide evidence, evaluate the evidence, and finally produce criticism of individuals. Thus, they seem to represent the sum of investigating detective, indictment writing prosecutor, and evidence-based judge. Criticism can appear arbitrary, and that it is difficult to defend against.

Given all the challenges in practice, private investigation science is a much needed field of research to supply knowledge to fraud examiners.

Internal or External Investigation

There are both internal and external fraud examiners. Especially in large multinational corporations, they will have a compliance department that moves into business areas in the corporation where there is suspicion of financial crime. The department may be labeled compliance, internal audit, internal control, or some other name.

If a business wants to examine facts, causes, and responsibilities for an event, it is normally free to determine how the investigation will be conducted. If external examiners are hired for the job, it may be justified by lack of internal competence, lack of internal resources, or lack of internal independence to investigate the case.

But if internal resources are available and competent, then examination in the company can be handled internally. Internal experts implement investigations to establish what happened, how it happened, who did what, and why it happened. This is called internal investigation.

Investigation in a business can also be carried out by external experts. They may come from professional service firms such as law firms, auditing firms, or consultants specializing in fraud examinations. A combination of internal and external experts is also possible.

In comparison to external examiners, internal examiners have the advantage that they have a thorough knowledge of the major areas of business. Based on their local knowledge, they can adapt the perspective and scope of an investigation based on the type of cause, severity, and who is involved. A disadvantage to external examiners may be that an internal examiner does not have a large enough number of cases to develop and maintain professional investigation practices.

Dervan (2012) stresses the importance of determining who will conduct the inquiry. Several options exist, including utilizing corporate human resources, internal compliance officers, in-house auditors, or outside examiners. Outside examiners can make investigative findings more credible, while at the same time potentially more expensive and less relevant.

Internal versus external assessment can be a matter of cost, if the enterprise has sufficient expertise among its staff and the relevant internal candidates have the necessary confidence, trust, and independence. It can also be a matter of disclosure. Although external examiners can work confidentially for the enterprise, it is probably safer with internal examiners, if the enterprise does not want the public to learn about the case. Fraud examinations become public in retrospect in those cases where police investigation and prosecution occur. Fraud examinations tend to become public when a government agency hires an external examination team, because journalists and also the public have a right to know based on transparency in the public sector.

The private investigation industry is growing. The number of private fraud examiners is rising, as these experts enjoy a substantial market for compliance services, investigation services, and detective work.

Examiners, Officers, Journalists

It is interesting to compare private fraud examiners, investigating police officers, and inquiring journalists. Investigative journalism is a form of journalism in which reporters deeply investigate a single topic of interest, such as serious crime incidents, political corruption, or corporate wrongdoing. An investigative journalist may spend months or years researching and preparing a report. Investigative journalism is a primary source of information. Most investigative journalism is conducted by newspapers, wire services, and freelance journalists. Sometimes this kind of journalism is labeled watchdog journalism or accountability reporting.

Journalists conduct background digging on their own initiative based on tips and own suspicion of a hidden and sensational misconduct. An investigative reporter may make use of one or more of these tools, among others, on a single story:

- Analysis of documents, such as lawsuits and other legal documents, tax records, government reports, regulatory reports, and corporate financial filings
- Databases of public records
- Investigation of technical issues, including scrutiny of government and business practices and their effects
- Research into social and legal issues
- Subscription research sources such as LexisNexis
- Numerous interviews with on-the-record sources as well as, in some instances, interviews with anonymous sources

Investigation as a concept can be defined either in its own right or as different from anything else. Here an *investigation* is defined as a concept or an activity both similar to and different from police investigations and investigative journalism.

Counselors are engaged in misconduct examinations, while police officers are involved in criminal investigations, and journalists are in the business of digging. This book is about fraud examination by private investigators, but both police criminal investigations and investigative journalism are discussed, because there are both similarities and differences between the three tasks.

Counselors in law firms, accounting firms, and consulting firms conduct examinations on behalf of private and public enterprises based on the principal's suspicion of misconduct. Counselors can be lawyers, accountants, economists, social scientists, and others in the consultant role. Complementary expertise in the investigation is law, economics, finance, accounting, psychology, social sciences, project management, organization, information technology, and forensic science.

Police officers in economic crime, environmental teams, and other aspects of the police conduct investigations on their own initiative based on police reports and reviews of suspected crime.

Fraud examination is in many ways the opposite of police investigation. An examination takes place in silence, the public does not know about it, no procedures must be followed, and a secret report is handed over to the client without the right of suspected individuals to see it. A police investigation, on the other side, is regulated, followed by a public trial in court, and the parties are heard in public.

Differences and similarities between the work of examining consultants, investigating officers, and digging journalists are important in this book, because private investigators can learn from both the police and the media in being professional detectives. A comparison between the three occupational groups is shown in Table 5.1. The table is divided into themes of initiation of inquiry, process of work, and result of inquiry for the three occupational groups.

Table 5.1 shows that the goal of fraud examiners is that the client is satisfied with respect to achieving an accurate as possible facts description based on the client's mandate for the investigation. The goal of police investigators is to find the truth, so that all pieces of the puzzle are identified and placed in position, the puzzle is thus solved, and the objective truth is found, so that the issue of innocence or guilt can be determined. The goal of watchdog journalists is to reflect community needs to know what kind of sensational misconduct events happen in society, and present these stories in a way that is part of edutainment.

According to the criminal procedure act, the purpose of police investigation is to obtain the information necessary to decide the question of prosecution, to serve as preparation for the court's treatment of the question of guilt and any question of determining the reaction, as well as to prevent or stop criminal actions. If a particular person is suspected, then the investigation will seek to identify both what speaks against him and what speaks in favor of him. The investigation shall be completed as quickly as possible and so that nobody is exposed to unnecessary suspicion or disadvantage.

If a fraud examiner suspects criminal offenses, it should be reported to the police. But this is not the way it works. The fraud examiner only passes on the information to the principal, and it is up to the principal to decide whether to hand information over to the police. The report is the principal's property, since the fraud examiner was paid for it. But the fraud examiner can indeed recommend to the principal to report crime suspicions to the police. The police can initiate an investigation and impose fines on companies or bring charges against individuals, if they find sufficient evidence. The court will decide whether people should be punished. A settlement between the community and the defendant for breach of the penal provisions is to happen in the courts.

But this is not always. Often a privatization occurs of the legal settlement between the community and individuals who have committed criminal acts. Fraud examination can easily result in such privatization. For example, a chairman can make an agreement with the CEO that he or she should resign and commit oneself to repay the embezzlement amount. Without the police

Table 5.1 Comparison of Fraud Examiners, Police Officers, and Watchdog Journalists

	Examination Consulting	Investigation Policing	Infomining Journalism
Characteristics of Profession	Fraud examiners conduct private investigations. Investigations by auditors, detectives, lawyers, accountants, psychologists, and other professionals.	Police officers conduct police investigations. Investigations by police detectives, forensic scientists, police auditors and other police professionals.	Journalists conduct investigative inquiries. Digging and excavation organized by journalists from different professional media backgrounds.
Initial starting point for professional inquiry	Suspected reprehensible act in a business. Assignment from business in the form of a mandate. External examination against payment of principal. Legitimacy given by the client within applicable laws and regulations, such as the working environment act.	Suspected criminal offense based on police reports, reviews, tips, and own sources. Authority to initiate investigation provided in the criminal code, the criminal procedure act, the police act, and other laws and regulations.	Suspected sensational irregularities among famous people and organizations based on tips and whistle-blowing. Possible misuse of public funds, serious incident, fundamental and principal case, current trends, and consequences of possible crime. Investigative journalism at its own initiative.
Work process for professional inquiry	Resources depending on the client and the investigating unit. Sources of information on a voluntary basis. Use of methods unregulated and subject to examiner's competence and client's mandate, and depending on appropriate examination steps. Unregulated in relation to society, concerned persons, and involved persons. Iterative working by comparing information and returning to the mandate. Uncovering a particular fact by collection and presentation of facts. Can include assessments, both legal and business issues.	Resources depending on priorities of police management and senior investigating officer. Sources of information both voluntary (talking) and forced (documents). Use of methods regulated by laws and dependent on investigative steps. Regulated in criminal procedure in relation to prosecution and courts. Iterative working by the choice of new investigative steps. Search, collect, and secure evidence that substantiates the accused's guilt as well as innocence. Uncovering a particular fact by collection and presentation of information. Can include assessments, both legal and business issues.	Resources depending on editor's priorities. Focus on a sensational chain of events, famous people and organizations, sensational in scope, and conflict between actors. Sources of information on a voluntary basis. Use of methods regulated by the press; beware poster. The official media poster that is followed by all media says, a.o. that the simultaneous refutation right is important, and previous statements do not negate the requirement for concurrency. Iterative working through the use of sources. Considering tips and sources in established networks.

(continued)

Table 5.1 Comparison of Fraud Examiners, Police Officers, and Watchdog Journalists (continued)

	Examination Consulting	Investigation Policing	Infomining Journalism
Result of inquiring work	Investigation report to the principal. The goal is a complete picture of facts that are objective and according to mandate for the examination. Avoid media criticism of the investigation. Avoid complaints from suspects and others subject to inquiry.	Conclusion on the dismissal or prosecution based on evidence that proves either innocence or guilt. Avoid miscarriage of justice. Case information registered in police investigation and intelligence systems. Avoid media criticism of the investigation.	Publication of news and reports about the case. The goal is sensational media coverage and follow-up stories stimulated by new sources coming forward. Methods report on the journalistic investigative procedure. Avoid criticism by the press complaints commission.
Evidence claims during inquiry process	Normally, most likely the facts. It is a question whether there should be stricter standards of proof when examiner concludes by objective events description that laws are violated and criminal act has occurred, since there is no formal trial as part of the fraud examination.	Facts that are the basis for dismissal or criminal prosecution. Guilt must be proven beyond a reasonable doubt. Evidence for police investigation needs to be organized in such a way that it verbally can be presented in court by the prosecutor.	Unclear evidence requirements. Journalists are in search of the most probable facts, but with secret sources and circumstantial evidence, not all material is reliable. In newspaper articles, journalists may tend to indicate rather than verify what happened.
Citations in the inquiry process	Open sources (although confidential) must be verifiable. Information about individuals is protected by the personal data act.	Open as well as secret police intelligence sources. Information about individuals is not protected by the personal data act.	Open as well as secret media sources. Protection of sources is important. Can cause problems with verifiability of information.
Contraction from suspects	Complete contradiction before the examination report is given to the principal.	Complete contradiction during police investigation.	Not complete contradiction, but simultaneous refutation of information elements.
Self-incrimination in the inquiry process	Complete protection against disclosure of information that could reveal own offenses.	Complete protection. A suspect has no obligation to explain or give information to the police. A prosecuted has obligation to meet in court.	No protection but the press must show special consideration for people who are not expected to be aware of the impact of their statements. Sources of information must be protected from themselves.
Deadline for the inquiry	Often short deadline as defined in the mandate by the principal.	No time limit, but to be completed as quickly as possible and so that nobody is exposed to unnecessary suspicion or disadvantage.	No time limit, but often editor pressure to get story published.

involved, the CEO will neither be prosecuted nor eventually be sentenced to prison. Without the police involved, the chairman is in full control of crime handling. Without the police involved, public attention is avoided, which potentially could have damaged corporate reputation.

Privatization of criminal justice is not unusual. Criminal offenses are not reported to the police because organizations deal with such matters internally. In a survey by a Norwegian security advisory board, 40% of responding business enterprises agreed with the statement that crime is not reported because they process such matters internally. Fifty-seven percent disagreed with the statement, while 3% did not know.

Privatization of law enforcement is unfortunate and may have several causes. One reason is that the police dismiss many cases. Asked whether the offense is not reported because the police usually dismiss the case, 75% agreed with the statement, 22% disagreed, while 3% did not know. Another reason may be that the business does not want the negative publicity that a prosecution of a former chief executive typically will entail. The business has no pleasure or benefit from a former CEO going to jail. Rather, the business is mainly interested in getting rid of the person and getting money back from the person.

Although fraud examination by private investigators is not supposed to deal with the criminal law, many investigations do it anyway, because the cases are not reported to the police. Fraud examination conclusion thus represents a private judgment or verdict, which has consequences for the suspected executive or employee. If the examiner did a bad job, it can have consequences for innocent people.

In some cases, watchdog journalists, fraud examiners, as well as police investigators have all been involved. An example is Finance Credit in Norway, where the chairman Torgeir Stensrud was sentenced to imprisonment for 7 years, while the CEO Tron Kristoffersen received a sentence of 9 years imprisonment. It all started with a watchdog journalist who revealed problems in the firm. Later, fraud examiners from Ernst & Young were hired by banks who had suffered heavy losses from the collapse of Finance Credit. The examination report was handed over to the police, and the two executives were prosecuted and sentenced in court (Eidsivating, 2013). The sequence here was first media detection, then private inquiry, and finally public prosecution.

In the Spitsbergen case, it started with contract examination by PwC without any concrete suspicion of criminal offenses. Next, TV journalists started to investigate and found surprising circumstances. Then, PwC was hired a second time to do a fraud examination, which led the board to report findings to the police. The sequence here was first private inquiry, then media detection, then private inquiry again, and finally public prosecution. Spitsbergen CEO Robert Hermansen was sentenced to 2 years in prison. He was released from Tromsø prison in March 2013 (Østerbø, 2013).

The Spitsbergen case is an example of a serious corruption incident that led to prosecution and conviction, which probably never would have led to police investigation and later punishment without the private fraud examination by PwC. In such cases, private consulting and investigation may be labeled preliminary inquiries in advance of police work. There are several examples of such cases, where both journalists (such as Finance Credit) and examiners (such as Spitsbergen Coal Mining) provided useful preliminary studies as basis for police work.

Consulting, policing, and digging are different when it comes to closing of a case. Fraud examiners will end when the client is unwilling to pay for more, or when the private investigation is completed. Police detectives will end when the case is resolved in terms of prosecution or dismissal, or when lack of resources means that the case is dropped. A police officer said to a newspaper in Norway that it is demoralizing to be dropping cases every day (Sætran, 2014). Investigating journalists will end when they cannot find any more sensational revelations. Often, journalists will retain a small contingency should something new emerge in the case that has already been covered.

Far more cases are examined privately than those that become publicly known, because there are all kinds of reasons for keeping an investigation report a secret. Similarly, far more cases are investigated by the police than those that become publicly known, because many cases are stopped before the stage of public prosecution. Also, journalists only publish a small fraction of stories based on a vast number of tips and whistle-blowing cases.

While the government distinguishes between police investigation, public prosecutor's indictment, and judge's verdict in court, the distinction is not as clear by private examination and digging journalism. Both examiners and journalists may fall into the trap of adopting all three roles more or less simultaneously. It does occur that a fraud examiner becomes a detective, a prosecutor, as well as a judge in the same case. For example, the suspect may be forced to leave his position; because of the private investigation, he may perceive no other choice but to sign his own resignation.

Private examiners take on cases where there is a paying client. Police detectives take on cases where there is strong suspicion of a serious law violation, and where the police have sufficient resources to investigate the matter. Investigative journalists take on cases that can be published as sensational news to create more readers, listeners, and viewers.

Private examinations are civil in nature with the opportunity for consecutive police report and judicial perspective. Police investigations are governmental in nature with a judicial perspective. Media journalism is civil in nature without a judicial perspective. Private investigations may be preliminary to police investigations, where revelations of misconduct are documented by fraud examiners and followed up by police detectives.

Fraud examiners can have a value creation and value-added role in relation to the principal and client by making proposals for action on how misconduct and crime can be avoided in the future. Some fraud examinations may be consider investments, where the organization not only pays for finding out what happened, but also pays for improvements in future practice. For example, an organization is de-bureaucratized and thus reduces costs, and at the same time transparency improves, thereby reducing opportunities for financial crime. Then the examination has made a contribution of value, and a cost-benefit analysis may prove that benefits exceed costs. As an investment, fraud examination is a cost today leading to benefits tomorrow for the client.

Police detectives have no value creation or value-added role in a criminal investigation. They have to find out what happened, and whether someone committed a crime that should be prosecuted in court. The value of their work is found in general in society's appreciation of law enforcement. The value of their work is also found in general in crime prevention, if they are successful in improving detection rates, as high detection rates have an impact on crime deterrence. Crime prevention—the goal of deterrence—is based on the assumption that criminals or potential criminals will think carefully before committing a crime if the likelihood of getting caught and the fear of swift and severe punishment are present. According to Comey (2009), deterrence works best when punishment is swift and certain.

Similarly, investigative journalists have no value creation or value-added role in media coverage of financial crime. However, they serve their readers with news and shed light on negative events in the community. The value of their work can be found in transparency, where people in society are educated about what is going on. Journalists have an informative role by presenting suspicions and facts to the public. The value of their work is also to detect and reveal negative incidents, which may have a deterrent effect on potential criminals.

Fraud examiners can assess people's responsibilities, but they are not supposed to judge them. Police investigators can conclude on people's violations of criminal law, but it is up to the courts to judge. Journalists can point out possible liability, but they should not conclude on criminal behavior. Neither examiners nor journalists are supposed to consider criminal liability, as it is the sole responsibility of the government's law enforcement functions of police, prosecution, and court.

Fraud examiners can approach problems in breadth and depth, and they can evaluate policies and procedures in companies. They may focus as much on activities and actions as on actors and players. The police, however, are restricted to focus on possible offenses and potential offenders, because they are to investigate suspicions of crime. Journalists can point out incorrect procedures and rule, but will typically have a strong personal focus in their headlines. Thus, the police are the most focused in their work, while fraud examiners have a wide focus, and journalists have a focus depending on what they find sensational and publishable.

Investigators may be both generalists and specialists. Fraud examiners tend to be generalists who were trained as economists, lawyers, accountants, or auditors. They are generalists who have learned about financial crime by doing consulting work in client organizations. Some of them may be former detectives, who know the steps in criminal investigations, but most of them have learned it by doing it.

Police officers have a formal education in criminal investigations, and some are specialized in financial crime investigations. In national police units, police officers are even more specialists. While some are experts on corruption, others are experts on insider trading, embezzlement, and tax evasion.

Journalists are generalists in all kinds of news reporting. In larger media organizations such as major newspapers and TV stations, journalists are allowed to become specialized. Some cover domestic news, while others cover news from abroad. In news-making criminology, journalists interpret, influence, and shape the representation of newsworthy items about crime and justice. News-making criminology is about how the media construct images of crime (Barak, 2007). According to Burns and Orrick (2002), research suggests that the media present a distorted image of crime by focusing on violent, sensational events that are atypical of crime in society. They argue that the media are neglecting coverage of corporate offenses, and that the media disproportionately focus on conventional crime while neglecting the impact of corporate misbehavior. Similarly, Goldstraw-White (2012) warns that journalist research is often biased, aimed at producing a good story rather than a factual report, and tends to highlight particular types of offenders, such as those regarded as famous.

Selection of a fraud examiner is based on celebrity status and recommendation from others, in addition to any general association to a professional service firm. Selection of a police detective is often based on geography, since most police forces are organized along the geographical axis rather than the skills or knowledge axis. Selection of a journalist is often based on personal interest and specialization in the field.

Fraud examination tends to have positive status, because the principal demonstrates willingness to fight financial crime in his or her own organization. Initiating fraud examination sends a signal that misconduct and crime are not acceptable. It is perceived as positive, because the goal is not just to identify and possibly get rid of suspect(s), but also to improve organizational controls, routines, structure, and culture. It has a positive status for the organization that it will handle suspicions, and that it has taken whistle-blowing seriously. Initiating fraud investigation may improve corporate reputation.

Police investigation, on the other hand, tends to have a negative status for the organization and cause damage to business reputation. Wrongdoing in the organization is investigated by the government. Authorities are coming from the outside with their powers to identify potential criminals. The organization itself has no control over what police detectives do, what seizures they make, and what leaders and employees are questioned. The police may use coercive measures such as putting suspects in custody. Custody is a power symbol in police investigations. Police enforcement measures include seizure, arrest, and eventual detention, search warrants, compulsory attendance, interception of communications, and covert surveillance.

Similarly, newspaper articles and TV coverage are outside the control of the business. Sensational stories are published that cause obvious damage to business reputation. However, while police investigation may cause damage in the longer run, media stories tend to be quickly forgotten. But the sensational and disproportionate media presentation can hit very hard in the short run, making employees embarrassed and customers reluctant. So while the investigated business is suffering, the newspapers and TV stations enjoy positive status, because media represent the community that will challenge the power and expose abuses of power by ensuring people's conscience.

Neither examiners nor journalists have coercive measures such as the police's custody. Nevertheless, both have considerable power. Private investigators can—with support from the principal—drive suspects from pillar to post. They can get suspects fired or make them resign. Journalists can hang out people with or without good reason.

Despite clear differences between police detectives, fraud examiners, and investigative journalists, there can be offsets between these groups depending on the resource situations. If the number of investigating police officers goes down, while the number of private investigators goes up, then in practice more detective work will be carried out by private examiners. Where the police do not have the capacity to undertake cases, private experts will take the job, as long as somebody will pay for it. Where businesses choose not to go to the police with allegations of financial crime, but instead to a professional service firm, then fraud examiners will take the job.

The relative resource position between finance police and fraud examiners is further aggravated by the leakage of best talents from public sector to private sector. A professional police detective or a prosecutor can make twice the amount of money by joining a professional service firm.

Examination, investigation, and excavation are compared here. Actually, one could distinguish between two types of examination: private investigation and judicial investigation. Judicial investigation is triggered by a shareholder at the general meeting. The court appoints a private examiner. While private investigation results in an examination report handed over to the principal, judicial investigation results in an examination report handed over to the court. The court passes the report to shareholders. Therefore, a private investigation is followed up by the organization, while a judicial investigation is followed up by the owners.

Examination after bankruptcy is also a special type of private investigation. The bankruptcy lawyer should only investigate suspicions of financial crime to the extent that it might benefit creditors, as it is the creditors' funds that are spent doing the investigation. The trustee shall, accordingly, be careful not to spend time or money to investigate circumstances that no longer have particular relevance for the bankruptcy. The bankruptcy team will therefore focus on offenses involving violations that have caused the creditors losses, including having been the reason for bankruptcy. The team will also focus on conditions that may reveal monetary claims that the team can pursue to provide additional assets to meet creditors' losses. Typically, violations of laws concerned with working environment, data management, and internal control procedures are not a priority of the trustee unless it is relevant to the asset position for creditors.

Examiners, detectives, and journalists are all examples of knowledge workers who perform knowledge work based on a variety of knowledge categories, such as finance, accounting, psychology, sociology, technology, economics, law, and organization. The purpose of knowledge work does vary, but the result of this work is information as a foundation for knowledge and understanding. Knowledge is defined as information combined with interpretation, refection, and context. In various knowledge categories, knowledge workers may have levels of knowledge in terms of know-what, know-how, and know-why.

References

Barak, G. (2007). Doing news making criminology from within the academy. *Theoretical Criminology*, 11(2), 191–207.

Burns, R.G., and Orrick, L. (2002). Assessing newspaper coverage of corporate violence: The dance hall fire in Gotenborg. *Critical Criminology*, 11, 137–150.

Comey, J.B. (2009). Go directly to jail: White collar sentencing after the Sarbanes-Oxley Act. *Harvard Law Review*, 122, 1728–1749.

Dervan, L.E. (2012). International white collar crime and the globalization of internal investigations. *Fordham Urban Law Journal*, 39(361), 101–127.

Eidsivating. (2013). Case LE-2013-5379, Eidsivating lagmannsrett (Eidsivating Court of Appeals). Verdict dated January 14.

Goldstraw-White, J. (2012). *White-Collar Crime: Accounts of Offending Behaviour.* Palgrave Macmillan, London.

Gottschalk, P. (2014). *Financial Crime and Knowledge Workers—An Empirical Study of Defense Lawyers and White-Collar Criminals.* Palgrave Macmillan, New York.

Grande, A. (2013). Nekter å betale gransker (Declines to pay examiner). *Dagens Næringsliv* (daily Norwegian business newspaper), November 12, p. 5.

Jaschke, H.G., Bjørgo, T., Romero, F. del B., Kwanten, C., Mawby, R., and Pogan, M. (2007). *Perspectives of Police Science in Europe*, Final Report. European Police College, CEPOL, Collège Européen de Police, Hampshire, England.

Kersten, J., and Burchard, A. (2013). Police science in Germany: History and new perspectives. *European Journal of Policing Studies*, 1(1), 21–39.

Kopon, A., and Sungaila, M.C. (2012). The perils of oversharing: Can the attorney-client privilege be broadly waived by partially disclosing attorney communications during negotiations? *Defense Counsel Journal*, July, 265–277.

Østerbø, K. (2013). Fengselet ble ikke den leirskolen jeg hadde trodd (Prison did not become the camp site I had expected). *Aftenposten* (Norwegian national daily newspaper), March 16, p. 20.

Sætran, F. (2014). Politijurist: Demoraliserende å henlegge saker hver dag (Police lawyer: Demoralizing to drop cases every day). *Aftenposten* (Norwegian national daily newspaper), February 10, p. 9.

Information Management 6

Fraud examiners in white-collar crime investigations are in the business of collecting information. Information is transformed and analyzed according to a procedure to confirm or disconfirm assumptions. Information is collected and assessed concerning potential fraud. Investigation is about obtaining the most reliable, accurate, and relevant information so that the client can make effective decisions. Fraud examiners need an information management strategy to make sure their approach to information management is optimal. Information is the raw material in private investigations like it is in police investigations.

In policing, Zhao et al. (2008: 3) argue that strategic planning in crime detection and prevention represents a departure from traditional, reactive police work:

> Strategic planning in police departments represents a significant departure from a traditionally reactive orientation to one that is more proactive in nature.

In our context of private investigations, we apply the term *private policing* to capture similarities with law enforcement.

Information management strategy is one of several strategies that investigation units develop and implement to improve white-collar crime detection and prevention. Intelligence is an important element of the strategy. An information management strategy defines management approaches to the organization, control, and application of information resources through coordination of people and technology resources in order to support strategies and processes. While knowledge management strategy focuses on personnel resources, and information systems strategy focuses on technology resources, information management strategy focuses on the identification, retrieval, storage, and application of information resources. Important issues in this strategy are information relevance and timeliness (Chaffey and White, 2011).

Managed together, the three resources of information, personnel, and technology must support organizational strategy, which typically is concerned with safety and security in the client organization. For information strategy, Chaffey and White (2011) cite the following 10 strategic issues:

1. Information relevancy
2. Organizational significance of information management

3. Legal and ethical compliance
4. Assessing information value
5. Information quality
6. Legal and ethical compliance with specific reference to information life cycle management
7. Information management skills
8. Information security including risk management
9. Maximizing value from information
10. Information systems strategy

Information systems strategy is treated as a separate strategy area in Chapter 9 of this book. For information management strategy, distinctions can be made between information policy, information audit, and information strategy. Information policy is concerned with what should be, as it defines principles for how information is to be managed. Information audit is concerned with what is, as it provides an evaluation of current practice. Information strategy is concerned with the future for a defined period ahead, as it defines objectives, targets, and actions to achieve them (Chaffey and White, 2011).

Chaffey and White (2011: 185) list three main criteria for information quality with subcriteria as follows:

- Content dimension
  - Accuracy: Information correct.
  - Relevance: Information can support decision making.
  - Completeness: No data items missing.
  - Conciseness: Information is not too detailed.
  - Scope: May be broad or narrow, internal or external to the organization.
- Time dimension
  - Timeliness: Available when needed. Immediate or real-time information is a common requirement. Alerts are also a requirement.
  - Currency: Information is up to date.
  - Frequency: Information supplied at appropriate regular intervals.
  - Time period: A time series covers the right period of time.
- Form dimension
  - Clarity: Information readily interpreted.
  - Detail: Both summary dashboard views and detailed drill-down views may be required.
  - Order: Data sorted in a logical order and can be modified.
  - Presentation: Tabulations and graphs.
  - Media: Hard copy (printouts) and soft copy (electronically stored and displayed).

Private investigators need to understand, interpret, discern what is important/not so important, retrieve, identify, safeguard, report, and document their findings (Bressler, 2011). An investigative team should collate all the initial facts that have come to light (Coburn, 2006).

Criminal Intelligence

A key feature of the process of growth in local and global financial crime has been a steep increase in the complexity involved, brought about by, among other things, numerous innovative mechanisms and instruments that have repeatedly blurred the boundaries between financial sectors (Kattan et al., 2009: 353):

> Innovative financial products and practices have more often than not generated new linkages among financial agents in different financial sectors. For example, the past 12 years have witnessed a steady growth in cross-sectorial risk transfer between reinsurance and capital markets.

New and complicated interrelations among financial sectors have a wide variety of consequences. On the one hand, they may enable and promote efficiency and effectiveness in the allocation of resources, both locally and globally. On the other hand, new connections often bind agents with competing interests, with differing degrees of access to information as well as different insights regarding the content of a variety of transactions. Intelligence is needed—from both inside and outside the financial sector—to combat financial crime occurring in novel and complicated interrelations among financial sectors.

Strategic criminal intelligence analysis aims to weigh a variety of crime types against each other in order to base priorities on a calculus of social harm. According to Sheptycki (2007), this implies for the police that strategic analysis attempts to compare different types of criminal activity, including violence, drug distribution and consumption, intellectual property theft, car theft and burglary, smuggling of guns, child pornography, trafficking in humans, stock market fraud, and the avoidance of health and safety legislation in food production. Similarly, fraud examiners can weigh a variety of financial crime types, such as embezzlement, tax evasion, insider trading, Ponzi schemes, etc.

Chaffey and White (2011) distinguish between the following six information management themes:

1. *Information value* representing the importance. Information can be prioritized in importance and better-quality sources identified so that improved information is delivered. Information value can be

assessed in terms of its fitness for policing purpose. Once information has been identified as valuable, plans can then be put in place to protect it from deletion or modification, share it within a defined audience, and improve its quality. Lower-value information can be either improved to increase its relevance to investigators or removed from detailed reports to produce summaries.

2. *Information quality* in terms of content, time, and form. The content dimension is concerned with accuracy (information correct), relevance (information can support decision making), completeness (no data items missing), conciseness (information is not too detailed), and scope (may be broad or narrow, internal or external to the organization). The time dimension is concerned with timeliness (available when needed, immediate or real-time information is common requirement, alerts are also a requirement), currency (information is up to date), frequency (information supplied at appropriate regular intervals), and time period (a time series covers the right period of time). The form dimension is concerned with clarity (information readily interpreted), detail (both summary dashboard views and detailed drill-down views may be required), order (data sorted in a logical order and can be modified), presentation (tabulations and graphs), and media (hard copy from printouts, and soft copy electronically stored and displayed).
3. *Information security* to safeguard from accidental and deliberate modification or deletion by people and events. Information and the media on which it is held may be destroyed by security breaches. Information security refers to protection of information and the systems and hardware that use, store, and transmit that information. The key features of information security are availability (only to those eligible), confidentiality (only to those eligible), and authenticity and integrity (safeguarding accuracy of information).
4. *Legal and ethical compliance* to handle sensitivity. Information is held about individuals on computer systems. Governments have developed many laws both to protect individuals and to give government agencies access to information that may be needed for law enforcement.
5. *Information resource* for knowledge management. Investigations units are collections of individuals that possess knowledge. Information becomes knowledge when it is interpreted by individuals and put into context. Knowledge is information combined with reflection, interpretation, and context, where skills and opinions are added to make sense of new insights. Knowledge becomes information when it is codified and stored in information systems.
6. *Information requirement* to technology. Information is handled electronically by computer systems. Technology support to achieve the

objectives of the information management strategy involves selecting relevant information systems applications and infrastructure.

Furthermore, Chaffey and White (2011) distinguish between the following five information management approaches:

1. *Structuring the information management function.* The need for a separate organizational structure with a clearly defined information management remit provides a focus for improving information management that everyone in the fraud examination team is aware of. The creation of this unit demonstrates a commitment to information management since they have empowered the group with the resource and responsibility to improve information management.
2. *Responsibilities.* In addition to creation of distinct overall responsibility for information management as a whole, there is a need for governance, stewardship, infrastructure, and usage. Governance responsibility represents management actions for overall direction. Stewardship responsibility involves activities such as information capture or creation, dissemination, and deletion. Infrastructure responsibility is concerned with creating the right environment for using information. Usage responsibility includes assessing information for quality and highlighting problems with quality.
3. *Resource analysis* includes information audit and information mapping. The purpose of information audit is for the organizational information resource to identify actual and potential users of information, information quality requirements for these users, types of information available, where information is held, how information is used, and cost of information usage. The purpose of information mapping is to help detectives manage information as a resource by cataloging, understanding, organizing, and navigating within information sources.
4. *Information policy* highlights the importance of information management to staff and details personnel responsibilities. It is a brief statement of intent of how information should be managed and used within an organization.
5. *Risk management* is used to identify potential risks in a range of situations and then take actions to minimize the risks. Risk management typically has these four steps: (a) identify risks, including their probabilities and impacts, (b) identify possible solutions to these risks, (c) implement the solutions targeting the highest-impact, most likely risks, and (d) monitor the risks to learn for future risk assessment.

Distinct information management strategy is developed for detective work to help exploit and protect information assets. An information management strategy may include six themes and five approaches as presented above.

Strategy Characteristics

Traditionally, intelligence was understood to mean information from criminals about criminal activity by a covert source. Today, intelligence is a systematic approach to collecting information with the purpose of tracking and predicting crime to improve law enforcement (Brown et al., 2004). Intelligence analysts investigate who is committing crimes, how, when, where, and why. They then provide recommendations on how to stop or curb the offenses. As part of this, analysts produce profiles of crime problems and individual targets, and produce both strategic (overall, long-term) and tactical (specific, short-term) assessments within the confines set by the investigative unit.

The aim of intelligence strategy is to continue to develop intelligence-led investigations. An intelligence strategy provides a framework for a structured problem-solving and partnership-enhanced approach, based around a common model. For example, the National Intelligence Model in the UK police is a structured approach to improve intelligence-led policing both centrally and locally in policing districts such as the South Yorkshire Police (SYPIS, 2007).

Intelligence-led policing is carried out in many law enforcement areas. For example, intelligence-led vehicle crime reduction was carried out in the West Surrey police area in the UK. Analysis of vehicle crime included identifying the following (Brown et al., 2004):

- Locations (hot spots, streets, car parks, postcodes, wards, etc.) of vehicle crime
- Sites where vehicles were dumped
- Times of offenses
- Prolific vehicle crime offenders
- Areas where prolific offenders were identified as offending
- Models of vehicles targeted for vehicle crime
- Type of property stolen in theft from vehicle offenses

The analysis resulted in problem profiles, which identified emerging patterns of crime. These patterns included vehicle crime occurring in beauty spot car parks and the theft of badges from cars. Such information was disseminated to local officers to act upon.

Intelligence-led policing is defined as a business model and a management philosophy according to Ratcliffe (2008: 89):

> Intelligence-led policing is a business model and managerial philosophy where data analysis and crime intelligence are pivotal to an objective, decision-making framework that facilitates crime and problem reduction, disruption and prevention through both strategic management and effective enforcement strategies that target prolific and serious offenders.

Intelligence-led methodology is a business model and managerial philosophy, where intelligence and data analysis are coupled with forensics to support situational awareness for decision makers.

An interesting case of intelligence-led policing in the UK was the project called Operation Gallant that led to a reduction of 17% in car thefts. Operation Gallant involved all basic command units (BCUs) in the collection and analysis of information (Brown et al., 2004: 2):

> In the case of Operation Gallant, the intelligence-led vehicle crime reduction approach involved the activity of officers from across a BCU. A crime analyst, dedicated solely to examine vehicle crime patterns and trends, developed a detailed picture of vehicle crime in the area, including analysis of time, location, vehicle type and known offenders. As a result of this strategic analysis, a number of interventions were planned, drawing heavily upon the Operation Igneous tactical menu. The most significant, in terms of resources devoted to the operation, involved a program of prolific offender targeting and crime prevention advice targeted towards the owners of high-risk vehicles.

The substantial decline in car crimes was accounted for in terms of the increased attention paid to this crime sector (Brown et al., 2004: 16):

> Given the fact that the first reduction coincides with the commencement of the planning process for Operation Gallant, this may also reflect an anticipatory effect in which the very act of planning and talking about an operation leads to a decline.

Classification of Information Sources

In intelligence work pertaining to investigating and preventing white-collar crime, a variety of information sources are available. Sheptycki (2007) lists the following information sources in policing for general corporate social responsibility work: victim reports, witness reports, police reports, crime scene examinations, historical data held by police agencies (such as criminal records), prisoner debriefings, technical or human surveillance products, suspicious financial transactions reporting, and reports emanating from undercover police operations. Similarly, internal investigation units in business organizations can apply intelligence sources. Intelligence analysis may also refer to the governmental records of other governmental departments and agencies, and other, more open sources of information may also be used in elaborate intelligence assessment. Most of the information used to prevent and investigate financial crime is sensitive, complex, and the result of a time-consuming process (Wilhelmsen, 2009).

However, Sheptycki (2007) found that most crime analysis is organized around existing investigation and prevention sector data. Intelligence analysis is typically framed in terms of preexisting institutional ways of thinking. He argues that organized crime notification, classification, and measurement schemes tend to reify preexisting notions of traditional policing practice.

According to this perspective, it is important for strategic criminal analysts to be aware of the variety of information sources available. In this book we have chosen to classify information sources into the following categories:

1. *Interview.* By means of *meetings* with witnesses, suspects, reference persons, and experts, information is collected on suspicions, misconduct, potential crime, potential criminals, times and places, organizations, criminal projects, activities, roles, etc. Records and documents do not speak for themselves and are often created to mislead. Interviews can elicit facts and uncover relevant leads. Testimony may explain records and transactions, clarify relationships, identify leads, and establish organizational structures. There is a difference between interview and interrogation. In an interrogation, the investigator has a single objective: to learn if the suspect committed the crime or is responsible for another instance the investigator is seeking to prove or disprove. In an interview, particularly a financial crime interview, the investigator attempts to develop a rapport with the witness and looks for detailed answers to collect as much relevant and high-quality information as possible.
2. *Network.* By means of *informants* within as well as outside the examined organization, information is collected on actors, plans, competitors, markets, customers, etc. Informants often have connections with persons that an investigating fraud examiner would be unable to formally approach. Informants represent a source of leads and intelligence.
3. *Location.* By *visiting* and analyzing potential and actual crime scenes and potential criminal scenes, information is collected on criminal procedures, preferences, crime evolution, etc. Hot spots and traces are found. Secret ransacking of suspicious places is one aspect of this information source. Pictures, in terms of crime scene photographs, are important information elements. Evidence can be obtained by a well-drafted and properly executed search. The seizure may be financial information, videotapes, transaction records, or many other

things. For example, a suspect may have a second computer in his office, where fraud examiners may find information that was not on the network or on the official workstation.

4. *Documents.* Studying documents obtained voluntarily or through management *confiscation* may provide information on ownership, transactions, accounts, etc. One such example is forensic accounting, which is the application of accounting tasks for an evidentiary purpose. Forensic accounting is the action of identifying, recording, settling, extracting, sorting, reporting, and verifying past financial data or other accounting activities for settling current or prospective legal disputes, or using such past financial data to project future financial data in order to settle legal disputes (Curtis, 2008). Documents allow the investigator to follow money flows through bank accounts, brokerage companies, asset purchases, nominee owners, shell companies, and private individuals. The discovery of one document may trigger a domino effect in which one piece of evidence flows directly to another lead and evidence.
5. *Observation.* By means of *anonymous personal presence*, both individuals and activities can be observed. Both in the physical and the virtual world, observation is important in financial crime intelligence. An example is digital forensics, where successful cybercrime intelligence requires computer skills and modern systems in policing. Digital forensics is the art and science of applying computer science to aid the legal process. It amounts to more than the technological, systematic inspection of electronic systems and their contents for evidence or supportive evidence of a criminal act; digital forensics requires specialized expertise and tools when applied to intelligence in important areas such as the online victimization of children. But also manual observation of individuals at certain places, at certain times, meeting certain people, and acting in certain ways can represent useful information to fraud examiners.
6. *Action.* For example, *provocation* and actions conducted by the investigating unit to cause reactions that yield investigation information. Since much of white-collar crime is opportunity based, providing suspects with new opportunities can reveal their misconduct. A misleading insider tip, an incomplete invoice, a fake invitation, or some other means can be applied to provoke somebody to act or to restrain from action. In the police, provocation is used frequently in some areas of crime. For example, in online victimization of children, online grooming offenders in a pedophile ring are identified and their reaction to provocation leads intelligence officers to new nodes (persons, computers) and new actual and potential victims. While the individual pedophile is mainly concerned with combining indecent image impression

and personal fantasy to achieve personal satisfaction, online organizers of sexual abuse of children do so for profit. Police initiate contact with criminal business enterprises making money from pedophile customers by claiming online to be a child of 9 years, for example. Undercover operations by police officers also belong to the action category of information sources. Undercover operations are also possible in fraud examinations. For example, if suspicions of embezzlement or other kinds of financial crime exist, a person from the investigation team can be hired temporarily from a manpower firm by the client organization into a regular job.

7. *Surveillance.* Surveillance (visual and auditory) of places by means of *video cameras* and microphones belongs to this information source. Many business organizations have surveillance cameras on their premises to control entrants and also other critical areas. It is possible for investigators to listen in on discussions in a room without the participants knowing. For example, the police in a district identified the room used by local Hells Angels members for crime planning and installed listening devices in the room. Harfield (2008: 64) argues that when surveillance is employed to produce evidence, the product is often considered incontrovertible (hence defense lawyers' focus on process rather than product when cross-examining surveillance officers): "An essentially covert activity, by definition surveillance lacks transparency and is therefore vulnerable to abuse by over-zealous investigators."
8. *Communication control.* Wiretapping in terms of *interception* belongs to this information source. Police listen in on what is discussed on a telephone or transmitted via a data line without the participants being aware. In the UK, the interception of communications (telephone calls, emails, letters, etc.), while generating intelligence to identify more conventional evidential opportunities, is excluded from trial evidence by law—to the evident incredulity of foreign law enforcement colleagues (Harfield, 2008). Public sector law enforcement agents and some regulators may obtain court authorization for telephone wire interception, based on probable cause to intercept telephone conversations under tightly restricted conditions.
9. *Physical material.* This is the investigation of material in order to identify, for example, *fingerprints* on doors or bags, or material to investigate blood splatters and identify blood type. Another example is legal visitation; this is an approach to identify illegal material. DNA is emerging as an important information source, and is derived from physical material such as hair or saliva from a person. One approach to physical material collection is police search.

10. *Internet.* As an *open source*, the Internet is as important for general information and specific happenings to corporate crime intelligence as to everyone else. It is important to note that use of open sources is by no means a new activity, and nor is it a new phenomenon of the Internet, which is in itself not a source; rather, it is a tool used for finding sources. Also, there are risks of using open sources such as self-corroboration. Facebook, Twitter, Instagram, and other open applications on the Internet are valuable sources for information about individuals who are subject to investigation.
11. *Policing systems. Police records* are readily available in most police agencies. For example, DNA records may prove helpful when DNA material from new suspects is collected. Similarly, corporate social responsibility units may collate and develop records that do not violate privacy rights. Corporate social responsibility (CSR) is a set of voluntary corporate actions designed to improve corporate behavior. These corporate actions not required by law attempt to further some social good and extend beyond the explicit transactional interests of the firm. The voluntary nature of CSR means that these activities can be viewed as gifts or grants from the corporation to the society in terms of preventing and detecting fraud.
12. *Employees.* Information from the *local unit* is often supplied in the form of tips to examiners, using open or anonymous tip lines. Similarly, a corporate social responsibility unit can receive tips from employees in various departments.
13. *Accusations.* Victimized persons and critical individuals file a *claim* with the corporate investigation unit or the unit for corporate social responsibility. While seldom of objective nature, information elements in accusations can be valuable in fraud examinations. A starting point is sometimes a whistle-blower, who blames someone for something. A whistle-blower is a person who was or still is in the organization. According to Kaplan et al. (2011), employee tips are the most common form of initial fraud detection, suggesting that employees frequently are aware of fraud before others professionally charged to detect fraud, such as internal and external auditors.
14. *Exchange.* In fraud examinations of corporate crime such as corruption, *investigation cooperation* includes exchange of intelligence information between investigators inquiring about different businesses in different countries. Trade organizations and other entities for business organizations create exchanges for financial crime intelligence. Professional associations such as the Association of Fraud Examiners create a platform for networking that can be useful in general and also in specific assignments.

15. *News media.* Investigative journalists can make contributions to an ongoing fraud examination by contacting sources that are not as available to private investigators. Some information sources prefer to remain anonymous, and they may feel better protected by journalists than by examiners. For example, in a corruption case, someone may contact a journalist and tell that the CEO did indeed know about the corruption many years ago and not just learned about it recently after whistle-blowing occurred. The person as a source might feel uncomfortable telling examiners about his or her own boss. The secret source may, for example, have a picture of the CEO with Libyan dictator Muammar Gaddafi before the company was allowed to build an oil refinery and after bribing the Gaddafi family. Newspapers very much appreciate pictures as evidence of participation in misconduct and crime.
16. *Control authorities.* Cartel agencies, stock exchanges, tax authorities, and other control authorities are both collectors and *suppliers of information* to the community. Fraud examiners can easily obtain information about who is registered as chairman, who are the shareholders, financial statements for several years, and other general business and personnel matters.
17. *External data storage.* A number of business and government organizations store information that may prove useful in financial crime intelligence. For example, telecom firms store data about traffic, where both the sender and the recipient are registered with date and time of communication. Electronic information of some investigative value is stored on or transmitted by an electronic device, usually in digital form. Electronic evidence is fragile since it can be altered, damaged, or destroyed by improper handling or examination. Therefore, it is essential that special precautions are taken to collect, document, examine, and preserve electronic evidence (Newman, 2009).

White-collar criminals, who have already been sentenced in court, represent a special kind of information source. They may be released from prison or still be in prison. They may want to tell their version to fraud examiners. They may want to tell that more people were involved in the crime. Prisons and other correctional environments are potential places for several information sources and production of intelligence useful to law enforcement. The total prison environment, including the physical plant, the schedule regimens of both staff and inmates, and all points of ingress and egress, can be legitimately tapped for intelligence purposes in countries such as the United States (Maghan, 1994). Since organized criminals are often sophisticated in terms of using, or exploiting, the corrections environment to their advantage, police and correction personnel need to be immersed in the intelligence operations and strategies of their respective agencies. Legal visitation and escape attempts are sources of information. Prisoners are reluctant to testify, and their credibility is easily attacked. Communication control is derived from inmate use of phones, visits, mail, and other contacts.

All 17 information sources listed above have different characteristics. For example, information sources can be distinguished in terms of the extent of trustworthiness and accessibility. Some people may be easily accessible but not very trustworthy. Others may be trustworthy but difficult to access.

The 17 information sources can be classified into two main categories. The first category includes all person-oriented information sources, where the challenge in fraud examination is communication with individuals. The second category includes all media-oriented information sources, where the challenge in fraud examination is the management and use of different technological and other media. This distinction into two main categories leads to the following classification of the 17 information sources:

A. Person-oriented information sources
   1. Interviewing in meetings
   2. Talking to informants in network
   5. Making anonymous observations
   6. Initiating provocation through action
   12. Receiving tips from employees
   13. Studying claims in accusations
   14. Exchanging external information

B. Media-oriented information sources
   3. Visiting locations as crime scenes
   4. Scanning documents
   7. Watching surveillance videos
   8. Listening to communication
   9. Studying physical material
   10. Searching social media and the Internet
   11. Requesting police information
   15. Reading news in the media
   16. Searching information from control authorities
   17. Looking up data stored externally

When an investigation is compared to a puzzle, the puzzle cannot be solved when a single piece is missing. Different puzzle pieces can be found by using different information sources. Therefore, a fraud examiner needs to master both interpersonal and technological challenges to be able to solve the puzzle.

Combinations of information sources are selected in investigation and intelligence according to the subject of white-collar crime incident. When forensic accounting is applied as document study, it is typically combined with interviews and observations, thereby integrating behavioral aspects into forensic accounting (Ramamoorti, 2008).

Forensic Accounting

Forensic accounting is concerned with identifying, recording, settling, extracting, sorting, reporting, and verifying past financial data. The focus of forensic accounting is upon evidence revealed by the examination of financial documents. The evidence collected or prepared by a forensic accountant may be applied in different contexts. For example, forensic accounting results can serve as evidence in an internal corporate investigation that leads either only to internal discipline or no action whatsoever (Curtis, 2008).

Forensic accounting as a discipline has its own models and methodologies of investigative procedures that search for assurance, attestation, and advisory perspectives in order to produce legal evidence. It is concerned with the evidentiary nature of accounting data, and as a practical field is concerned with accounting fraud and forensic auditing; compliance, due diligence, and risk assessment; detection of financial statement misrepresentation and financial statement fraud (Skousen and Wright, 2008); as well as tax evasion, bankruptcy and valuation studies, violations of accounting regulations, nonstandard entries, structured transactions, records tampering, and earnings mismanagement.

Forensic accountants apply decision aids as well as professional judgment in their work (Chan et al., 2008). Decision aids comprise technology and systems that offer the potential to improve detection of white-collar crime in accounting. Hughes et al. (2008) argue that strong corporate control environments are critical to responsible and reliable detection of misconduct.

Forensic results can also serve as evidence in a professional disciplinary hearing or other administrative proceedings, such as an administrative enforcement procedure by financial authorities. As with evidence in some phases of a criminal action, the weight that a testimony carries will depend on a number of factors, the most important, according to Curtis (2008), being whether the forensic accountant can be qualified an expert, and thus whether the opinion of the accountant actually qualifies as an expert opinion. When forensic accounting is applied as document study, it is typically combined with interviews and observations, thereby integrating behavioral aspects into forensic accounting (Ramamoorti, 2008). Forensic accounting is emerging as a specialist discipline (Kranacher et al., 2008).

Financial crime such as fraud can be subject to forensic accounting, since fraud encompasses the acquisition of property or economic advantage by means of deception, through either misrepresentation or concealment.

Forensic examinations include consideration of digital evidence, including communications (Curtis, 2008).

To develop investigative knowledge in the area of forensic accounting, Kranacher et al. (2008) suggest a model curriculum consisting of several concepts, such as basic accounting, basic auditing, transaction processing, business law, business communication, and computer skills. The purpose of such a curriculum is to build up knowledge, skills, and abilities in forensic accounting in order to combat white-collar crime.

Accounting, in general, and forensic accounting, in particular (Baird and Zelin, 2009), are important investigative tools for the detection of white-collar crime. However, Carnegie and Napier (2010: 360) found that society's perception of the legitimacy of the accounting profession and accounting professionals has suffered following scandals such as Enron:

> The unexpected collapse of Enron and the bewildering demise of Arthur Andersen in the aftermath sent shock waves through the accounting profession worldwide. The impact of Enron's collapse was greater because it was closely followed by the bankruptcy of WorldCom in the USA, while scandals and collapses involving companies such as HIH Insurance in Australia, Parmalat in Italy, Royal Ahold in the Netherlands and Equitable Life Assurance Society in the UK showed that this was not just a US phenomenon. "Enronitis" became a label associated with highly questionable accounting and auditing practices. Although these practices were widely condemned as they became public knowledge, they sharply undermined confidence in corporate financial reporting and auditing as well as corporate regulation.

As a consequence, accountants have to deal with an increasing variety of new rules on corporate governance, audit independence, and financial reporting. Carnegie and Napier (2010) applied legitimacy and social contract theory to portray the consequences of this for the accounting profession after Enron. According to the legitimacy theory, business organizations are part of a broader social system and do not possess an inherent right to own or use resources, or even to exist. Society confers legitimacy upon an organization, whereby legitimacy is defined as a condition or status that exists when an entity's value system is congruent with the value system of the larger social system that the entity is a part of. Under social contract theory, the basic morality is adherence to uniform social accords that serve the best interests of those entering into agreement. Social contract theory is concerned with showing how individual and social group rights and liberties are founded on mutually advantageous agreements between members of society.

The Madoff scandal in the United States is an interesting example in forensic accounting. Bernard Madoff was awarded the maximum possible prison sentence of 150 years in 2009 after pleading guilty to 11 felony charges:

securities fraud, investment advisor fraud, mail fraud, wire fraud, money laundering, false statements, and others. Ragothaman (2014) argues that there are a number of lessons to be learned in forensic accounting based on the Madoff debacle. He suggests that a number of red flags (fraud risk factors) were indeed present and should have been visible for many years. For example, there were many complaints. The earliest complaint was in 1992, while Madoff was arrested in 2008.

Forensic accounting is dependent on a link between accounting information and intelligence management. Despite calls that management accounting should generally be linked more closely to management, Hall (2010) found that there is still a great deal to be learned concerning the role of accounting information in managerial work. Similarly, there is much to be learned about the role of forensic accounting in white-collar detection, prevention, and strategy in business enterprises.

Crime Intelligence Analysis

For Innes et al. (2005: 41), crime analysis is concerned with insight and understanding:

> There has been a move away from an ad hoc, intuitive and largely unstructured mode of analytic work, to a more ordered, rationalized approach, based upon specific methodologies, on the basis that this provides a more 'objective' perspective on patterns of crime and offending. This has raised the profile and status of intelligence analysis within policing, and seen new techniques and technologies introduced, which should, at least in theory, allow police a better understanding of how, when and why crimes are occurring.

The Council of Europe (2002) described crime analysis as a law enforcement function whereby data relating to crime are collected, collated, analyzed, and disseminated. Crime analysis is the study of crime patterns and trends in an attempt to solve crime cases or prevent their repeat occurrence.

A distinction can be made between operational/tactical analysis and strategic analysis. Operational analysis is directed toward a short-term law enforcement goal with an immediate impact in mind, e.g., arrest, seizure, and forfeiture. The goal of strategic crime analysis is to develop or implement a policy, or to evaluate a policy based on insights regarding the nature of a type of crime or criminal and the scope and projections of growth in types of criminal activities. However, strategic analysis need not be restricted to crime; methods of strategic analysis can be used in principle for all kinds of security and safety issues. Strategic analysis can deal with crime as well as with other security issues like traffic problems and public order maintenance.

According to the Council of Europe (2002), it departs from the question of which information is needed and which data are lacking. A structured plan has to be developed and discussed. The next step is the detection of a problem, the consideration of a new phenomenon, and the gathering of information.

Examples of strategic crime analysis include:

- *Crime pattern analysis*: Examination of the nature and distribution of crime within an area, in order to identify emerging and current trends and patterns, linked crimes or incidents, and hot spots of activity. This includes crime trend identification, crime series identification, general profile analysis, and hot spot analysis, alongside examination of the nature and scale of crime within a defined area and within a time frame.
- *Crime control methods analysis*: Evaluation of investigative or preventive methods and techniques with the aim of establishing their future usefulness.
- *General profile analysis*: Identification of the typical characteristics of perpetrators of certain crimes.
- *Results analysis*: Evaluation of the effectiveness of law enforcement activities.
- *Demographic/social trends analysis*: Examination of the nature of demographic changes and their impact on criminality, as well as the analysis of social factors (e.g., unemployment), which might underlie changing trends in offending patterns. Also, statistical description of the constitution of the population of a given area and the associated economic indicators with reference to law enforcement requirements.
- *Criminal business analysis/profile*: The examination of how illegal operations/businesses and techniques work, in detail.
- *Market profile*: A survey of the criminal market around a given commodity (e.g., illicit drugs, stolen vehicles). It can include crime pattern analysis and network analysis.
- *Strategic analysis*: A category of types of crime analysis designed to aid the formation or evaluation of crime policy. The aims are to provide information that can depict a phenomenon, and which can identify trends in criminality upon which management can base their decisions.

The UN has made illicit businesses a target of law enforcement. This is important, because besides violating human rights, illicit businesses preclude proper economic development and collectively make up as much as 10% of the global economy. Byrne (2011) argues that given the scope of this complex ethical problem, it is fortuitous that law-making institutions, including the UN, have been clarifying the issues at stake.

Examples of tactical/operational crime analysis include:

- *Specific profile analysis*: Identification of the specific characteristics of perpetrators of certain crimes. This entails construction of a hypothetical picture of the perpetrator of a serious crime or series of offenses, on the basis of crime scene data, witness statements, and other available information.
- *Offender group analysis*: Examination of the structure of a group of suspects, the significance of each member, and their involvement with criminal activities.
- *Investigations/operations analysis*: Evaluation of the effectiveness of activities that are undertaken within the context of an investigation.
- *Case analysis*: Establishment of the course of events immediately before, during, and after a serious offense.
- *Comparative case analysis*: Identification of a series of crime cases with common offenders by seeking similarities between offenses.
- *Operational crime analysis*: Category of types of crime analysis designed to support the investigation of one particular crime or one specific series of crime incidents with common offender(s). It aims to provide an understanding of the information collected during a specific investigation.
- *Network analysis*: Provision of a detailed picture of the roles played by individuals, the nature and significance of the links between people, and the strengths and weaknesses of the criminal network.

Whistle-Blowers as Informants

According to Kaplan et al. (2011), employee tips are the most common form of initial fraud detection, suggesting that employees frequently are aware of fraud before others professionally charged to detect fraud, such as internal and external auditors. The willingness of employees who learn about fraud to report this information varies with several factors. For example, if the executive, to whom misconduct should be reported, is not trusted, employees will tend not to report. Whistle-blowing decisions are dependent on information, trust, security, predictability, and organizational culture in general.

Johnson (2005) has the following definition of *whistle-blowing*:

> Whistle blowing is a distinct form of dissent consisting of four elements: (1) the person acting must be a member or former member of the organization at issue; (2) his or her information must be about nontrivial wrongdoing in that

organization; (3) he or she must intend to expose the wrongdoing; and (4) he or she must act in a way that makes the information public.

Vadera et al. (2009) has the following definition of *whistle-blowing*:

> Whistle blowing is the disclosure by organizational members (former or current) of illegal, immoral, or illegitimate practices under the control of their employers, to persons or organizations that may be able to effect action.

Vadera et al. (2009) identified the following characteristics of whistle-blowers and whistle-blowing:

- Federal whistle-blowers were motivated by concern for public interest, were high performers, reported high levels of job security, job achievement, job commitment, and job satisfaction, and worked in high-performing work groups and organizations.
- Anger at wrongful activities drove individuals to make internal reports to management. Retaliation by management shifted individuals' focus away from helping their organizations or victims and toward attaining retribution.
- Whistle-blowing was more likely when observers of wrongdoing held professional positions, had more positive reactions to their work, had longer service, were recently recognized for good performance, were male, were members of larger work groups, and were employed by organizations perceived by others to be responsive to complaints.
- Whistle-blowing was more frequent in the public sector than in the private.
- Whistle-blowing was strongly related to situational variables, with seriousness of the offense and supportiveness of the organizational climate being the strongest determinants.
- Inclination to report a peer for theft was associated with role responsibility, the interests of group members, and procedural perceptions.

In 2001, Sherron Watkins, an employee in the American energy company Enron, notified her chief executive officer Kenneth Lay about a perceived accounting scandal. Watkins did so hoping Lay would act. He did not, and was later arrested due to his involvement in the wrongdoings, because she blew the whistle.

Negative consequences after whistle-blowing, suffered by some whistle-blowers, are labeled retaliation. Retaliation implies to take an undesirable action against a whistle-blower, who reported wrongdoing internally or externally, outside the organization. Retaliation can be defined as taking adverse action against an employee for opposing an unlawful employment practice or participating in any investigation, proceeding, or hearing related to such a practice (Bjørkelo and Matthiesen, 2011).

Thus, fraud examiners have two issues to consider when dealing with whistle-blowers as an information source. First, not all that is said and not all accusations from a whistle-blower are necessarily true. Therefore, information from a whistle-blower has to be carefully checked and verified. Second, a whistle-blower may be in danger of retaliation, making it a requirement for fraud examiners to protect the whistle-blower. Fraud examiners have to make sure that a whistle-blower participating in an investigation does not experience negative consequences.

Arranging the Interview

The main source of information in a white-collar investigation is people an investigator talks to. The talk takes place in the form of an interview for a fraud examiner or an interrogation for a police detective. An interview is questioning of victims and cooperative witnesses to obtain testimony and evidence or proof of significant omissions. An interrogation is questioning of suspects and uncooperative witnesses for the purpose of obtaining testimony and evidence or proof of significant omissions (Williams, H.E., 2006).

Interview planning often begins with a background check of the person to be interviewed. Previously filed reports, intelligence files, and criminal history records may give the investigator an insight into the character and motives of the interviewee as witness or the interrogated as suspect. Before conducting an interview, the investigator will review all the information available (Williams, H.E., 2006). In fraud examinations, the interview takes place in the form of a meeting, where the examiner as an interviewer opens up broad issues before going into detailed questioning of the interviewee.

The determination of whether an interviewee is telling the truth is always a consideration. If untruthfulness is suspected, the investigator must be prepared with facts to refute the untruthfulness. H.E. Williams (2006) finds it often smart to allow the interviewee to continue to talk, on the assumption that by confronting the interviewee with his own falsities, he may push the interviewee into giving valuable information.

References

Baird, J.E., and Zelin, R.C. (2009). An examination of the impact of obedience pressure on perceptions of fraudulent acts and the likelihood of committing occupational fraud. *Journal of Forensic Studies in Accounting and Business*, 1(1), 1–14.

Bjørkelo, B., and Matthiesen, S.B. (2011). Preventing and dealing with retaliation against whistleblowers. In Lewis, D., and Vandekerckhove, W. (eds.), *Whistleblowing and Democratic Values.* International Whistleblowing Research Network.

Bressler, L. (2011). The role of forensic accountants in fraud investigations: Importance of attorney and judge's perceptions. *Journal of Finance and Accountancy*, 1–9.

Brown, R., Cannings, A., and Sherrif, J. (2004). *Intelligence-led vehicle crime reduction: An evaluation of Operation Gallant,* Home Office Online Report 47/04, http:// www.homeoffice.gov.uk/rds/pdfsolr4704.pdf.

Byrne, E.F. (2011). Business ethics should study illicit businesses: To advance respect for human rights. *Journal of Business Ethics*, 103, 497–509.

Carnegie, G.D., and Napier, C.J. (2010). Traditional accountants and business professionals: Portraying the accounting profession after Enron. *Accounting, Organizations and Society*, 35, 360–376.

Chaffey, D., and White, G. (2011). *Business Information Management*, 2nd ed. Prentice Hall, London.

Coburn, N.F. (2006). Corporate investigations. *Journal of Financial Crime*, 13(3), 348–368.

Council of Europe. (2002). *Crime Analysis: Organized Crime—Best Practice Survey No. 4.* Economic Crime Division, Department of Crime Problems, Directorate General I—Legal Affairs, Council of Europe, Strasbourg, France.

Curtis, G.E. (2008). Legal and regulatory environments and ethics: Essential components of a fraud and forensic accounting curriculum. *Issues in Accounting Education*, 23(4), 535–543.

Hall, M. (2010). Accounting information and managerial work. *Accounting, Organizations and Society*, 35, 301–315.

Harfield, C. (2008). Paradigms, pathologies, and practicalities—Policing organized crime in England and Wales. *Policing*, 2(1), 63–73.

Hughes, K.E., Louwers, T.J., and Reynolds, J.K. (2008). Toward an expanded control environment framework. *Journal of Forensic Accounting*, 9, 115–128.

Innes, M., Fielding, N., and Cope, N. (2005). The appliance of science: The theory and practice of crime intelligence analysis. *British Journal of Criminology*, 45, 39–57.

Innes, M., and Sheptycki, J.W.E. (2004). From detection to disruption: Intelligence and the changing logic of police crime control in the United Kingdom. *International Criminal Justice Review*, 14, 1–24.

Johnson, R.A. (2005). Whistleblowing and the police. *Rutgers University Journal of Law and Urban Policy*, 1(3), 74–83.

Kaplan, S.E., Pope, K.R., and Samuels, J.A. (2011). An examination of the effect of inquiry and auditor type on reporting intentions of fraud. *Auditing: A Journal of Practice and Theory*, 30(4), 29–49.

Kattan, W., King, W., and Ramella, M. (2009). Handling conflicts of interest within financial innovation—The case of regulation and supervision of Bermuda sidecars. *Journal of Financial Crime*, 16(4), 353–363.

Kranacher, M.J., Morris, B.W., Pearson, T.A., and Riley, A. (2008). A model curriculum for education in fraud and forensic accounting. *Issues in Accounting Education*, 23(4), 505–519.

Maghan, J. (1994). Intelligence gathering approaches in prisons. *Low Intensity Conflict and Law Enforcement*, 3(3), 548–557.

Newman, R. (2009). Computer forensics fraud investigations. *Journal of Forensic Studies in Accounting and Business*, Winter, 69–81.

Ragothaman, S.C. (2014). The Madoff debacle: What are the lessons? *Issues in Accounting Education*, 29(1), 271–285.

Ramamoorti, S. (2008). The psychology and sociology of fraud: Integrating the behavioral sciences component into fraud and forensic accounting curricula. *Issues in Accounting Education*, 23(4), 521–533.

Ratcliffe, J.H. (2008). *Intelligence-Led Policing*. Willan Publishing, Devon, UK.

Sheptycki, J. (2007). Police ethnography in the house of serious and organized crime. In Henry, A., and Smith, D.J. (eds.), *Transformations of Policing*. Ashgate Publishing, Oxford, pp. 51–77.

Skousen, C.J., and Wright, C.J. (2008). Contemporaneous risk factors and the prediction of financial statement fraud. *Journal of Forensic Accounting*, 9, 37–62.

SYPIS. (2007). South Yorkshire Police Intelligence Strategy 2007—Breaking the Chain. South Yorkshire Police, UK. www.policereform.gov.uk

Vadera, A.K., Aguilera, R.V., and Caza, B.B. (2009). Making sense of whistle-blowing's antecedents: Learning from research on identity and ethics programs. *Business Ethics Quarterly*, 19(4), 553–586.

Wilhelmsen, S. (2009). Maximising Organizational Information Sharing and Effective Intelligence Analysis in Critical Data Sets. Dissertation for the degree of philosophiæ doctor (PhD), University of Bergen, Norway.

Williams, H.E. (2006). *Investigating White-Collar Crime*. Thomas Publisher, Springfield, IL.

Williams, S., and Williams, N. (2003). The business value of business intelligence. *Business Intelligence Journal*, Fall, 30–39.

Zhao, J.S., Thurman, Q.C., and Ren, L. (2008). An examination of strategic planning in American law enforcement agencies. *Police Quarterly*, 11(1), 3–26.

Knowledge Management 7

The core of any investigation is to have competent professional skills in a team. They must have the resolve to work hard and complete the investigation in a tight time frame. Having the right skills mix is a key factor in a successful investigation team. Coburn (2006) argues that the most appropriate team will usually consist of an investigative lawyer, a forensic accountant, and a seasoned financial investigator. They have relevant knowledge than can be applied to investigative tasks.

Knowledge is defined as information combined with interpretation, reflection, and context. It is about understanding and gaining insights from facts. It is about thinking. It is about reflecting and combining pieces of information and understanding those pieces in their possible relationships. While information can be stored and available on computers, knowledge exists only in the heads of individuals. Knowledge is processed information that exists in tacit form within the individual's head. Knowledge is shared among individuals through communication between them or via computers where knowledge is codified as information.

The working definition of knowledge suggested by Chaffey and White (2011: 209) is as follows:

> The combination of data and information, to which is added expert opinion, skills and experience, to result in a valuable asset which can be used to aid decision making. Knowledge may be explicit and/or tacit, individual and/or collective.

Explicit knowledge refers to details of processes or procedures that have been codified or captured and recorded. Explicit knowledge can be readily detailed in procedural manuals and databases. Examples include records of meetings, records of interviews with suspected white-collar criminals, and management reports. Tacit knowledge is less tangible than explicit knowledge. It refers to experience on how to react to an investigation situation when many different variables are involved.

Tacit knowledge is generally unspoken knowledge that distinguishes the more expert individual in a particular domain and that reflects the practical ability to learn from experience (Taylor et al., 2013). It is more difficult to encapsulate this knowledge, which often resides in the heads of employees. Techniques for sharing this knowledge include learning stories and histories.

Examples include knowing how to react when changes occur in an interview situation or at client management change (Chaffey and White, 2011).

Knowledge Management

Knowledge management is concerned with knowledge sharing and knowledge creation in organizations. Knowledge management activities include creation, acquisition, identification, storage, sharing, and application of knowledge (Heisig, 2009). Some knowledge management activities contribute to exploration (i.e., discovery of new knowledge), while others contribute to exploitation (i.e., application of what is already known). Exploitation refers to solution reuse, while exploration refers to solution innovation. Exploitation leverages existing knowledge through the application of preestablished procedures, technologies, and policing approaches. Exploration can lead to new investigative approaches and new examination procedures (Durcikova et al., 2011).

Knowledge management efficiency in an organization is dependent on capabilities such as collective skills, abilities, and general expertise of the organization. Expertise in any profession is a hard-won combination of many factors and typically includes advanced knowledge, skills, and abilities developed through years of experience. Within the investigation profession, expert investigators are individuals who possess innate traits and abilities supplemented with knowledge gained through formal training in areas such as forensic accounting and computer forensics, and on-the-job training (Taylor et al., 2013).

Where knowledge deficits exist in private investigations, incomplete information and know-how give rise to uncertainties that obscure prediction and execution. Performance risk and execution risk are lowered through knowledge transfer mechanisms developed to avoid and handle uncertainties. Such knowledge transfer permits knowledge reuse, and the recombination of existing knowledge is an important contribution to uncertainty resolution (Mitchell, 2006).

Knowledge management strategy focuses on personnel resources, where the knowledge of each fraud examiner, as well as the combined knowledge in the investigation team, represents resources that are to be explored and exploited for professional inquiry work. The knowledge management strategy process includes developing a working definition of knowledge, developing a working definition of knowledge management, doing a knowledge audit, defining knowledge management objectives and strategy approaches, and implementing strategy with quality measures (Chaffey and White, 2011).

However, despite the opportunities presented by knowledge management, its integration to the investigation sector has been somewhat troublesome.

Even when the term *knowledge management* is applied in investigations, it often implies facts-based inquiry rather than knowledge-based inquiry. Facts-based investigation ignores important aspects of knowledge-based investigation, such as interpretation of facts by colleagues, reflection around facts by combining information pieces, and contextual factors that influence the meaning of facts. Too often, facts in terms of numbers and names represent only pieces of a reality that need to be mapped into a complete picture of knowledge (Luen and Al-Hawamdeh, 2001).

Private investigations represent an interesting and unique field of knowledge management for several reasons. A possible white-collar crime has occurred, and examiners are to figure out what, how, who, and why. It is a puzzle of information pieces that has to be solved. If one piece is missing in a puzzle of thousands of pieces, the crime will never be solved. Second, knowledge cannot be shared freely. Knowledge has to be applied in a sequence of investigative steps, where witnesses and suspects are involved to the extent that the investigation makes progress. Colleagues in the firm and executives in the client organization only get to know about a current investigation to the extent that they have a role to play in it. A senior investigating person plays the role of a knowledge manager, who monitors information flows. Only when the private investigation is completed is knowledge from the case to be shared in the broader field of stakeholders and spectators.

Thus, any discussion regarding the role of knowledge management within the context of private investigations must necessarily begin with an overview of the specific nature of the typical investigating unit. Effective knowledge management is dependent on a knowledge-centered culture, which may or may not exist in different units in both the investigating firm and the investigated firm. For knowledge management to thrive within the investigative context, the organizational environment must be conducive to its success. If knowledge work is regarded as shuffling papers or attending formal meetings, it is little valued and carries no prestige within teams of that kind. Two significant factors that hinder the integration of knowledge management in the inquiry context seem to be the secrecy structure and the competitive nature of many organizations (Dean et al., 2006; Seba and Rowley, 2010; Seba et al., 2011).

The issue of knowledge management in private investigations is not a question of whether or not it might be useful. It is a question of how it can be implemented, which is the contingent approach to management. There is no universal knowledge management strategy. Rather, a strategy is based on the situation in the organization, such as a law firm. Factors that make the investigative context special include power in terms of client board support, active information collection in terms of intelligence, and the need for high-quality information that can serve as evidence in the final report.

Strong knowledge management capabilities require processes that apply resources in particular ways and structures that embody and support distinct values. Distinct values are found in the organizational culture, while organizational structure is the pattern of interactions, coordination, and control that shape behavior and outcomes.

Knowledge management is dependent on both organizational structure and organizational culture. Structure and culture define the framework within which knowledge management takes place. Barriers to and enablers of knowledge management in the investigation unit can be found both in the organizational structure and in the organizational culture. This has been the topic of several research studies of detective work. Other research studies have focused on management approaches, intelligence for knowledge, and knowledge integration.

Private investigations are heavily dependent on information, intelligence, and knowledge. The amount of information an investigator comes in contact with in the course of his or her work is often astounding. With a more proactive and preventive approach to crime identification, detectives have increasingly relied on information and knowledge and associated information technology in terms of knowledge management systems to improve their performance. Accordingly, the management of knowledge is a crucial aspect of investigation work to promote knowledge development and sharing.

Knowledge is indispensable to modern investigations. Investigative ability to create, identify, share, and apply knowledge directly affects investigations' competitive advantage (Choi et al., 2010). Of special importance is financial crime knowledge among fraud examiners. Investigation and prevention of financial crime requires that board members and executive managers have knowledge about crime categories and motives. Executives need to be knowledgeable about contexts, complexities, and also connections. Bevan and Gitsham (2009) argue that such knowledge can be developed through leadership development programs, whereby the appropriate knowledge and skills are sought when recruiting new talent into the organization, and these knowledge and skills are subsequently built upon through career development planning and succession planning, while ensuring that performance management and incentive systems enable and reward the building and acquisition of such knowledge, and that such knowledge is developed through individual as well as collective competency frameworks.

Collier (2006) argues that effective knowledge management is as important to investigating and preventing crime as it is to any other public or private sector organization in terms of improving performance. Over the past 10 years, there has been a shift from a reactive, response-led approach to a proactive, intelligence-led style of law enforcement. In the UK, Norway, Sweden, and many other countries, the intelligence-led approach has been developed into a systematic approach by national criminal intelligence services. The intelligence used in both strategic and tactical assessments is derived from a number of knowledge and information sources, and the production of assessments represents knowledge work as well.

Wilhelmsen (2009) found that since knowledge and experience often are obtained with great personal and work-related costs, the individual or the organization can develop emotional ownership to the information and not be willing to share all he or she knows. However, sharing knowledge in suspected crime cases is vital because misleading or false information can have unfortunate and harmful consequences.

In knowledge collaboration, teams are considered to be an important building block in today's knowledge-based organizations. An important factor affecting team performance is sociocognitive processes. A key problem underlying the sociocognitive process in teams is the uneven distributed knowledge among individuals in the team. In particular, Choi et al. (2010) argue that a sociocognitive structure called the transactive memory system plays a particularly important role in a team's ability to leverage team members' knowledge in team performance. A transactive memory system refers to a specialized division of cognitive labor that develops within a team with respect to the encoding, storage, and retrieval of knowledge from different domains. The cognitive labor implies that team members know who knows what and who knows who knows what.

One of the main challenges in managing an organization's knowledge is transferring knowledge from its source to its destination where it is needed. Unlike tangible assets, the investigation unit often does not know if they have access to relevant knowledge and where it potentially is located. Furthermore, they do not know how much it is worth to them, as compared to the value of office buildings (Liu et al., 2010).

Professional Service Firms

Many fraud examiners work in professional service firms such as accounting firms, auditing firms, law firms, and consulting firms. Professional firms differ from other business enterprises in at least two distinct ways. First, they provide highly customized services and thus cannot apply many of the management principles developed for product-based industries. Second, professional services are highly personalized, involving the skills of individuals. Such firms must therefore compete not only for clients, but also for talented professionals. To compete for clients, knowledge management is important. To compete for professionals, knowledge management is important as well, since talents are attracted by modern organizations.

Knowledge management is a critical issue in professional service firms (Palte et al., 2011). Human resources determine firm performance (McClean and Collins, 2011). While knowledge management has become a strategic success factor and differentiator in professional firms (Hansen et al., 1999), these firms are emerging as the typical organization in the knowledge-based economy. A professional service firm is any organization reliant on a workforce with substantial expertise—that is, a definition similar to a knowledge-intensive firm or knowledge-based organization (Nordenflycht, 2010). The central characteristic associated with professionals is their mastery of a particular expertise or knowledge base. For professional service firms such as consultants, accountants, auditors, lawyers, architects, and engineers, knowledge is a capacity to act.

Nordenflycht (2010) identified three distinctive characteristics of the professional service firm: high knowledge intensity, low capital intensity, and a professional workforce. For professional firms, the main asset is intellectual capital, and they have to seek new ways to leverage their intellectual capital on a continuous basis. The core business of these firms is to provide sophisticated knowledge-based services grounded on the existence of intellectual assets (Swart and Kinnie, 2003).

Lawrence et al. (2012) studied transformations of professional service firms. They examined the roles of episodic and systemic forms of power in radical organizational change. They found that episodic power is able to initiate and energize radical change when it represents a significant break from traditional authority structures and is legitimated through appeals to traditional organizational values. Furthermore, systemic power was found to be able to institutionalize radical change when the systems associated with it are legitimated by the skilled use of language by key actors and then left to operate independently by those actors.

Lawrence et al. (2012) argue that professional service firms have been experiencing both institutional and market pressures that have challenged the traditional partner management style, pushing the firms toward a more business-like managed professional business form. The latter embraces corporate-style governance, a separation of management and professional tasks, more centralized and coordinated decision making, greater functional and professional differentiation, a more elaborate hierarchy, and the introduction of formal control systems.

To create radical change in professional firms, Lawrence et al. (2012) argue that power is needed. Power is the dimension of a relationship through which behavior, attitude, or opportunity of an actor is affected by another actor, system, or technology. Episodic power refers to relatively discrete acts of mobilization initiated by self-interested actors. Episodic power exists in its exercise and is expressed in relationships. Systemic power is the form of power that works through routine, ongoing practices, and decision processes.

The concept of systemic power is rooted in social and cultural systems, rather than in individual actors.

Nordenflycht's (2010) three distinctive characteristics of professional firms led him to develop an explicit theory of such firms' distinctiveness. First, knowledge intensity is perhaps the most fundamental distinctive characteristic. Knowledge intensity indicates that production of a firm's output relies on a substantial body of complex knowledge. The firm relies on an intellectually skilled workforce. There are two key managerial challenges that result from knowledge intensity:

- Cat herding: One challenge arising from an intellectually skilled workforce is retaining and directing those skilled employees. It requires alternative incentive mechanisms.
- Opaque quality: This refers to situations where the quality of an expert's output is hard for nonexperts to evaluate, even after the output is produced and delivered. It requires mechanisms to signal quality.

Next to knowledge intensity is low capital intensity as a characteristic. It indicates that a firm's production does not involve significant amounts of nonhuman assets, such as inventory, factories, and equipment, and even intangible nonhuman assets like patents and copyrights. Low capital intensity is not a necessary implication of knowledge intensity, as many companies require both an intellectually skilled workforce and significant nonhuman assets. Examples are hospitals and oil companies.

A final characteristic of professional firms is a professionalized workforce. A profession is characterized by a particular knowledge base, regulation and control of that knowledge base and its application, as well as ideology, which refers to the professional codes of ethics as well as less explicit norms that define appropriate behavior for professionals.

An additional characteristic of many professional firms is no outside ownership. Ownership of the firm is allocated exclusively to professionals who work for the firm and not to any outside investors (Nordenflycht, 2010).

Intelligence for Knowledge

Luen and Al-Hawamdeh (2001) found that the amount of information that police officers come into contact with within the course of their work is astounding. This and the vast knowledge that police officers need in order to perform their normal duties suggest the need for police officers to be proficient knowledge workers, being able to access, assimilate, and use knowledge effectively to discharge their duties. The same is certainly true for private investigators as well; thus, we continue here the analogous treatment of police investigators and private investigators as knowledge workers.

While data are numbers and letters without meaning, information is data in a context that makes sense. When combined with interpretation and reflection, information becomes knowledge, while knowledge accumulated over time, as learning, is wisdom. In this hierarchical structure we find that intelligence amounts to more than information and less than knowledge. Intelligence is analyzed information, as illustrated in Figure 7.1.

The word *intelligence* can refer to a product, a process, the individual organization that shapes raw data into a finished intelligence product, and also the larger community containing these organizations. The word *intelligence* also often refers to the military or to agencies like MI5 (the Security Service) or MI6 (Secret Intelligence Service) in the UK. However, in this chapter, intelligence relates to suspicion of criminal actions and is defined as a goal-oriented gathering, systematization, and analysis of information (Wilhelmsen, 2009).

Data are considered the raw material from which information develops. As is the case with notes, information is data endowed with relevance and purpose. The same can be said of intelligence, in that it is a form of insight to which some relevance has been attached through an attempt to offer an organized analysis of the information received by a crime analyst/intelligence officer. Accordingly, on the above continuum, intelligence is placed between

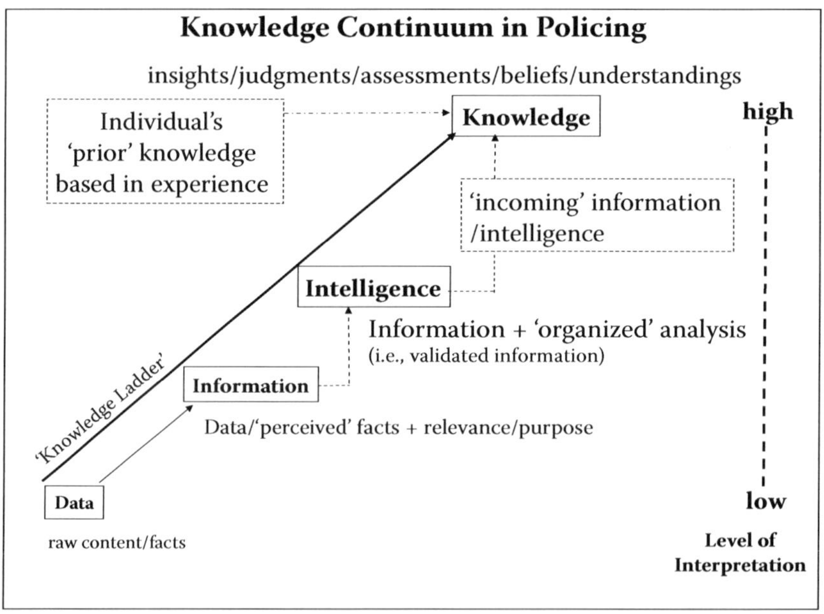

Figure 7.1 Hierarchy of investigation and prevention insight expressed as a continuum.

information and knowledge as ideally (as argued) intelligence represents a form of validated information.

Information is the lifeblood of an investigation. An investigation goes nowhere if information is not forthcoming concerning an incident. Information is the raw material, which breathes life into an investigation. It comprises ordinary rank-and-file employees, either working in human resource departments and accounting departments or sitting at a computer conducting searches, background checks, or more sophisticated crime mapping and intelligence analysis reports and collecting and collating information.

Information and, to a similar extent, intelligence thereby consist of facts and other data that are organized to characterize or profile a particular situation, incident, or crime and the individual or group of individuals presumed to be involved. This organizing of data into meaningful information necessarily involves some level of interpretation of the facts as presented. However, the role of interpretation here in information is relatively minor in comparison to its role in terms of knowledge construction. In this regard, the role of interpretation in intelligence is greater and more explicit than it is in terms of information, but not as extensive as in the making of knowledge.

Knowledge helps one develop relevant meaning to information in intelligence work (Innes and Sheptycki, 2004: 6):

> The distinction between information and intelligence is well established, but can be difficult to grasp. Information consists of bits of data that, when combined and viewed together with relevant background knowledge, may be used to produce intelligence, which informs the actions and decisions of policing organizations.

As implied, knowledge operates at a higher level of abstraction and consists of judgments and assessments based on personal beliefs, truths, and expectations regarding the information received and how it should be analyzed, evaluated, and synthesized—in short interpreted—so that it may be used and implemented into some form of action.

Knowledge Integration

In knowledge management, the theory of absorptive capacity is important. Absorptive capacity is viewed as a dynamic capability of processing knowledge that enhances organizational innovation (Joshi et al., 2010). More specifically, absorptive capacity is an organization's ability to identify, assimilate, transform, and apply valuable external knowledge (Roberts et al., 2012). Through their investigative practice, investigators develop collective knowledge about certain areas of crime, criminals, behaviors, and motives. This knowledge base enhances the unit's ability to identify and value both internal and external knowledge. However, sheer exposure to related external knowledge is not sufficient to ensure that the unit will absorb it successfully. The knowledge must be assimilated or transformed into the organization's knowledge base. While a knowledge base enables the associative connections needed for insights into new white-collar crime cases, the organizational assimilation of new knowledge depends more so upon the transfer of knowledge across and within units. Investigators apply their newly absorbed knowledge in a variety of ways, for example, to replenish their knowledge base, to forecast suspect behaviors, to reconfigure existing capabilities, and to create innovative inquiry services.

Access to external knowledge enables the importation of new knowledge coupled with the recombination of existing knowledge. Recombination avoids the inside view, which refers to an insular approach to investigations, where intuition and knowledge of current cases are used to forecast future case outcomes. Bold forecasts are reduced when investigation leaders adopt an outside view, which refers to an active search of complementing and contradicting knowledge. The outside view avoids distortion related to historic bias (Mitchell, 2006).

There are three assumptions underlying absorptive capacity (Roberts et al., 2012):

- Absorptive capacity depends on prior related knowledge. Without some prior related knowledge, the investigator will not be able to accurately determine the potential value of external knowledge. This implies that absorptive capacity is domain specific.
- An organization's absorptive capacity depends on the absorptive capabilities of its individual members. However, it is not simply the sum of its members' absorptive capacities. Rather, it depends on the links between individuals as well. Thus, the organization's absorptive capacity is formed from an overlap in individual members' knowledge across and within units. These overlaps imply that absorptive capacity is unit specific and case specific.
- An organization's absorptive capacity is path dependent. Accumulating absorptive capacity in one period will permit its more efficient accumulation in the next. Likewise, in an uncertain environment, absorptive capacity affects expectation formation, permitting the investigators to predict more accurately the nature and potential of new knowledge. These two features of absorptive capacity—cumulativeness and its effect on expectation formation—imply that its development is path dependent.

According to Roberts et al. (2012), organizational scholars have viewed absorptive capacity from two general perspectives: as a stock of prior related knowledge and as an ability to understand new knowledge. When viewed as an asset, absorptive capacity is referred to as the level of relevant prior knowledge possessed by the unit. When viewed as an ability, absorptive capacity is referred to as the extent to which the unit is able to change according to new knowledge.

Within absorptive capacity Mitchell (2006) stresses the importance of knowledge integration. The knowledge integration process involves social interactions among individuals using internal communication channels for knowledge transfer to arrive at a common perspective for problem solving. Where organizational units hold specialized knowledge, interunit linkages are the primary means of transferring knowledge.

Transferring knowledge among experts in the firm is not the only possible approach to knowledge integration. An alternative approach is a combination of specialized, differentiated, but complementary knowledge. As the problem of knowledge integration is usually conceived as a consequence of the benefits of specialization, it may not be surprising that many definitions characterize knowledge integration as a process/activity whereby such specialized knowledge is combined—rather than shared and transferred. This means that when studying and conceptualizing knowledge integration at the level of people and processes, projects and partnerships, and strategies and outcomes, the fundamental problem of knowledge integration lies in understanding the process involving the combination of specialized knowledge bases embodied in individuals. To be successful, a minimum of common knowledge has to be present to enable knowledge integration of completely specialized knowledge.

When integration of knowledge is conceptualized as a combination of expert knowledge, the core argument developed by Söderlund and Bredin (2011) is that knowledge integration depends on the individual actors' abilities to participate in knowledge integration processes, and hence that the individuals' behavior and skills are central for the analysis of such processes. It is at this level that different areas of expertise and problem-solving cycles typically are being integrated. This is perhaps especially true for complex criminal investigations such as white-collar crime, where expert knowledge of finance, organization, management, psychology, law, communication, and sociology is often needed in a well-integrated process. If knowledge collectivities are playing an increasingly important role for knowledge integration and problem solving in investigative work, it seems imperative to address how individual investigators relate to less developed groups and new organizational contexts, and how they cope with increasingly higher demands for flexibility and mobility.

Knowledge in Analytical Work

Private investigators are referred to as knowledge workers. White-collar crime inquiry largely revolves around creation, acquisition, identification, storage, share, and use of knowledge in meaningful ways (Heisig, 2009), so as to identify elements of know-what, know-how, and know-why as they relate to suspicion of white-collar crime. Knowledge management processes in investigations are applied to ensure inquiry personnel are more cognitively sophisticated by promoting the creation of new knowledge and the sharing of existing knowledge.

Innes and Sheptycki (2004: 6) argue that intelligence is value added to information:

> The distinction between information and intelligence is well established, but can be difficult to grasp. Information consists of bits of data that, when combined and viewed together with relevant background knowledge, may be used to produce intelligence, which informs the actions and decisions of policing organizations.

As law firms, auditing firms, and consulting firms worldwide constantly strive for competitive advantage, major approaches and tools in pursuing their objectives are knowledge management and information technology. The attention for a knowledge-based perspective on organizations has led to much scientific as well as practical interest in organizing firms with the help of knowledge management. The importance of knowledge to organizations has been extensively established in the business and management literature as being the basis of future sustainable competitive advantage. Knowledge is the stock in trade for law firms and other professional firms.

This chapter applies the knowledge-based view of the firm as its main theoretical perspective. The knowledge-based view is part of the resource-based view of the firm, which views the firm as a collection of productive resources. The knowledge-based view considers knowledge as the critical input in production of legal services in the law firm. Knowledge is the primary source of value of the firm. Based on the assumption of bounded rationality, this view assumes that individuals will never possess identical stocks of knowledge. Since each firm has its unique set of human resources in terms of lawyers as knowledge workers, there will always be knowledge asymmetries between law firms (Dibbern et al., 2008).

Knowledge management (KM) is introduced to help companies create, share, and use knowledge effectively. Some knowledge organizations such as law firms have introduced the role of the chief knowledge officer (CKO), which is not so much to provide KM facilities and services as to enable the organization to learn, to innovate, and to gain from entrepreneurship. CKOs have to discover and develop law firms' implicit vision of how KM will make a difference.

In this chapter we studied professional service firms as the case of a knowledge organization. The increased efforts in most firms to improve their KM are related to a number of changes in the consulting industry. First, there is a shift from paper-based to electronically based information and documents that consultants work on. Second, advances in information and communication technology enable storing, transfer, and exchange of information electronically, as a supplement to meetings and phone calls. Electronic services available on the Internet make consultants interact with a number of external service providers electronically rather than through internal functions. Globalization of consulting services requires professional firms locally to act globally for corporate clients that are doing business in several parts of the world.

Fraud examiners are specialists rather than generalists. A specialist is a person who knows a lot about a little, while a generalist is a person who knows a little about a lot. The drive toward specialization needs to be combined with generalization, where specialists share their understanding with other specialists as well as clients. Merging expert advice and sometimes translating it into something understandable for the layman is enabled in KM by putting together electronic pieces of text, images, videos, and sound tracks.

Strong KM capabilities require processes that apply resources in particular ways and structures that embody and support distinct values. KM capabilities are based on two fundamental assets: people and technology. To the extent a professional firm can develop firm-specific resources that are not easily replicable by competitors, it can better protect its knowledge investments.

KM is not at all something completely new to professional firms. Knowledge firms and knowledge workers have been doing knowledge work, and KM, ever since professional consulting work first began. In every advice, in every transaction, in every call of a colleague to share an opinion or critique an idea, in every training session, in every practice team meeting, and in every work-related break room conversation, lawyers, accountants, auditors, and detectives have been building and sharing knowledge for centuries. Yet KM has not always been a success in professional firms, and KM has become a challenge to firms that had half a dozen employees, while they now have hundreds and even thousands of employees.

References

Bevan, D., and Gitsham, M. (2009). Context, complexity and connectedness: Dimensions of globalization revealed. *Corporate Governance*, 9(4), 435–447.

Chaffey, D., and White, G. (2011). *Business Information Management*, 2nd ed. Prentice Hall, London.

Choi, S.Y., Lee, H., and Yoo, Y. (2010). The impact of information technology and transactive memory systems on knowledge sharing, application, and team performance: A field study. *MIS Quarterly*, 34(4), 855–870.

Coburn, N.F. (2006). Corporate investigations. *Journal of Financial Crime*, 13(3), 348–368.

Collier, P.M. (2006). Policing and the intelligent application of knowledge. *Public Money and Management*, April, 109–116.

Dean, G., Filstad, C., and Gottschalk, P. (2006). Knowledge sharing in criminal investigations: An empirical study of Norwegian police as value shop. *Criminal Justice Studies*, 19(4), 423–437.

Dibbern, J., Winkler, J., and Heinzl, A. (2008). Explaining variations in client extra costs between software projects offshored to India. *MIS Quarterly*, 32(2), 333–366.

Durcikova, A., Fadel, K.J., Butler, B.S., and Galletta, D.F. (2011). Knowledge exploration and exploitation: The impacts of psychological climate and knowledge management system access. *Information Systems Research*, 22(4), 855–866.

Hansen, M.T., Nohria, N., and Tierney, T. (1999). What's your strategy for managing knowledge. *Harvard Business Review*, 77(2), 106–116.

Heisig, P. (2009). Harmonisation of knowledge management—Comparing 160 KM frameworks around the globe. *Journal of Knowledge Management*, 13(4), 4–31.

Innes, M., and Sheptycki, J.W.E. (2004). *From detection to disruption: Intelligence and the changing logic of police crime control in the United Kingdom*. International Criminal Justice Review, 14, 1–24.

Joshi, K.D., Chi, L., Datta, A., and Han, S. (2010). Changing the competitive landscape: Continuous innovation through IT-enabled knowledge capabilities. *Information Systems Research*, 21(3), 472–495.

Lawrence, T.B., Malhotra, N., and Morris, T. (2012). Episodic and systemic power in the transformation of professional service firms. *Journal of Management Studies*, 49(1), 102–143.

Liu, D., Ray, G., and Whinston, A.B. (2010). The interaction between knowledge codification and knowledge-sharing networks. *Information Systems Research*, 21(4), 892–906.

Luen, T.W., and Al-Hawamdeh, S. (2001). Knowledge management in the public sector: Principles and practices in police work. *Journal of Information Science*, 27(5), 311–318.

McClean, E., and Collins, C.J. (2011). High commitment HR practices, employee effort, and firm performance: Investigating the effects of HR practices across employee groups within professional service firms. *Human Resource Management*, 50(3), 341–363.

Mitchell, V.L. (2006). Knowledge integration and information technology project performance. *MIS Quarterly*, 30(4), 919–939.

Nordenflycht, A.V. (2010). What is a professional service firm? Towards a theory and taxonomy of knowledge-intensive firms. *Academy of Management Review*, 35(1), 155–174.

Palte, R., Hertlein, M., Smolnink, S., and Riempp, G. (2011). The effect of a KM strategy on KM performance in professional service firms. *International Journal of Knowledge Management*, 7(1), 16–34.

Roberts, N., Galluch, P.S., Dinger, M., and Grover, V. (2012). Absorptive capacity and information systems research: Review, synthesis, and directions for future research. *MIS Quarterly*, 36(2), 625–648.

Seba, I., and Rowley, J. (2010). Knowledge management in UK police forces. *Journal of Knowledge Management*, 14(4), 611–626.

Seba, I., Rowley, J., and Delbridge, R. (2011). Knowledge sharing in the Dubai Police Force. *Journal of Knowledge Management*, 16(1), 114–128.

Söderlund, J., and Bredin, K. (2011). Participants in the process of knowledge integration. In Berggren, C., Bergek, A., Bengtsson, L., Hobday, M., and Söderlund, J. (eds.), *Knowledge Integration and Innovation—Critical Challenges Facing International Technology-Based Firms*. Oxford University Press, Oxford, pp. 96–121.

Swart, J., and Kinnie, N. (2003). Sharing knowledge in knowledge-intensive firms. *Human Resource Management Journal*, 13(2), 60–75.

Taylor, T.Z., Elison-Bowerrs, P., Werth, E., Bell, E., Carbajal, J., Lamm, K.B., and Velazquez, E. (2013). A Police Officer's Tacit Knowledge Inventory (POTKI): Establishing construct validity and exploring applications. *Police Practice and Research*, 14(6), 478–490.

Wilhelmsen, S. (2009). Maximising Organizational Information Sharing and Effective Intelligence Analysis in Critical Data Sets. Dissertation for the degree of philosophiæ doctor (PhD), University of Bergen, Norway.

Configuration Management

8

An investigation plan is drawn up, and tasks are completed in a sequential as well as iterative procedure. Tasks are based on the plan that might include information about what are the facts to date, what is the best strategy to investigate this matter, what is the contravention/internal concern, who are the targets, who are the witnesses, what documents should be obtained, who should be interviewed, who will be of assistance, who will not be of assistance, where to keep documents/control procedures, and relevant bank accounts (Coburn, 2006). Investigative work is carried out by a team from a law firm or another professional service firm.

Law firms, accounting firms, and other professional service firms have always been pure knowledge businesses, always conscious of the fact that their sustainable advantage is the expertise and knowledge of their consultants, and their firms, rather than any physical factors of service production (Susskind, 2013). The growing awareness of knowledge and its value in organizations from the last decade of the 20th century, coupled with the changes in the business environment, has resulted in progressive firms finding alternative ways of providing cost-efficient and high-quality services that may sharpen their competitiveness and broaden their influence within the investigation services industry and the global economy.

The Big Four are the four largest international professional services firms, offering audit, assurance, tax, consulting, advisory, actuarial, corporate finance, and legal services. They handle the vast majority of audits for publicly traded companies as well as many private companies. The Big Four are Deloitte, PricewaterhouseCoopers (PwC), Ernst & Young, and KPMG.

The legal industry is faced with many changes in the business environment. Some of the major changes are mergers and acquisitions in the industry, new information technology for knowledge management (KM), globalization of legal services, increased specialization in the practice of law, more knowledgeable and demanding clients, and increased profit orientation among partners. As an example of a professional service firm involved in fraud examination, law firms are discussed in this chapter.

Law Firm Business

A law firm is a business entity formed by one or more lawyers to engage in the practice of law. Law firms apply legal knowledge to client's unique problems to provide a solution. In its core the practice of law is the provision of specialized knowledge and services in a variety of ways. The primary service rendered by a law firm is to advise clients (individuals, corporations, or authorities) about their legal rights and responsibilities, and to represent clients in civil or criminal cases, business transactions, and other matters in which legal advice and other assistance is sought.

Many law firms represent large corporate enterprises, organizations, or entrepreneurs with a need for continuous and specialized legal services that can only be supplied by a team of lawyers. The client is a customer of the firm, rather than a customer of a particular lawyer. Relationships with clients tend to be enduring. Such repeat clients are able to gain benefits from the continuity and economies of scale and scope enjoyed by the firm.

A law firm is generally composed of lawyers, paralegals, managers, support personnel, and administrators. Most law firms use a partnership form of organization. In such a framework, lawyers who are highly effective in using and applying knowledge in fee earning are eventually rewarded with partner status, and thus own stakes in the firm. These diverse occupations have distinct functions, yet these individuals must work together to achieve the desired outcome of adding value to the firm. Lawyers represent their clients in legal matters by presenting evidence and legal arguments and provide counsel to clients concerning their legal rights and obligations.

Lawyers are competent in general legal principles and procedures and in the substantive and procedural aspects of the law and have the ability to analyze and provide solutions to legal problems. Lawyers are knowledge workers, which we will explore in this chapter. They are professionals who have gained knowledge through formal education (explicit) and through learning on the job (tacit). After completing their advanced educational requirements, most law students enter their careers as associates in law. In this role, they continue to learn, and thus they gain significant tacit knowledge through learning by doing.

Legal Knowledge

A law firm is an organization specialized in the application of legal knowledge to client problems. The client may want to prevent a problem or solve a problem. In law firm work of prevention and solution, lawyers in the firm apply a variety of knowledge categories such as declarative knowledge and procedural knowledge. One important element of expertise is knowledge, which Taylor et al. (2013) divide into explicit or declarative knowledge and implicit or tacit knowledge. For lawyers, declarative knowledge is explicit knowledge of the law, court sentences, and other legal premises.

Many law firms have transformed themselves from a professional model to a corporate business model. Knowledge is perceived as the resource on which the business is based. Unique, nonimitatable, combinable, and exploitable knowledge provides competitive advantage. Thus, their primary resources stem from the human capital and social capital of the individuals employed within them.

Senior fee earners care more for the overall success of the firm, because they are either partners or senior associates responsible for driving business to the firm. They see the benefit of KM when they can task more junior fee earners on matters, and they can do the job quicker, or because they themselves use the know-how systems more and understand the necessity for KM. Senior fee earners have had more contact with KM, as they have been around the firm longer and found it valuable. In order to earn higher fees, they need to be more efficient and therefore tap into reusable know-how more frequently.

Personal service as the main driver of value perception is closely associated with dedicated KM lawyers. Therefore, the human component in KM is very important. Most lawyers spend several hours a day answering queries, also the type of queries you cannot really capture or look up in a know-how database.

As part of the execution of knowledge processes by lawyers in law firms, we find that these knowledge workers can decide for themselves and are free to decide whether and what knowledge they need, what knowledge they want to develop, communicate, implement, and evaluate. There is an independence of professionals working together, which might be characterized as collective individualism or individualistic collectivism that makes the sharing of knowledge difficult. Employees with a lot of autonomy are free to choose an individual approach to knowledge processes, knowledge needs, knowledge storage, knowledge access, knowledge sharing, knowledge application, knowledge creation, and knowledge evaluation. Autonomy of the performance is an important structural feature that can promote knowledge processes, since such autonomy encourages individuals to develop new knowledge.

Individuality of lawyers may be encouraged, as lawyers can only be managed to the extent they consent to be managed. Furthermore, individuality expresses itself in law firms as lawyers, being professionals, have specialized knowledge and have been trained as an elite member. Some practice groups within law firms may have such specialized practices that their knowledge primarily is of interest to themselves only. This is another example of the individuality of lawyers, as it creates a problem of so-called information silos to the extent that information is not being shared firm-wide.

Law firms often provide expert advice, and knowledge is the foundation and intrinsic value of the expert. Paid to think, consult, and communicate, lawyers are an elite group that makes money commensurate to the value of their knowledge, individually and collectively.

Knowledge Resources

Lawyers in a law firm consult each other, challenge each other, and make friends with each other. They meet during lunch, in front of the coffee machine, in the hallway, or during a formal meeting. This behavior supports the personalization strategy of KM. The codification strategy of KM finds support when lawyers search internal databases, websites, and communicate online. Because of an increased availability and use of IT, it has become so much easier to publish massive amounts of information and knowledge. This creates both an opportunity and a problem. The opportunity is that relevant information is most likely out there; however, to find it is another story. Effective and efficient knowledge sharing could help to relieve this information overload. Furthermore, law firms have grown. Law firms merge or form networks with (inter)national firms.

Because of this growth, the structure and overview of the firm becomes more complex, and so it becomes harder for lawyers to find relevant experts and expertise. We also see that clients want more quality and service in shorter time, and so sharing knowledge within the firm becomes essential. Last but not least, we see that new legal problems emerge, as well as new laws and regulations, for example, as a consequence of new development on the Internet. Having the right knowledge at the right time to deal with new developments is another example of why it is not a surprise that researchers and law firms have become more interested in KM generally and knowledge sharing in particular.

Law firms and lawyers cannot afford to spend time reinventing the wheel every time a client has a similar problem. Because several individuals in different departments within an organization possess knowledge, sharing it is a requirement for the combination and development of knowledge. Sharing knowledge between lawyers improves the economic benefits a law firm can realize from the knowledge of its lawyers. Sharing of knowledge is becoming increasingly important because a network of lawyers can significantly come up with better legal advice than any individual lawyer. Cooperation without hiding important knowledge will result in more productivity and innovation than anyone could reach individually.

Law Firm Clients

Law firm clients are now expecting law firms to use information technology. Law firms in Japan are facing the broader organizational changes brought about by the increased use of information networks by their clients (Nottage, 1998). Du Pont made the Detroit law firm Dickinson Wright provide quick access to information.

Some expect that the transformation of law firms is likely to be wholly positive as far as the clients are concerned. There will be more legal information more widely available, and that information will be available more quickly and efficiently than before. Susskind (2013) expects that both clients and lawyers will be better off—the client will have access to better legal information, and the lawyer will find clients needing more legal services.

Becker et al. (2001) argue that clients no longer need big, expensive firms to conduct ambitious research projects speedily and comprehensively. Powerful Internet-based research facilities make it unnecessary for clients in the US to engage prestigious Washington, DC, firms to help them find out what is happening in federal regulatory agencies and on Capitol Hill. Email and virtual workrooms have reduced the cost and time needed to transmit information and to conduct business. Furthermore, the Internet is likely to intensify competition among law firms by making prices more transparent. Only firms that are distinctive and offer a high degree of expertise will escape the ensuing downward pressure on fees (Becker et al., 2001).

According to Jones (2000), for law firms that have already embraced KM, the next wave will likely include a stronger focus on client-facing extranets and the development of expert systems. Extranets are essential for ensuring lasting relationships with clients, not only because they increase a client's access to their counsel, but also because the firm gets linked tightly with the client that it'll never let go. Expert systems are showing huge potential efficiency returns and hold promise for much of the transactional work tax matters, real estate closings, and financial closings that make up the bulk of legal services.

Susskind (2013) has suggested three generations of websites by law firms. The third and final generation is the most significant and useful. These are sites that offer services. These may be client relationship systems or online legal services. In either event, the common theme is that they go much further than simply providing bodies of relatively unanalyzed information. Instead, they provide more distilled and tailored services, suited to particular users' particular needs.

In contrast to the reactive advice clients receive today, they will receive proactive and more generic legal advice. This advice will not be completely customized but will be good enough to meet client needs and far cheaper than one-on-one legal advice. This proactive advice will reach the latent legal market of people who are unable to benefit from the legal input they require because conventional legal services are too expensive or impractical in the circumstances. Low-end legal advice will become a low-cost, high-volume commodity, and only specialist lawyers will continue to advise in person.

Legal publishers or large accounting firms may "muscle in" on providing legal information services, blurring the line between legal advice and legal publishing and taking over much of the market for legal services from lawyers. The movement toward client-facing software (software that addresses the needs of clients as opposed to the needs of lawyers) will shift billing practices away from hourly rate billing and toward value-based and project billing (Mountain, 2001).

The Internet allows clients to access freshly updated online legal advice from anywhere at any time. Because of this disruptive potential, to focus on the current lack of correlation between law firm technology capabilities and profitability is shortsighted (Mountain, 2001). With the emergence of the World Wide Web, it is possible for clients to gain access to increasingly sophisticated online facilities (Susskind, 2013).

Hokkanen (2000) finds that the legal KM world can (and should) overlap a lot with the new Internet models of business because the legal business model is knowledge based. While the Internet model is concerned with innovation in the offerings to new clients and the creation of new value chains to external customers, the KM model is concerned with innovation in internal processes. When considering client-centric extranets and legal e-business opportunities, it is clear that the two worlds actually converge.

Value Shop Work

This chapter is about configuration management for knowledge-intensive professional firms. Investigation and prevention of white-collar crime have the value configuration of a value shop. As can be seen in the figure, five activities of a value shop are interlocking, and although they follow a logical sequence (much like the management of any project), the difference from a knowledge management perspective arises in terms of the manner in which knowledge is used as a resource to create value in terms of results for the organization. Hence, the logic of the five interlocking value shop activities in this example pertains to an investigation unit and the manner in which it carries out its core business of conducting reactive and proactive investigations.

The value shop configuration is very different from the value chain configuration. The value chain is typically found in manufacturing industries where physical goods are produced in a sequence of activities. The value chain configuration is characterized by a sequential and nonreversible stream of activities. The value shop configuration, on the other hand, is characterized by iterations.

The sequence of activities commences with problem understanding, moves into alternative investigation approaches, investigation decision, and

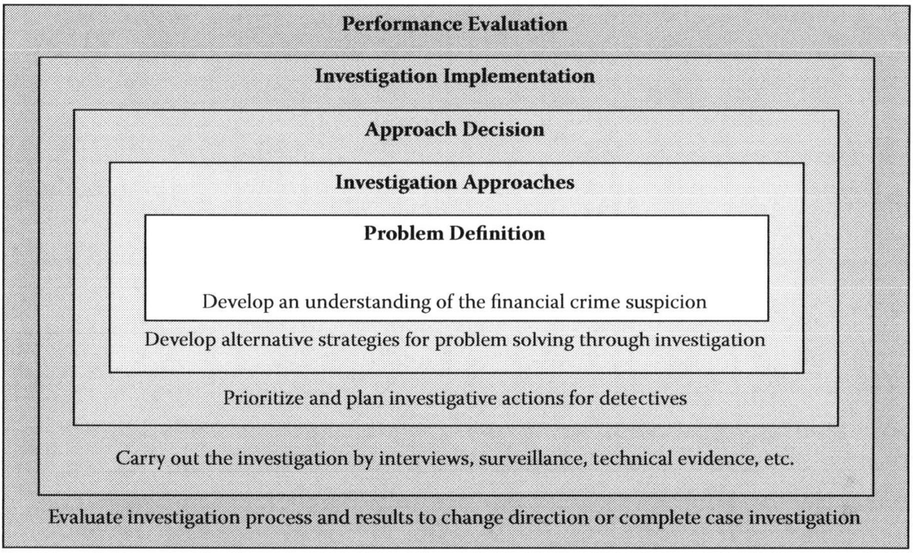

Figure 8.1 The knowledge organization of investigation and prevention units as value shop activities.

investigation implementation, and ends up with criminal investigation evaluation. However, these five sequential activities tend to overlap and link back to earlier activities, especially in relation to activity 5 (control and evaluation) in examination units, when the need for control and command structures is a daily necessity due to the legal obligations that investigation unit authority entails. Hence, Figure 8.1 is meant to illustrate the reiterative and cyclical nature of these five primary activities when it comes to managing the knowledge collected during, and applied to, a specific investigation in a value shop manner.

Furthermore, Figure 8.1 illustrates the expanding domain of the knowledge work performed in financial crime investigations, starting in the center with problem understanding and ending at the periphery with evaluation of all parts of the investigation process.

The five primary activities depicted above of the value shop in relation to a financial crime investigation and prevention unit can be outlined as follows:

1. *Problem definition.* This involves working with parties to determine the exact nature of the crime and hence how it is to be defined. For example, depending on how responding officers perceive or choose to define it, a physical assault in a domestic violence situation can be either upgraded to the status of grievous bodily harm to the spousal victim or downgraded to a less serious, common, garden variety assault and defined as a case where a bit of rough handling took place

toward the spouse. This concept of making crime, a term denoting how detectives choose to make incidents into a crime or not, is highly relevant here and accounts for why this first activity has been changed from the original problem-finding term used in the business management realm to a problem definition process here in relation to investigative work. Moreover, this first investigative activity involves deciding on the overall investigative approach for the case not only in terms of information acquisition, but also (as indicated in Figure 8.1) in terms of undertaking the key task, usually by a senior investigative officer in a serious or major incident, of forming an appropriate investigative team to handle the case.

2. *Investigation approaches.* This second activity of identifying problem-solving approaches involves the actual generation of ideas and action plans for the investigation. As such it is a key process, as it establishes the direction and tone of the investigation and is very much influenced by the composition of the members of the investigative team. For example, the experience level of investigators and their preferred investigative thinking style might be a critical success factor in this second primary activity of the value shop.
3. *Approach decision.* This solution choice activity represents the decision of choosing between alternatives generated in the second activity. Despite being the least important primary activity of the value shop in terms of time and effort, it might be the most important in terms of value—in this case, trying to ensure, as far as is possible, that what is decided upon is the best option to follow to achieve an effective investigative result. A successful solution choice is dependent on two requirements. The first is that alternative investigation steps were identified in the problem-solving approaches activity. It is important to think in terms of alternatives; otherwise, no choices can be made. Second, the criteria for decision making have to be known and applied to the specific investigation.
4. *Investigation implementation.* As the name implies, solution execution entails communicating, organizing, investigating, and implementing decisions. This is an equally important process or phase in an investigation, as it involves sorting through the mass of information coming into the incident room concerning a case and directing the lines of inquiry as well as establishing the criteria used to eliminate a possible suspect from further scrutiny in the investigation. A miscalculation here can stall or even ruin the whole investigation. Most of the resources expended on an investigation are used here in this fourth activity of the value shop.
5. *Performance evaluation.* Control and evaluation involve monitoring activities and the measurement of how well the solution solved

the original problem or met the original need. This is where the command and control chain of authority comes into play for investigation and prevention units, and where the determination of the quality and quantity of the evidence is made in terms of whether or not to ask the police to charge and prosecute an identified offender in a court of law.

References

Becker, W.M., Herman, M.F., Samuelson, P.A., and Webb, A.P. (2001). Lawyers get down to business. *McKinsey Quarterly*, 2, 45–55.

Coburn, N.F. (2006). Corporate investigations. *Journal of Financial Crime*, 13(3), 348–368.

Hokkanen, J. (2000). Knowledge management as Internet strategy. *Law Technology News*. http://www.lawtechnews.com/may00/

Jones, E. (2000). Remaking the firm: How KM is changing legal practice. *Knowledge Management Magazine*. http://www.kmmag.com/

Mountain, D. (2001). Could new technologies cause great law firms to fail? *Journal of Information, Law and Technology*, 1. http://elj.warwick.ac.uk/jilt/01-1/mountain.html

Nottage, L. (1998). Cyberspace and the future of law, legal education and practice in Japan. *Journal of Current Legal Issues*. http://webjcli.ncl.ac.uk/1998/issue5/

Susskind, R. (2013). *Tomorrow's Lawyer.* Oxford University Press, Oxford.

Taylor, T.Z., Elison-Bowers, P., Werth, E., Bell, E., Carbajal, J., Lamm, K.B., and Velazquez, E. (2013). A Police Officer's Tacit Knowledge Inventory (POTKI): Establishing construct validity and exploring applications. *Police Practice and Research*, 14(6), 478–490.

Systems Management 9

Information technology is vital to fraud examinations in two respects. First, information is found in systems regarding transactions and other activities. Second, the examination puzzle is solved by using computers. In this chapter, information technology for fraud examination is described in terms of the stages of growth model.

Stages of growth models have been used widely in both organizational research and information technology management research. According to King and Teo (1997), these models describe a wide variety of phenomena—the organizational life cycle, product life cycle, biological growth, and so forth. Organizational stages have been proposed for corporate social responsibility. Corporate social responsibility (CSR) normally takes place through organizational change processes, whether incremental or transformational, which depend on the organization's situation (Maon et al., 2010).

These models assume that predictable patterns (conceptualized in terms of stages) exist in the growth of organizations, the sales levels of products, the diffusion of information technology, and the growth of living organisms. These stages are (1) sequential in nature, (2) occur as a hierarchical progression that is not easily reversed, and (3) involve a broad range of organizational activities and structures.

Stages of Growth Models

Stage models specifically focus on organizational developments from a dynamic, long-term perspective, which assumes that organizations demonstrate different levels of acceptance, understanding, and integration of issues, principles, and activities at different points in time. These models emphasize the dynamic and evolutionary nature of development processes, during which initiatives become more integrative, sophisticated, and demanding. Even if the evolution might be perceived as a continuum, the continuum is clustered into a number of discrete stages, which can characterize the spectrum of possible developments. Typically, later stages represent greater consideration and higher maturity than earlier stages. Each stage model relates to distinct and often connected theoretical or methodological choices (Maon et al., 2010).

These stage models assert that organizations vary in their reactions and actions to important issues and exhibit various levels and stages of development. Stage models rely on organizational growth theory, which implies that organizations move through stages of growth and require appropriate strategies and structures for each of them. According to this theory, organizational development results from a series of predictable events that prompt responses, which in turn move the organization forward. Beyond these differences, the key characteristics of the successive stages seem similar across models, but may differ significantly on specific dimensions (Maon et al., 2010).

Benchmark variables are often used to indicate characteristics in each stage of growth. A one-dimensional continuum is established for each benchmark variable. The measurement of benchmark variables can be carried out using Guttman scales (Nunnally and Bernstein, 1994; Frankfort-Nachmias and Nachmias, 2002). Guttman scaling is a cumulative scaling technique based on ordering theory that suggests a linear relationship between the elements of a domain and the items on a test.

Embodying such characteristics, organizational learning and innovation diffusion theory can be applied to explain stages of growth models. Organizational learning is sometimes placed at the center of the innovation diffusion theory through a focus on institutional mechanisms that lower the burden of organizational learning related to IT adoption. Organizations may be viewed, at any given moment, as possessing some bundle of competence related to their current operational and managerial processes. In order to successfully assimilate a new process technology, an organization must somehow reach a state where its bundle of competence encompasses those needed to use the new technology (Fichman and Kemerer, 1997).

Innovations through stages of growth can be understood in terms of technology acceptance over time. Technology acceptance has been studied for several decades in information systems research. Technology acceptance models explain perceived usefulness and usage intentions in terms of social influence and cognitive instrumental processes. For example, Venkatesh and Davis (2000) found that social influence processes (subjective norm, voluntary, and image) and cognitive instrumental processes (job relevance, output quality, result demonstrability, and perceived ease of use) significantly influenced user acceptance. Furthermore, they identified determinants of perceived ease of use, a key driver of technology acceptance, adoption, and usage behavior.

Stage Model for Systems

Technology is sometimes labeled IT (information technology) or ICT (information and communication technology). Stages of knowledge management technology is a relative concept concerned with IT's ability to process information for knowledge work. IT at later stages is more useful to knowledge work than IT at earlier stages. The relative concept implies that IT is more directly involved in knowledge work at higher stages, and that IT is able to support more advanced knowledge work at higher stages.

Knowledge management is concerned with simplifying and improving the process of sharing, distributing, creating, capturing, and understanding knowledge. Information technology can play an important role in successful knowledge management initiatives. The extent of information technology can be defined in terms of growth stages for knowledge management systems.

The knowledge management technology stage model presented in this chapter is a multistage model proposed for organizational evolution over time. Stages of knowledge management technology are a relative concept concerned with information and communication technology's (ICT) ability to process information for knowledge work. The knowledge management technology stage model consists of four stages. In terms of the application to private investigations in this chapter, the stages are labeled investigator to technology, investigator to investigator, investigator to information, and investigator to application, as illustrated in Figure 9.1.

This model was developed by one of the authors after extensive empirical research into information systems applied in Norwegian knowledge

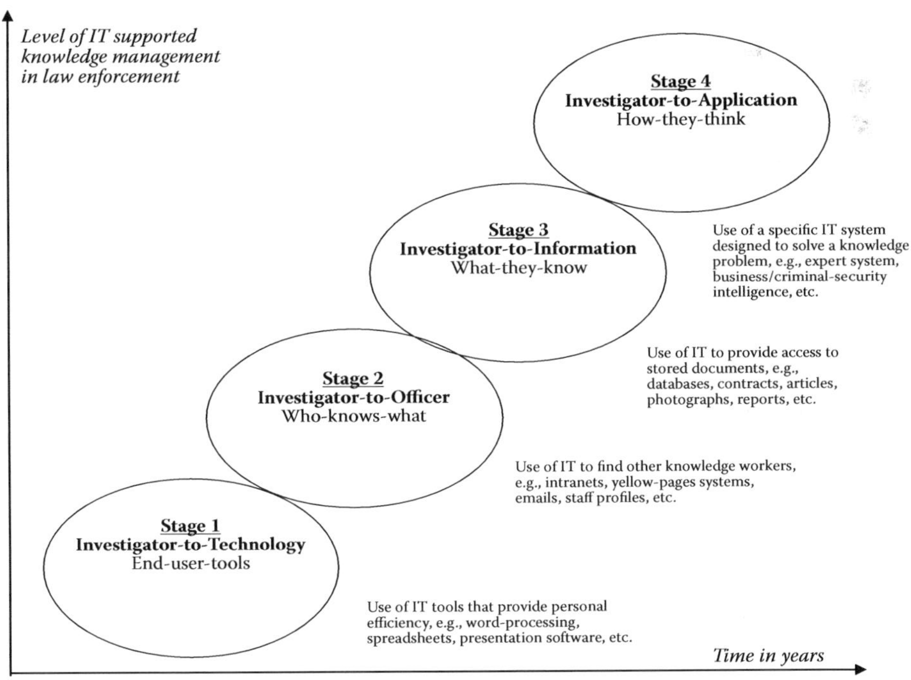

Figure 9.1 The knowledge management systems stage model for investigations.

organizations. While most knowledge organizations have systems at all four levels, the extent decreases along the axis of IT-supported knowledge management in private investigations and other areas of work.

Stages of knowledge management technology are such that ICT, in its later stages, is more useful to knowledge work than it is at earlier stages. The relative concept implies that ICT is more directly involved in knowledge work at higher stages, and that ICT is able to support more advanced knowledge work at higher stages, as illustrated Figure 9.1.

Here, a model consisting of four stages is presented: investigator-to-technology systems, investigator-to-investigator systems, investigator-to-information systems, and investigator-to-application systems, as illustrated in the figure.

1. *Investigator-to-technology stage*: Tools for end users are made available to knowledge workers. In the simplest stage, this means a capable networked PC on every desk or laptop in every briefcase, with standardized personal productivity tools (word processing, presentation software) so that documents can be exchanged easily throughout a company. More complex and functional desktop infrastructures can also be the basis for the same types of knowledge support. Stage 1 is characterized by widespread dissemination and use of end user tools among knowledge workers in the firm. For example, in this stage, investigators in a consulting firm will use word processing, spreadsheets, legal databases, presentation software, and scheduling programs.

   Most knowledge workers rely on office systems, such as word processors, voice mail, email, and presentation tools, which are designed to increase worker productivity. Some knowledge workers require highly specialized knowledge work systems with powerful graphics, analytical tools, and document management capabilities.

   Stage 1 can be labeled *end user tools* or *people to technology*, as information technology provides knowledge workers with tools that improve personal efficiency.
2. *Investigator-to-investigator stage*: Information about who knows what is made available to all people in the firm and to target outside partners. Search engines should normally facilitate work with a thesaurus, since the terminology in which expertise is sought may not always match the terms (and hence search words) the expert uses to classify that expertise. The aim is to record and disclose who in the organization knows what by building knowledge directories. Often called yellow pages, the principal idea is to make sure knowledgeable people in the organization are accessible to others for advice, consultation, or knowledge exchange. Knowledge-oriented directories are not so

much repositories of knowledge-based information as gateways to knowledge, and the knowledge is as likely to be tacit as explicit.

The creation of corporate directories—also referred to as the mapping of internal expertise—is a common application of knowledge management technology. Because much knowledge in an organization remains not codified, mapping the internal expertise is a potentially useful application of technology to enable easy identification of knowledgeable persons.

Here we find the cartographic school of knowledge management, which is concerned with mapping organizational knowledge. It aims to record and disclose who in the organization knows what by building knowledge directories.

At stage 2, firms apply the personalization strategy in knowledge management. The personalization strategy implies that knowledge is tied to the person who developed it and is shared mainly through direct person-to-person contact. This strategy focuses on dialog between individuals: knowledge is transferred mainly in personal email, meetings, and one-on-one conversations.

Electronic networks of practice are computer-mediated discussion forums focused on practice problems that enable individuals to exchange advice and ideas with others based on common interests. Electronic networks have been found to support organizational knowledge flows between geographically dispersed coworkers and distributed research and development efforts. These networks also assist cooperative open-source software development and open congregation on the Internet for individuals interested in a specific practice. Electronic networks make it possible to share information quickly, globally, and with large numbers of individuals.

3. *Investigator-to-information stage*: Information from knowledge workers is stored and made available to everyone in the firm and to designated external partners. Data mining techniques can be applied here to find relevant information and combine information in data warehouses.

   On a broader basis, search engines are web browsers and server software that operate with a thesaurus, since the terminology in which expertise is sought may not always match the terms used by the expert to classify that expertise.

   At stage 3, firms apply the codification strategy in knowledge management. The codification strategy centers on information technology: knowledge is carefully codified and stored in knowledge databases and can be accessed and used by anyone. With a codification strategy, knowledge is extracted from the person who developed it, is made independent from the person and stored in the form of interview guides, work schedules, benchmark data, etc., and then searched and retrieved and used by many employees.

An important part of stage 3 systems is enterprise content management systems that belong to enterprise-wide knowledge management systems. Enterprise-wide knowledge management systems are general purpose business-wide efforts to collect, store, distribute, and apply digital content. Enterprise content management systems help organizations manage business-wide content. Such systems include agency repositories of documents, reports, presentations, and best practices, as well as capabilities for collecting and organizing semi-structured information such as email. Email as a tool at stage 1 is developing into a content provider of information for knowledge sharing at stage 3.

Some organizations develop a knowledge database. For example, the Norwegian consulting firm ISI applies a knowledge base to increase ability of organizational learning. The knowledge base contains methods, techniques, white papers, concept notes, best practices, practice presentations, components, library references, policies, quality systems, process descriptions, routines, strategy documents, ISI presentations, and CVs for all investigators.

Using databases includes determining the frequency of certain documents consulted. This information about the use of databases gives an impression of what knowledge is needed and what knowledge is less needed. An employee can share his or her knowledge through databases containing information and knowledge capture, and a colleague who might perhaps use that knowledge to explain exactly where this knowledge can be found. There are three opportunities of knowledge sharing in organizations: between individuals, between individuals and knowledge repositories (e.g., download a report or a document repository to store a report in the repository), and between existing knowledge repositories. While the first opportunity can be found at stage 2, the other opportunities are found at stage 3.

Stage 3 can be labeled *what they know* or *people to docs*, as information technology provides knowledge workers with access to information that is typically stored in documents. Examples of documents are contracts and agreements, reports, manuals and handbooks, business forms, letters, memos, articles, drawings, blueprints, photographs, email and voice mail messages, video clips, scripts and visuals from presentations, policy statements, computer printouts, and transcripts from meetings.

4. *Investigator-to-application stage*: Information systems solving knowledge problems are made available to knowledge workers and solution seekers. Artificial intelligence is applied in these systems. For example,

neural networks are statistically oriented tools that excel at the application of data to classify cases into categories. Another example is expert systems that can enable the knowledge of one or a few experts to be used by a much broader group of workers. Investigator-to-application systems will only be successful if they are built on a thorough understanding of procedures in private investigations.

Artificial intelligence (AI) is an area of computer science that endeavors to build machines exhibiting human-like cognitive capabilities. Most modern AI systems are founded on the realization that intelligence is tightly intertwined with knowledge. Knowledge is associated with the symbols we manipulate.

Artificial intelligence as well as database technology provides a number of intelligent techniques that organizations can use to capture individual and collective knowledge and to extend their knowledge base. Expert systems, case-based reasoning, and fuzzy logic are used for capturing knowledge from knowledge workers and making information representations and procedures available to other knowledge workers. Neural networks and data mining are used for knowledge discovery. They can discover underlying patterns, categories, and behaviors in large data sets that could not be discovered by intelligence investigators alone or simply through experience.

Knowledge-based systems deal with solving problems by exercising knowledge. The most important parts of these systems are the knowledge base and the inference engine. The former holds the domain-specific knowledge, whereas the latter contains the functions to exercise the knowledge in the knowledge base. Knowledge can be represented as either rules or frames. Rules are a natural choice for representing conditional knowledge, which is in the form of if-when statements. Inference engines supply the motive power to the knowledge. There are several ways to exercise knowledge, depending on the nature of the knowledge. For example, backward-chaining systems work backward from the conclusions to the inputs. These systems attempt to validate the conclusions by finding evidence to support them. In private investigations this is an important system feature, as evidence determines whether a person is charged or not for a crime.

Case-based reasoning systems are a different way to represent knowledge through explicit historical cases. This approach differs from the rule-based approach because the knowledge is not complied and interpreted by an expert. Instead, the experiences that possibly shaped the expert's knowledge are directly used to make decisions. Learning is an important issue in case-based reasoning, because with the mere addition of new cases to the library, the system learns. Private investigators are looking for similar cases to learn how they were handled in the past, making case-based reasoning systems an attractive application in private inquiries into suspicions of white-collar crime.

In fraud examinations, private investigators will apply information technology at all four levels in their knowledge work, depending on the challenges ahead. Systems may be accessed in the client organization as well as in the professional service firm to which the fraud examiners belong.

Seven C Knowledge Framework

In terms of the seven C knowledge framework for knowledge organizations, knowledge management in private investigation units might and should adopt these recommendations as follows, where information systems may play an integral part:

1. *Connect*: In the hierarchy of partners versus nonpartners, and in the network of partners, different methods of connections are required. Nonpartners are supervised by partners, while partners among themselves share and exchange tasks openly, since they at the end of the year share the total profit of the firm. More importantly, connect is concerned with access to relevant information, where information is the raw material in knowledge work performed by investigators. Connect is defined in terms of access to information at stages 2 to 4 in the stage model for information technology-supported knowledge management.
2. *Competencies*: Knowledge categories and knowledge levels have to be made explicit in firms involved in private investigations, such as law firms. Investigators are competent in general legal principles and procedures and in the substantive and procedural aspects of the law and have the ability to analyze and provide solutions to legal problems. However, as defense investigators, they need to be competent not only in substance defense, but also in symbolic defense and information control versus the prosecution. More importantly, competencies are concerned with exploitation and exploration of knowledge, where successful investigators as knowledge workers are able to develop new perspectives and new strategies for their clients. When two parties in a legal fight are represented by two different law firms, the winner is often the client who is helped to argue his or her case in an innovative manner.
3. *Contacts*: Law firms have grown so large that nobody knows what all the others are doing in the firm. Senior fee earners have had more

contact with knowledge management as they have been around the firm longer and found it valuable.

4. *Communication*: The stages of growth model for knowledge management systems to support knowledge work suggests explicit systems for investigator-to-investigator communication at stage 2 of the model. This is the who-knows-what systems stage, where knowledge workers find each other by searching for areas of common interest. Often, an attorney will search for colleagues who may have worked on a similar case successfully, such as a merger or an acquisition, in the past.
5. *Catalysts*: The managing partner in a law firm should install leadership and strategy that shows and supports an active engagement in exploitation and exploration of knowledge. Investigators should be encouraged to tell what they do not know, so that colleagues might help, without judging the questioning colleague.
6. *Culture*: A culture of knowledge sharing is created when nobody fears negative reactions when exposing previous work to colleagues. A culture of knowledge creation occurs when colleagues are allowed to make mistakes. More importantly, shared mental models are needed in a law firm, where successful law firms have a shared understanding of client-attorney relationships as well as colleague-colleague relationships. Investigators in successful law firms share an ambition of making money by contributing a significant difference to their clients. By working iteratively in problem solving, rather than sequentially, investigators mentally think that relationships rather than transactions should be the way of solving client problems.
7. *Capability*: Unique IT systems are created at all levels of the stages of growth model for knowledge management support, but most importantly, in terms of uniqueness, are case-based reasoning systems. Such systems enable the inexperienced investigator to compare a large number of previous cases with the current client case. Generally, successful law firms have unique, nonreplaceable, and valuable knowledge management systems. A knowledge management system is created of the six other Cs, and the interaction between them is difficult to imitate and replicate. Of special importance are vertical and horizontal interactions. Vertical interactions occur when data and information are available to investigators as individual knowledge workers where they apply their wisdom in legal actions. Horizontal interactions occur when investigators in the law firm interact with each based on the unique firm-level knowledge management system.

Capability is illustrated in Figure 9.2, where distinctions are made between data, information, knowledge, and wisdom. Data are numbers and

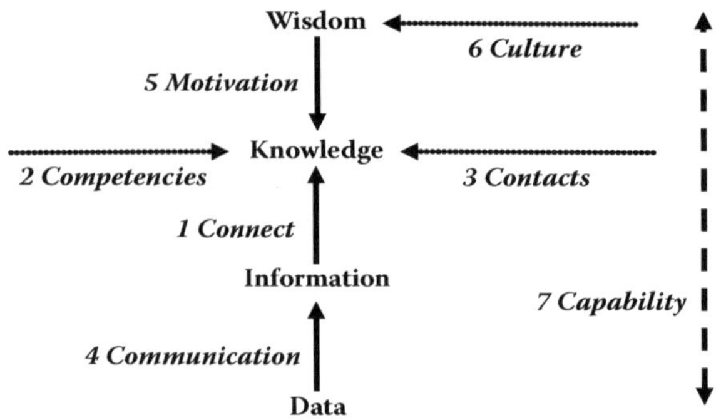

Figure 9.2 Seven Cs in a value hierarchy of insight elements for knowledge management.

other elements without meaning to investigators. Information is data in a context making sense to investigators. An example is the number 62, which at the data level might be the age or the weight of an individual. Information about the age of 62 years becomes knowledge when the investigator reflects on whether this is an old person, by reflecting on client age in a context of interpretation. Wisdom in the figure is defined as accumulated learning over time based on knowledge. However, knowledge is more important than wisdom since knowledge causes the investigator to act.

Most complex in the hierarchy as illustrated in Figure 9.2 is wisdom. Most valuable is knowledge, as knowledge leads investigators and other knowledge workers to actions.

Competition among law firms is intensifying. As clients reward firms that have distinctive depth and breadth of expertise in their most valuable practices, the firms must be more and more willing to pay a premium to attract and retain partners in those specialties. More senior investigators are going in-house to assume increasingly influential positions and to escape the pressures of client development and the tyranny of the billable hour. Senior partners are the ones who have the most to gain if their firms are able to leverage intellectual assets in ways that keep lucrative clients on board and draw in new ones through new services and efficiencies. One measure of senior management's receptivity to KM can be found in its commitment to technology in general, and in its commitment to communication with clients using technology in particular.

For knowledge management approaches to succeed in private investigations, frameworks chosen must reflect the special role of the investigator as an internal or external expert in search of truth in a critical or possibly criminal occurrence. At the same time, both organizational structure and culture need to open up to benefit fully from knowledge sharing and knowledge creation. One starting point might be the individual investigator by defining that person as a knowledge worker.

Knowledge work refers to organizational activities and occupations that are characterized by an emphasis on theoretical knowledge, creativity, and use of analytical and social skills. Knowledge work encompasses both what is traditionally referred to as professional work and more contemporary types of work. In these kinds of work, knowledge acts as the main input into the work, the major way of achieving the work, and the major output (Newell et al., 2009).

The term *knowledge worker* encompasses, then, both professionals and those with other discipline-based knowledge or more esoteric expertise and skills, whose major work tasks involve the creation of new knowledge or the application of existing knowledge in new ways. Knowledge workers typically have high levels of education and specialist skills combined with the ability to apply these skills in practice to identify and solve problems (Newell et al., 2009).

The relevance of each of the seven C factors to investigation units does vary depending on the inquiry tasks that we study. Here we have emphasized private detectives who are knowledge workers trying to solve crime cases. In terms of catalysts, detectives have to be specialists. In terms of connect, competencies, and communication, detectives need to keep a tactical mindset in terms of sharing knowledge with colleagues. Furthermore, the need-to-know principle causes restrictions on access to examination databases.

Business Intelligence

One method of detecting improper activities in corporations where financial crime is suspected is through the use of information technology. Most organizational information is usually created and managed electronically. Computer forensics allows private investigators to uncover more of the facts, support otherwise unsubstantiated information, confirm or refute allegations, and analyze competing theories in relation to those facts. Computer forensics involves identifying, collecting, analyzing, and protecting large amounts of data and peripheral evidence (Newman, 2009).

Business intelligence (BI) systems provide the ability to analyze business information in order to support and improve management decision making across a broad range of business activities (Elbashir et al., 2008). For example, Staffordshire Police in Great Britain uses a series of custom-made applications, including crime recording, custody recording, file preparation, courts administration, and an intelligence system. A small number of criminals commit most of the crime, and detailed BI analysis of data reveals information about offenders and leads to their eventual prosecution. Functions in the system include general queries, property queries, statistical searches, crime profiling queries, and prolific offender queries (Williams and Williams, 2003).

BI is neither a product nor a system. It is architecture and a collection of integrated operational as well as decision support applications and databases that provide an investigator access to data.

Computer forensics is defined as a scientific, systematic inspection of the computer system and its contents for evidence or supportive evidence of a crime or other computer use that is being inspected. It includes the art and science of applying computer systems to aid the inquiry process. Additionally, analytical and investigative techniques are used to examine this evidence and data that are magnetically stored or encoded using the binary number system. The computer might have been the target of some illegal activity, the medium through which the illegal activity is committed, incidental to the commission of the illegal activity, or a combination of the previous three (Newman, 2009).

Data mining is about extracting information from large databases (Srinivasa et al., 2007: 4295):

> Data mining is a process of extracting nontrivial, valid, novel and useful information from large databases. Hence, data mining can be viewed as a kind of search for meaningful patterns or rules from a large search space that is the database.

Forensic ToolKit tells about its products in this way (http://www.access-data.com/products/digital-forensics/ftk):

> FTK is a court-accepted digital investigations platform built for speed, stability and ease of use. It provides comprehensive processing and indexing up front, so filtering and searching is faster than with any other product. This means you can zero in on the relevant evidence quickly, dramatically increasing your analysis speed. The database-driven, enterprise-class architecture allows you to handle massive data sets, as it provides stability and processing speeds not possible with other tools. Furthermore, because of this architecture, FTK can be upgraded easily to expand distributed processing and incorporate web-based case management and collaborative analysis.

Some caution is needed before getting too excited about data mining, according to Lind et al. (2007):

> Whenever huge masses of personal data are stored at one place, and especially when tied to a system with the intelligence to tailor this data, there is enormous privacy risk. The idea is that strict access control surrounds the data. Will that be the case? We can only hope. We see a risk of abuse from corrupted personnel and from hackers or other intruders. Also, there is a risk that data be overly interpreted as true, and that end users be wrongly accused. With the ease in accessing

and perhaps performing data mining on huge amounts of personal data, the risk that a police investigation might take the wrong turn is much greater.

We are now ready to propose a stage model for application of business intelligence in private investigations of white-collar crime. We suggest a four-stage model as visualized in Figure 9.3:

Stage 1: *Big data* is a term for a collection of data sets so large and complex that it becomes difficult to process them using on-hand database management tools or traditional data processing applications. Big data analytics refers to technologies that are grounded mostly in data mining and statistical analysis. Since the late 1980s, various data mining techniques have been developed by researchers from artificial intelligence, algorithm, and database communities (Chen et al., 2012; Hu et al., 2012).

Stage 2: *Environmental scanning* is a term for goal-oriented collection of new data sets from external data sources that can be included in

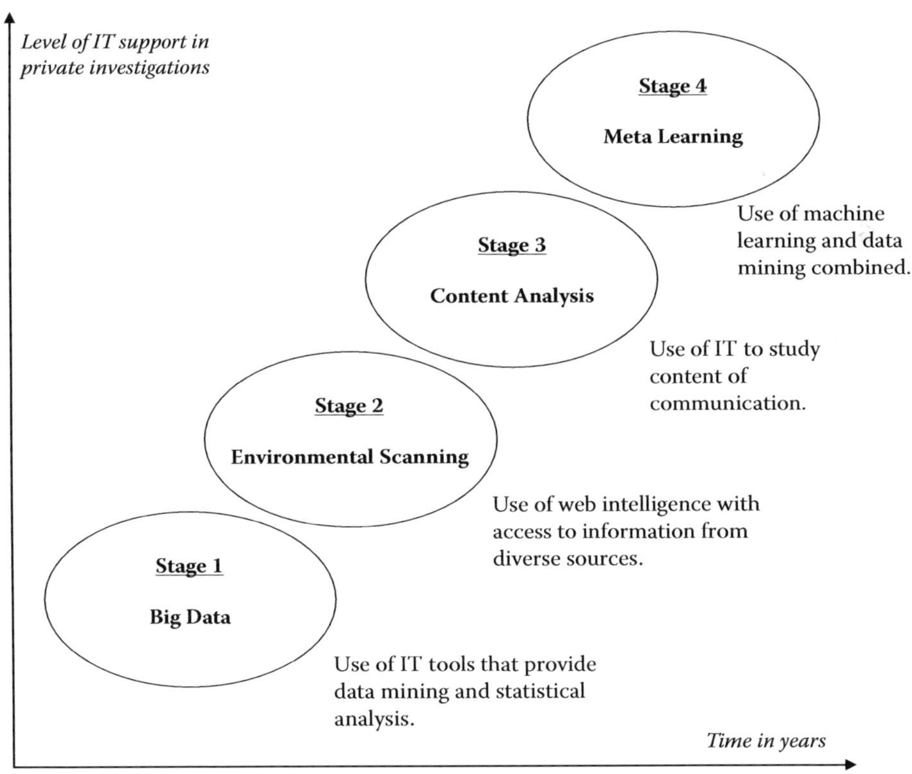

Figure 9.3 Stage model for application of business intelligence in private investigations.

data analytics. Online environmental scanning provides investigators with opportunities to tap into collective web intelligence to develop better insights about factors that may belong in the crime puzzle. Web business intelligence enables access to information from diverse sources. Sentiments and business relations can be extracted from financial news (Lau et al., 2012).

Stage 3: *Content analysis* or textual analysis is a methodology in the social sciences for studying the content of communication. For example, Chau and Xu (2012) examined the contents of blogs to ascertain whether and to what degree certain words were relevant to a topic of interest. As a preliminary analysis, they measured the relevance by looking at the number of times (word frequency) that words were mentioned in each collected blog. Then they filtered out similar blogs.

Stage 4: *Meta-learning* is a specialized form of machine learning that uses the expertise acquired through machine learning or data mining processes to increase the quality of results obtained in future applications. While machine learning provides a multitude of algorithms to complete a task without offering guidance about which particular algorithms to use in a given context, in contrast, meta-learning provides a way to learn about the learning process itself to obtain knowledge about which underlying features and algorithms can be most efficiently applied (Abbasi, et al., 2012).

Abbasi et al. (2012) applied meta-learning to detection of financial fraud. In light of the need for more robust identification methods, they used a design science approach to develop MetaFraud. To evaluate the framework, they conducted a series of experiments on a test bed encompassing thousands of legitimate and fraudulent firms. The results reveal that each component of the framework contributes to its overall effectiveness.

Abassi et al. (2012) demonstrate an approach at the highest level of the stages of growth model. Their approach is at the experimental level, and thus not relevant to practicing fraud examiners and financial crime specialists of today. But their work shows the way forward, and what can be expected in the future. Consistent with design science, they used a series of experiments to rigorously test each component of their MetaFraud framework, as well as to compare the framework to existing state-of-the-art methods. The experimental results revealed that the framework was indeed effective, with legitimate and fraud recall of over 80% for different settings.

References

Abbasi, A., Albrecht, C., Vance, A., and Hansen, J. (2012). MetaFraud: A meta-learning framework for detecting financial fraud. *MIS Quarterly*, 36(4), 1293–1327.

Chau, M., and Xu, J. (2012). Business intelligence in blogs: Understanding consumer interactions and communities. *MIS Quarterly*, 36(4), 1189–1216.

Chen, H., Chiang, R.H.L., and Storey, V.C. (2012). Business intelligence and analytics: From big data to big impact. *MIS Quarterly*, 36(4), 1165–1188.

Elbashir, M.Z., Collier, P.A., and Davern, M.J. (2008). Measuring the effects of business intelligence systems: The relationship between business process and organizational performance. *International Journal of Accounting Information Systems*, 9, 135–153.

Fichman, R.G., and Kemerer, C.F. (1997). The assimilation of software process innovations: An organizational learning perspective. *Management Science*, 43(10), 1345–1363.

Frankfort-Nachmias, C., and Nachmias, D. (2002). *Research Methods in the Social Sciences*, 5th ed. Arnold, London.

Hu, D., Zhao, J.L., Hua, Z., and Wong, M.C.S. (2012). Network-based modeling and analysis of systemic risk in banking systems. *MIS Quarterly*, 36(4), 1269–1291.

King, W.R., and Teo, T.S.H. (1997). Integration between business planning and information systems planning: Validating a stage hypothesis. *Decision Science*, 28(2), 279–308.

Lau, R.Y.K., Liao, S.S.Y., Wong, K.F., and Chiu, D.K.W. (2012). Web 2.0 environmental scanning and adaptive decision support for business mergers and acquisitions. *MIS Quarterly*, 36(4), 1239–1268.

Lind, H., Hjelm, J., and Lind, M. (2007). Privacy Surviving Data Retention in Europe? Presented at W3C Workshop on Languages for Privacy Policy Negotiation and Semantics-Driven Enforcement. www.w3.org

Maon, F., Lindgreen, A., and Swaen, V. (2010). Organizational stages and cultural phases: A critical review and a consolidative model of corporate social responsibility development. *International Journal of Management Reviews*, 20–38.

Newell, S., Robertson, M., Scarbrough, H., and Swan, J. (2009). *Managing Knowledge Work and Innovation*, 2nd ed. New York: Palgrave Macmillan.

Newman, R. (2009). Computer forensics fraud investigations. *Journal of Forensic Studies in Accounting and Business*, Winter, 69–81.

Nunnally, J.C., and Bernstein, I.H. (1994). *Psychometric Theory*, 3rd ed. McGraw-Hill, New York.

Srinivasa, K.G., Venugopal, K.R., and Patnaik, L.M. (2007). A self-adaptive migration model genetic algorithm for data mining applications. *Information Sciences*, 177, 4295–4313.

Venkatesh, V., and Davis, F.D. (2000). A theoretical extension of the technology acceptance model: Four longitudinal field studies. *Management Science*, 46(2), 186–204.

Williams, S., and Williams, N. (2003). The business value of business intelligence. *Business Intelligence Journal*, Fall, 30–39.

Evaluation of Investigations

10

Financial crime investigation is a growing business area for law firms, auditing firms, consulting firms, and other professional service firms. Financial crime specialists in these firms investigate suspicions of corruption, insider trading, embezzlement, tax evasion, and other kinds of financial crime. Their clients are organizations wanting to investigate facts, causes, and responsibilities for an incident or general misconduct. Financial crime specialists apply intelligence, investigation, examination, analysis, and hypotheses to establish facts. They perform fact-finding, causality study, change study, and suspect identification (Machen and Richards, 2004; Morgan and Nix, 2003; Wells, 2003).

Evaluation of private investigations by fraud examiners is needed to establish whether or not practice is in accordance with guidelines and expectations. Evaluation involves collecting, analyzing, and disseminating information to determine if an investigation did what it was intended to do. Ideally, evaluations should assess both the implementation of the investigation (called the process or formative evaluation) and the actual effect of the investigation (called the impact, outcome, or summative evaluation).

Process and Impact

When most people think of evaluation, they usually think of an impact evaluation, which is meant to address such questions as follows:

- How successful has the investigation been?
- Has the investigation met its objectives?
- Has the investigation made a difference? If so, how much of a difference can be attributed to this investigation (as opposed to other factors)?
- What are the factors behind the success of this investigation?
- What factors may have inhibited the success of this investigation?
- What modifications should have been made to improve the effectiveness of the investigation?

A process evaluation, on the other hand, focuses on whether an investigation has been implemented effectively. A process evaluation is as important as an impact evaluation, because how an investigation is implemented can determine its success or failure. In other words, if an impact evaluation determines that an investigation has not met its objectives, it may be because it was implemented ineffectively, which can be revealed by process evaluation.

Some questions that are answered in a process evaluation include the following:

- Was the investigation implemented according to plan? Was it implemented competently and effectively? Was it implemented in a manner that would help achieve ultimate goals?
- Were there sufficient resources available for proper implementation?
- What influence did investigation implementation have on investigation outcome? To what extent did investigation implementation have an impact on the ability of the investigation to meet (or not meet) its objectives?
- What were some of the factors involved in the implementation of an investigation that contributed to its success (or lack of success)?
- What specific problems were encountered as part of the implementation that may limit the impact of this investigation?

The purpose of this chapter is to present results from an exploratory study of private investigations by fraud examiners in Norway. Specifically, the purpose of this article is to present results from a study of investigation reports produced by law firms, auditing firms, and other firms for clients in both the private and the public sector.

This research is important, as the business of private investigations is both challenging and supporting police work. It is challenging police work, as evidence can be harmed and prosecution of criminal offenses can be carried out by private actors rather than public authorities. Private investigations can sometimes challenge the rule of law by taking on all three roles of law enforcement: police investigator, public prosecutor, and court judge. There is a danger of privatization of court settlement that should occur between the community and the criminal.

On the other hand, private investigations can support police work by confirming or disconfirming suspicions of financial crime. Private and public organizations pay the bills from professional firms to establish the facts.

This chapter is concerned with evaluation of fraud examinations. It is interesting to study how cases were solved, whether examiners found out what actually happened, what evidence was collected, whether witnesses support conclusions, and whether the examination in general can be characterized as professional. A suggestion could be that many of the investigations might have had a different outcome with a different and perhaps more qualitative or quantitative investigation method based on more advanced styles of thought. Some fraud examinations might have been carried out as a court process with examination of witnesses during a trial. Such an approach is neither suitable nor acceptable. It is the professionally qualified private investigation that eventually has brought forth the facts that later may be presented by justice authorities as evidence presented in court.

Evaluation Defined

By evaluation is meant a systematic study of work done or work in progress. Here we limit evaluation to studies of work completed. Evaluation methods generally may include quantitative research, qualitative research market research, material testing, product certification, test techniques, statistical research, experiments, quality auditing, and statistics. Here we limit evaluation to studies of examination reports, i.e., studies of documents where we search for information about elements that are related to our criteria. Criteria must be developed for an evaluation before the evaluation can be performed.

An evaluation will look for answers to questions listed above. An evaluation is concerned with both impact and process. Were the objectives achieved? How were objectives achieved?

However, the objective of a private investigation may have been inadequate or misleading. Therefore, it is not necessarily sufficient to study the extent of goal achievement, if one chooses to include the objective as main criteria for evaluation. Rather, an evaluator may question objectives given in the mandate, because the mandate is either incomplete or misleading. The evaluator should take an independent stand to evaluate the mandate from the principal, in terms of both completeness and relevance. A badly formulated mandate is not a good criterion for evaluating the actual fraud examination.

In addition to goal achievement, an evaluation may include, for example, efficiency, process, and results. If a fraud examination leads to nothing, to neither change nor learning, it is obviously hard to justify in the aftermath. Evaluation can also include appropriateness of the investigation in terms of being initiated in a given situation, as well as organization and instruments of investigation, actors' roles in the investigation, and resource consumption during investigation. Evaluation may include study of information management, knowledge management, configuration management, as well as systems management.

Evaluation is a systematic data collection, analysis, and assessment of a planned, ongoing, or completed activity, business, instrument, or sector. Evaluations can be conducted before an action is taken, during the implementation, or after the project is completed. Here we restrict the evaluation to investigations that are completed.

Colloquially, the term *evaluation* implies assessing or estimating the value of something. In the scientific literature, evaluation is a systematic process that is planned with a purpose, and the goal of evaluation is to develop knowledge that is sufficient to judge a completed fraud examination.

Evaluation is to assess the implementation of a project or a program. Evaluations are initiated when someone wants to make up his or her mind about the extent of success or failure of an initiative. Evaluations can thus be characterized as a form of feedback.

Evaluation is a systematic and objective assessment of activities. To stay objective and trustworthy, nobody from the fraud examination team should be involved in the examination evaluation. Evaluation should include the design (starting point), implementation (workflow), and results (examination impact and resource consumption). Evaluations need to be performed by competent people who are objective and independent of control from those who were responsible for the examination. Evaluations should satisfy certain quality requirements, such as openness about sources, triangulation of data (same information from multiple sources), documentation, and conclusion. Upon evaluation, it is to consider not only whether things are done right, but also whether the right things are done.

Either an evaluation can be performed of one specific fraud examination, or a sample of fraud examinations can be evaluated. If the latter approach is chosen, which we do later in this chapter, then there is limited additional information available, making triangulation difficult. The empirical study of a cross section of fraud examinations will be solely based on publicly available examination reports.

Evaluation is a research-based, systematic collection and assessment of knowledge as opposed to an impulsive judgment, which is more or less random and thus imprecise. *Research-based evaluation* and *evaluation research* can be used as synonyms.

Evaluations are always carried out in the aftermath of activities. It is to describe and judge an activity that has taken place. It involves a systematic collection of information, turning information into knowledge, and searching for links between elements and pieces of information. One such search is often for causal relationships, where some pieces of information may describe causes, while other pieces of information may describe effects. Evaluations are designed for each case depending on the context it is implemented in, what interests it covers, and what the focus should be.

To evaluate is to describe, discuss, and conclude. The description takes place within a framework that specifies procedures for data collection, analysis, and drawing conclusions from data. The discussion involves appreciating the findings and analyzing core information elements related to objectives. The conclusion is to be arrived at in a transparent procedure, in terms of both information and criteria relevant for the final judgment of the fraud examination. Selection of criteria for judgment is the outcome of priorities, and thus a question of values associated with the examination. Disagreement about priorities can exist, leading to disagreement about criteria applied to evaluate a private investigation.

Evaluations can be divided into two categories. Formative inquiry is assessment focusing on progression, and it takes place as the activities progress. Summative inquiry is assessment focusing on completed activities. It is summative evaluations of fraud examinations, which is the subject of this book.

Another classification of evaluations is the distinction between goal evaluation and process evaluation. Goal evaluation is an assessment of one or more targets achieved, while process evaluation assesses activities carried out from start to finish. Both forms of evaluation are the subject of this book.

It is important to distinguish between self-assessment and stranger assessment. Self-assessment is when investigators themselves evaluate their own fraud examination. Self-evaluation is useful to assess whether the job is done or more activities have to be completed. Self-evaluation is also useful for learning to improve work in future examination assignments. Stranger assessment is external evaluation where someone else evaluates investigators' work. This is usually an independent assessment, as presented in this book. Stranger evaluation is useful in providing feedback to investigators who may learn from the feedback to improve work in future examination assignments. Stranger evaluation is also useful in educational settings, where students and practitioners can learn from other people's fraud examination work.

The assessment can be made by comparison of evaluation findings to:

- An ideal (goal, policy, wishes, needs)
- Other similar activities, examinations, or organizations
- Development of activities over time

In our context, the comparison might be in relation to an ideal, a goal, or another investigation. Evaluation is thus about relative measures, where the investigation is compared to something else, where something else can be criteria, other investigations, or goals.

An evaluation does always have a purpose. An example is the evaluation of laws, which purpose is to study effects of laws, and where distinctions are made between rule-based evaluation, goal-based evaluation, and context-based evaluation.

Earlier in this book we have used the term *evaluation* in conjunction with the value shop configuration, where evaluation is the fifth and final primary activity. The fifth primary activity is to evaluate the quality of the professional investigation work in the case, evaluate the quality of legal work in the case, involve in the evaluation all who participated in the investigation so far, evaluate how the investigation of the case was headed, control the use of resources so far, and learn from the case work so far. Here the investigators themselves evaluate their own work. This is self-evaluation as opposed to external stranger evaluation. In the self-evaluation within the value shop, the result may be that the investigation has to be continued, that the investigation has to be stopped, or that the investigation has to use more or less resources in the future. Perhaps the result of self-evaluation is that the investigation must continue, because the quality of work is not good enough, and because the investigator did not come to the bottom of the case. The iterative feature of the value shop is characterized by investigators having to complete a new round of work through the primary activities. Investigators may have to return to the very first primary activity of better understanding the problem at hand in terms of suspicion of white-collar crime. Then they may have to move on to select new investigative steps.

Unlike self-evaluation in the value shop, this chapter is concerned with external evaluation of a completed fraud examination. Independent evaluators have to be assigned the task. An evaluation team will judge and consider the value of the work of an investigation team. Therefore, an evaluation sets requirements for systematic and methodological procedure that is transparent. It implies that someone stands outside and looks into the work that has been done, with more or less distance. An evaluation assumes that there is a factual basis, or other sufficiently specific information, that defines what should be measured and what is good or bad. Again, typical purposes of an evaluation of the investigation are to find out whether the investigation met its objectives and what were the effects of the investigation.

Evaluation of examinations is essential to developing fraud examination as a discipline. Evaluation as a discipline in itself should satisfy certain quality requirements, such as openness about sources, triangulation of information, documentation of work and results, as well as a clear conclusion.

Evaluation Procedure

An evaluation can involve either a variety of investigations or a particular investigation. By a range of investigations it is natural to compare them to each other. By a particular investigation it is natural to compare it with predefined criteria. Later in this book we do both based on a sample of fraud examinations in Norway.

It is appropriate to evaluate an investigation that is publicly known, so that the reader largely for himself or herself can check the claims, arguments, and conclusions of the evaluation. We choose a fraud examination, which has been featured in the media, where it was suspicion of economic crime. We start by evaluating why the investigation was initiated. Then we describe the criteria we will use to evaluate the investigation, and how we will collect information about the investigation. Then we can reproduce the main points of the investigation, before we conduct our analysis using criteria as already defined. Finally, we conclude with some recommendations to investigators.

Thus, procedure for the evaluation as well as contents of a potential evaluation report becomes as follows:

1. Introduction about fraud examination, how fraud examination is conducted, what is meant by evaluation, and why it is important to evaluate.
2. Description of the case that was the subject of examination, why the investigation was initiated, what was the investigators' mandate, and what resources were available to them.
3. Development of criteria to evaluate the investigation, including evaluation criteria for the investigators' choice of information strategy, knowledge strategy, value configuration (value chain or value shop), and systems strategy. Strategy choice depends on situational factors; therefore, there is a need for a description of characteristics of the investigative situation.
4. Development of a procedure for evaluation work, how to collect information about the investigation for evaluation. It may, for example, be appropriate to conduct content analysis in terms of document study and interviews with examiners. Fraud examination processes are often extremely closed processes for others than those directly affected. Media coverage is often telling stories incorrectly, because reporters did not obtain information directly from neither investigators nor client. Much of what is referred to in the media about an investigation may be incorrect or misleading. Therefore, evaluators need at this step to discuss source credibility and quality of information to be obtained.
5. Description of how the investigation was conducted, including considerations that were taken into account, and what mindset the examiners might have had. At step 5 there is a need for a theoretical discussion of the suspected white-collar crime, as well as a theoretical discussion of the fraud examination. For example, the relationship between fraud examiner as an agent and client as a principal can be discussed by agency theory. There is no need for a repetition of the investigation report.
6. Evaluation of the investigation by applying evaluation criteria to the actual examination performance, including evaluation of the investigation report. Here grades are given to different aspects of the evaluation, and justification for the grading should be produced. Consequences of the examination should be discussed, whether individuals have been affected by the fraud examination. Cost-benefit

analysis of the examination might be estimated based on assumptions of possible positive contributions and added value from the investigation.
7. Conclusion with recommendations concerning what examiners might learn from the evaluation.

Evaluation will involve the use of general criteria that apply to all possible investigations, as well as the use of specific criteria adapted to the investigation that is being evaluated. As regards the general criteria, they can be divided into five groups:

1. *Start.* How well suited was the starting point for the investigation? How well prepared was the investigation? How relevant was the starting point for the investigation? How long ago did the incident occur? Was the mandate clearly stated? Was the mandate focused rather than diffuse? Was the mandate suited to solve the case? Were activities in the examination clearly defined in the mandate? Were targets for the examination clearly defined in the mandate? How could the starting point have been even better? Did anyone have a hidden agenda for initiating or participating in the investigation? Was the mission rooted in a dynamic principal who was willing to take the consequences of the investigation? Did investigators have any role in the subject matter? Was the investigation mission taken seriously by control authorities? Were support staff identified and accessible for assistance in the work if required? Were financial constraints resolved so that investigators found the budget comfortable to solve the examination task? Was a precise scope for the investigation defined in terms of organizational units, aspects of business, and time horizon defined? Was it clear whether investigators would only report facts or also provide reviews of responsibilities and legal issues? Was the mandate so limited that one might question motives for hiding some relevant aspects from examination? A mandate can be particularly problematic if several different examinations about the same case are carried out in parallel, and when the private examination occurs in parallel or in advance of police investigation. When the police have strict evidence requirements, parallel work by private investigators can cause investigators not to review parts of the case that are highly objectionable, because they do not hold in terms of evidence in a criminal case.
2. *Process.* How well was the investigation conducted? How professional were the examiners? How well did information, knowledge, method, configuration, and systems strategy work? How well was contradiction and non-self-incrimination performed? Was everybody offered

contradiction at an early point in time, given sufficient information to respond, and given sufficient time to respond? Was self-incrimination consistently avoided? How could the work process have been performed in a better way? Was the work process sequential as a value chain or iterative as a value shop? Was impartiality considered and disqualified persons avoided? Was confidentiality handled in a proper way? Did investigators obtain confidential information, and how was this information handled? Have investigators, consciously or unconsciously, overlooked important information, even when it should have been included according to the mandate? Is everybody involved in the process happy with it? Could reasonable progress be observed without signs of strain?

3. *Result.* Did examiners get to the bottom of the case? Answer all questions in the mandate? Who had done what? Are all investigation goals achieved? Do people involved agree with the conclusions? Is the examination report accurate, relevant, complete, and concise, and characterized by clarity, detail, order, and is it easy to read? How relevant were the results of the investigation? Did investigators find out what actually happened? Were they able to identify and describe the sequence of events? Did examiners answer all questions, both those in the mandate and those that had caused the investigation? Did investigators find errors and reasons for errors? Were labor law consequences considered? Were relevant public authorities informed of eventual wrongdoings? Is the investigation report useful to the client? How could the investigation report have been formulated to be more useful to the client? Does the investigation report contain any errors or misrepresentations? Does the investigation report contain discussion of matters and accusations for which suspects were later never charged? How successful was the investigation as a project? Are choices of investigative methods and procedures explicitly described in the examination report so as to give the reader a transparent picture of the investigation? Credibility for the investigation is created when others would get to the same conclusions if they followed the same procedures and applied the same methods—is this possible with the current examination report?
4. *Impact.* Did the client or principal read the report? Did they agree with it? Did they understand it? What did they do with it? What consequences did the examination have for individuals, the organization, products, and the environment? Were people displaced or fired? Were individuals reported to the police? Was the business reorganized? Were new control procedures implemented? Were opportunities for white-collar crime reduced by limiting executive powers and degrees of freedom in business transactions? To what extent did

the client implement changes that were not part of the recommendations from examiners? Did the organization learn from negative incidents? Were suspected individuals left with suspicion without any excuse from client and examiner, when the suspicion could not be confirmed in terms of evidence? Was the blame game avoided? Did the benefits of the examination exceed costs?

5. *Resource.* How big was the consumption of resources in terms of money, key persons, and competence? Did the project complete within agreed cost and schedule? Were relevant skills used in the investigation? The term *resource* comes from a word that means to make something possible. A resource is thus an enabler. What was enabled by the use of resources? What resources were applied in the form of knowledge? What resources should have been used in the form of knowledge? How could resource consumption have been reduced?

These five dimensions of evaluation are used in the examples in Chapter 11. In general, the characteristics of a successful investigation include:

- As appropriate as possible description of facts
- As good as possible judicial reviews
- As excellent as possible legitimacy for and trust in both process and results
- As complete as possible answers to the mandate
- As relevant as possible learning from the examination
- As correct and relevant work procedure as possible
- As considerate behavior as possible
- As optimal resource allocation as possible
- As effective progress as possible in accordance with the announced schedule

Contributors to Evaluation

An evaluation of an examination is a process of using many of the same sources of information and methods of investigation that the investigators did. Evaluation is an examination of the examination. Evaluation is an investigation into the investigation. But the purpose is different. The examination was launched to find facts in a case where rumors and accusations were spreading. The evaluation is launched to judge whether the examination was fair, successful, and made a contribution. An evaluation is simply to find out whether the examination made sense or was a waste of time and money.

Perhaps informants are in a unique position to succeed with an evaluation. Previously, informants were described as a key source of information in private investigations. People who would tell something, especially whistle-blowers, are often the key to get to the bottom of a case. Similarly, informants can tell how the examination was experienced and what consequences, if any, the examination led to. Like in the investigation itself, informants are a source of information, while the treatment of informants is a matter of investigative or evaluative methods. Confrontation in an interview is one method, while collaboration in the same interview is another method.

Informants are persons who are in possession of or who have access to information that is of interest. The availability of this information is called access. Informants often have some motivation to provide information. One can distinguish between relationship-oriented informant handling as a method and transaction-oriented informant treatment. Relationship-oriented informant handling involves developing cooperation with a person in the relevant milieu or having generally good contacts in that milieu. Transaction-oriented informant treatment involves establishing and terminating contact for the sole purpose of information retrieval and transfer. There is no involvement other than information transaction, while a relationship includes discussions that can release new insights based on information as a raw material for the communication.

An evaluation of a fraud examination is a kind of case study. Evaluation can thus be defined as case study research. Case studies are intensive qualitative studies of one or more investigation units. The term *case* comes from Latin *casus*, which emphasizes the importance of the individual case. The case as the unit of analysis—in our context an investigation as the unit of analysis—is seen as a complex whole, where many subunits and their relationships to each other are brushed in detail. What characterizes a good case study raises questions about validity and reliability. Internal validity is about quality and credibility. External validity is a question of how representative these findings are for a larger population. The extent of generalization has to be considered. Reliability is about trustworthiness of measurements.

Informants are often interesting because they may help to shed light on events and issues that go beyond their own experiences. Informants possess knowledge about issues, situations, relationships, and context that is not widely available. Informants' knowledge wealth and experience can also contribute to unifying descriptions and interpretations of great value to evaluators. Evaluators may continuously seek to utilize interviews to test their own assumptions as well as assumptions for the informant's observations, while at the same time avoiding control or command of responses in a particular direction.

Informants can provide conflicting information. The problem is not always that informants deliberately withhold information or choose a biased angle when presenting information and interpretations. There are also a number of unconscious mechanisms that affect the informant's representation of what has happened. His or her reliability varies with the attitudes and experiences, issues, situations, time spans, and institutional contexts. An important element of each evaluation interview is to establish facts that cannot be subject to interpretation. As far as possible, one should establish the sequence of events, pinpoint critical events, and then who was present and what was said. This provides a structure for questioning.

Secrecy of Investigations

In order to evaluate an investigation by fraud examiners, access must be granted by the principal or client of the investigation. The exceptions are investigations that are publicly known, and where the investigation report is available to the public. Sometimes, investigation reports are leaked to the media, and thus make investigations publicly known. Only publicly known investigation reports can be evaluated in research that is to be published in scholarly journals.

Chapter 11 is based on publicly known fraud examination reports in Norway. However, so many more examination reports exist that are never made available or leaked to the public. The secrecy limits researchers' possibility to evaluate investigations for learning and knowledge development purposes.

There may be good reasons to hold an investigation report secret. The report may contain information that can benefit competitors, and thus may hurt the company in its markets. The report may contain more or less baseless accusations against individuals, thus getting the blame, without being able to defend themselves. Less acceptable reasons to keep an investigation report secret may be that investigators did not really succeed, they did not find the truth, they did a poor job with contradiction and failed on other quality requirements, or the report is poorly written. Some argue that corporate reputation may suffer if the contents of the examination report are made publicly known.

Many factors associated with a private fraud examination can lead to secrecy and confidentiality with regard to the contents of an investigation report. Here are some reasons experienced in Norway for the secrecy of investigation reports:

1. *Damage.* The examination report contains business secrets that competitors might take advantage of, and thus cause damage to the business in its markets. A number of sensitive business issues can be covered in the report, which can harm the organization far beyond what the investigation is all about, if it becomes publicly known. It might even be stock exchange-sensitive information, and then it is for sure important that nobody or everybody receive the same information at the

same time. Refusal to receive the report on Veidekke (a construction company) by Ernst & Young, for example, was reasoned by sensitive information that the company did not want third parties to get in their possession. The examination can result in unjustified conclusions that will harm corporate reputation and be damaging for future activities. It might, for example, become difficult to achieve government contracts. The organization does not have the chance to argue its case and defend itself in court, if allegations are not investigated by authorities and there is no prosecution. A published report not only harms the organization, but also can cast suspicion on management and employees in the firm. Deteriorating reputation can make it difficult to recruit qualified personnel to the firm, and clever experts will leave the firm to join the competition. If the firm becomes known for corruption or other kinds of financial crime, then fewer experts will want to work for the firm. Refusal to receive the report on Hadeland og Ringerike Bredbånd (a communication company) was explicitly reasoned by the danger of bad reputation.

2. *Confidentiality.* Lawyers are subject to confidentiality similar to medical doctors and psychologists. What is included in the attorney's confidentiality will not be presented even in court, unless the protected party agrees to have information disclosed. Similar regulations do not apply to auditors and others, unless they are working in support of lawyers. Fraud examiners belong to professions not regulated by confidentiality, but it can nevertheless be arranged between the client and the investigator. When law firm Wiersholm investigated Yara (a fertilizer company) for corruption, lawyers kept all secrets.
3. *Suspicion.* Some investigation reports are very comprehensive and also describe circumstances for which the suspect was never prosecuted. This was the case for the CEO in a bakery chain who was investigated by PricewaterhouseCoopers (PwC). Persons who are interviewed in private fraud examinations are not under oath as in court. Some interviewees may tend to include others in their statements and even put the blame on others to reduce their own guilt. Publishing such a resulting report will harm individuals who are not at all responsible for misconduct and illegal actions by the organization. Publication may be a pillory for people who did not commit any crime or misconduct.
4. *Error.* Some investigation reports have serious flaws, mistakes, errors, and shortcomings. This was the case with the investigation of Store Norske Spitsbergen, which is the northernmost mining company in the world. The CEO was later sentenced to 2 years in prison because of fraud and corruption. But the investigation report had several errors in it, which were corrected by the subsequent police

investigations by the Norwegian National Authority for Investigation and Prosecution of Economic and Environmental Crime, and also by investigative journalists at a TV station (TV 2). The private fraud examination at Spitsbergen was carried out by PwC.

5. *Accusation.* The investigation report has a number of unfounded accusations against individual persons, who receive the blame, without being able to defend themselves. The report describes persons and their activities that are not true. Persons are never prosecuted in court, so they have no legal frame within which to have their defense. Private investigation reports sometimes represent examination, prosecution, as well as sentence. These powers are strictly separated in the authorities: while the police conduct investigations, the prosecutor makes decision whether to prosecute, and the judge makes decision whether to sentence someone to prison. If these three roles are combined in one single person, the private investigator, serious mistakes can be made, especially when the financial crime specialist has done a mediocre job. Very often, investigation reports receive much more legitimacy and power than formal and institutional conditions can support. For example, journalists tend to read reports as sentences from a court. A report can criminalize individuals without providing them a reasonable opportunity to deny and refuse the case. Some situations can end up in personal tragedy, including suicide. Family and friends become victims as well. Financial and psychological ruin can follow. Chief executives have a tendency to blame persons further down the line, if at all possible. When the World Bank discovered that Norwegian engineering company Norconsult was bribing officials in Africa, top management was successful in blaming local Norwegians who had arranged corruption. Similarly, when Norwegian construction company Veidekke was caught in cartel activities, top management was successful in blaming a middle manager. Top-level executives let the blame move down the organization and even provide names of employees who were not necessarily guilty and maybe not even involved at all. People can be referred to in the investigation report because they were close to the matter, yet were innocent. If names of innocent individuals get into the public domain, there is a great danger that the names of these people are remembered. This is contrary in practice to the presumption of innocence in which everyone is innocent until proven guilty. Presumption of innocence is the fundamental principle of the rule of law that any doubt should benefit the accused. After law firm Wiersholm had examined Yara (a fertilizer company) for corruption, the Norwegian National Authority for Investigation and Prosecution of Economic and Environmental Crime charged a total

of four executives in the firm. After further police investigations, the charge against one of the executives was dropped. By then, however, everybody in the public knew the names of not only three, but four Yara executives in the case. The innocent executive's defense attorney commented that his client had unlawfully been drawn into the case by both private examiners as well as the police. The attorney for another executive, who was still charged, argued that his client had been a whistle-blower who brought the whole affair to light.

6. *Failure.* The private investigation by fraud examiners was unsuccessful and a failure. Investigators did not find answers to the questions that initiated the inquiry, and they did not solve problems as expected by the client. Some investigations found no facts and no truth. Some investigations added nothing new. This was probably the case with the investigation by Deloitte of government-owned Norsk Tipping, a betting enterprise, where the Office of the Auditor General did find evidence, while the private investigators did not.
7. *Misconduct.* The private investigation was a failure because investigators showed misconduct in their work. Their procedure was flawed and undocumented. Maybe examiners forgot about or ignored the interviewed persons' rights for contradiction and other quality measures of an investigation. Maybe the report is misleadingly written and emerges as a commissioned work with conclusions as required by the client.
8. *Packaging.* Some private investigation reports are simply not readable. Maybe the report is too long or too short. Perhaps the report is simply unintelligible. The packaging or wrapping of the investigation is complete garbage. Sentences do not make sense. Some reports are characterized by the complete absence of focus. Some reports are just a listing of issues with no explanations or links between them. The examination report about Troms Kraft (a public utility company) of 663 pages by consulting firm Norscan is simply too long. There is no way a reader can keep focused through such a large document, and it indicates that the investigators were lacking focus themselves. On the other hand, a report of only 14 pages by PwC in the Turkey case (smuggling of children home to Norway from Turkey) probably does not say much at all. Somewhere in between, maybe around 100 pages might be relevant to state clearly: (a) what the investigation was about, (b) how the investigation was carried out, (c) what major findings were made in the investigation, and (d) what might be the consequences of the investigation in terms of recommendations.
9. *Disagreement.* Among owners of the organization, there might have been agreement to conduct a private investigation, but agreement can be lacking afterwards concerning publication of the investigation

report. In the electric power company Troms Kraft, investigated by Norscan, two major owners disagreed what should happen next. In the fertilizer company Yara, investigated by law firm Wiersholm, one large shareholder required the chairman to resign, while other owners remained silent.

10. *Termination.* Like all other kinds of projects, some investigation projects are terminated before completion. One reason for early termination is the lack of relevance to the organization. Another reason is that the project was premature. A third reason might be that the project went on in a completely wrong direction. In all these circumstances, an unfinished document is all there is as an investigation report. When the Norwegian Football Association discovered that a specific court case was dismissed, it lost interest in the private investigation into player transitions. The investigation was conducted by the law firm Lynx.
11. *Protection.* Many individuals have provided valuable and sensitive information to private detectives under the assumption and with the promise that their information will never be disclosed. They were promised confidentiality and maybe even anonymity. Since there is no obligation to provide information to private investigators beyond the loyalty of helping one's employer, publication at a later point in time will be a serious breach of trust. It can cause serious, unwanted, and unexpected damage to interviewed individuals. Trust in future investigations, and trust in fraud examiners in general, will deteriorate. In the Yara case, investigated by law firm Wiersholm, the company accepted a substantial fine for corruption, while four prosecuted executives denied participation in corruption in Libya, India, and Russia. As long as there were no court hearings yet, it would be damaging to them if the investigation report became public. It would violate the presumption of innocence, which is common for all nations of justice. It could also be detrimental to an upcoming trial. Similarly, in addition to errors and inaccuracies, Store Norske Spitsbergen, investigated by PwC, had to protect individuals who had provided personal and confidential information to investigators.
12. *Evidence.* Sometimes, private investigations are followed by police investigations, which may or may not lead to prosecution and court ruling. If important evidence is leaked to the public, it can harm the court trial, both for the prosecutor and for the defendant. The police may be interested in private detectives keeping secret until a final legal decision has been made. Evidence is legally what is presented by the parties in a lawsuit. Maybe one reason for keeping the Yara investigation by law firm Wiersholm a secret is the police not wanting evidence to be harmed or destroyed.

13. *Workload.* Some argue that it would be too much work involved in making an examination report available to the public. The Norwegian Parliament's administration used this rationale for its refusal, when access to an examination report was denied. The administration argued that it would be too much work involved in censorship of the report written by Professor Kjønstad about some former members of Parliament who had received too much in pension payments.
14. *Discretion.* Another reason for not publishing the investigation report is to provide discretion for executives and key people who have influential friends. They are protected from negative public exposure. A publicly funded examination of the collapse of a publicly owned road construction company was kept secret to protect some important politicians and bureaucrats in an Oslo municipality. However, another examination carried out by law firm Kvale was published, where accusations mainly were aimed at management of the construction firm.
15. *Sensitivity.* The investigation report contains sensitive personal data that must not go astray. Either such information can be censored while the rest of the report is published or the entire report can be kept secret. Many of the examination reports evaluated in Chapter 11 are partly censored to conceal certain names and sensitive information. Examples are Gassnova, a utility enterprise examined by auditing firm BDO; Halden municipality, examined by law firm Hjort; Moscow school case, examined by auditing firm Ernst & Young; Norwegian Football Association, examined by law firm Lynx; Norwegian public betting firm, examined by auditing firm Deloitte; Oslo municipality, examined by auditing firm PwC; another Oslo municipality case, examined by auditing firm PwC; the Norscan examination of utility firm Troms Kraft; and the law firm Kvale examination of public road construction bankruptcy in Oslo.
16. *Property.* The organization hiring a private investigator to conduct a fraud examination pays for the work and becomes the owner of the examination report. It is the property of the client or principal. The owner sees no reason why the organization should tell the environment in society what examiners did find or did not find in a case of financial crime suspicion. Society is no stakeholder in the case and should therefore not get access to the report. An example is the military equipment manufacturer Kongsberg Group, which was investigated by PwC for possible corruption in Romania.

It is suggested that it should be agreed upon in advance of a private investigation whether or not a resulting investigation report is to be kept secret or shared with the public. However, as indicated by some of the issues above, depending on the success or failure of the examination, clients, investigators, participants, as well as others may change their mind in the course of the investigation.

There are probably many more reasons or excuses for not publishing a fraud examination report. The reasons are more or less good from a transparency perspective and corporate social responsibility perspective. Not all reasons for secrecy are equally acceptable, and certainly not honorable. If an investigation was poorly conducted, it may well be public, as long as personal information and other sensitive information has been removed or censored. It is not always acceptable to invoke lawyer privilege of confidentiality, because the investigation is not traditional attorney work. Particularly worrisome is when auditors and detectives are hiding behind attorneys' professional secrecy in the same firm, as they define themselves in the role of legal helpers. Here it should be cleaned up so that some lawyer roles do not necessarily imply secrecy. An investigation can clearly be distinguished against traditional legal advice from lawyer to client.

In general, it seems that many are claiming confidentiality even when there is no factual basis for it. Cheating with confidentiality is not uncommon to avoid disclosure of unpleasant news. Cheating as a reason not to show openness, dialog, and strive to cultivate transparency is a tempting option to avoid negative publicity. A type of cheating is when attorneys and their helpers in roles of private investigators claim the attorney-client privilege of complete secrecy. Another type of cheating is when companies invoke the need to take into account a possible subsequent police investigation and therefore must remain silent. A third type is to claim interests of the parties concerned. Society needs greater transparency in financial transactions in order to have confidence in the actors and organizations in general. Therefore, openness and transparency rather than secrecy and confidentiality are desirable and necessary.

When it becomes known that an investigation has taken place, followed by police investigation and prosecution indictment, there is a natural pressure toward the company to publish the private fraud examination report, which can harm the company or cause any of the other above-mentioned problems. The danger may be that parts of the report start to leak, thereby creating a false impression of the investigation. Individuals' involvement in negative events that are critically discussed in the report will make those individuals appear guilty. Individuals who do not get criticized in the report may, on the other hand, be interested in the report being published. Publication should, however, be clarified before the investigation begins, so that all involved know what they are part of.

If regulation of the private investigation business should lead to requirements concerning disclosure, it may cause a reduction in private fraud examinations being initiated and carried out. Businesses are fast to comply with current regulations, and if rules do not fit, then new approaches and solutions are quickly found. In the area of sociology of the law, an important topic is how laws work in society and how actors change behavior, if they do not like the law. If regulations are not in accordance with what businesses want, in an area where there is freedom of choice, this can easily lead players to choose other options than private investigations.

A number of reasons for secrecy were presented above. Similarly, one can think of many reasons for the disclosure of investigation reports to all stakeholders and to the public. It will act as a deterrent for others who have opportunities to do something illegal in terms of white-collar crime. They will see the consequences of their misconduct being publicly known. Disclosure may deter others thinking of committing economic crime, or who are affected to stop crime. Publication directs focus toward ethics and morale, where it becomes visible as to what boundaries to respect and what businesses can afford in the business context. Disclosure increases the degree of transparency and openness in society. An investigation report can contribute to learning in other business enterprises, where they will allocate resources and focus to prevent similar negative events. An investigation report can more easily be disclosed if personal and confidential information is hidden.

When there was discussion in Norway about disclosure of the law firm Wiersholm's report on corruption in Yara, a global fertilizer manufacturer, an argument for disclosure was that this was a case that had already been widely discussed in the media, and that it therefore was of great public interest. Yara is a well-known company to many in Norway, not least because of its roots in Hydro, another global player based in Norway. The public could become aware of how the corruption cases in Gadaffi's Libya and other countries were actually handled by Yara top management in the past. Disclosure may generally provide greater insights into the causes of economic crime, and thus raise awareness about ethical issues of misconduct and crime. By raising public awareness, businesses may become better prepared to prevent financial crime in the future.

Disclosure of internal investigation reports may also serve as an inspiration for potential whistle-blowers. Fraud examinations caused by whistleblowers inspire others to blow the whistle when they observe and experience misconduct and crime, especially above themselves in the organization. Their fear of what might happen can be reduced by reading what happened in similar cases in other organizations.

Last but not least, disclosure and publication of fraud examination reports enable empirical research into private investigations. Such research, as presented in Chapter 12, is much needed, since little is known about what is actually going on compared to what should be going on in private investigations. Only research and knowledge sharing can enable the business quality of fraud examinations to move forward. Research is important to prepare the foundation for future teaching of the art and science of fraud examinations in colleges and universities.

Disclosure to Law Enforcement

Fraud examiners in white-collar crime investigations and their clients not only prevent disclosure of private investigation reports to stakeholders, media, researchers, and the public. Often they also prevent disclosure to law enforcement such as the police, even when there is clear evidence of penalty law violations. This is a serious problem in democratic societies, where violations of state laws are to be investigated by the police, indicted by a state prosecutor, and a possible sentence decided by a judge in court.

Several reasons can be found to explain why the police do not get to know about private investigations of white-collar crime suspicions and potential evidence:

1. *Control.* One possible reason could be that the client organization loses control over the subject matter. By hiring examiners from an auditing firm or law firm, the client organization pays for the investigation and is owner of the investigation report. Thus, the client has complete control over information flows to and from the investigation. The client has complete control regarding following steps or no steps at all. The client can decide to terminate the investigation, or let an investigation report rest on the shelf. The client can decide whether or not to disclose investigation results. If investigation results are handed over to the police, the client loses control over information and what happens next. When the police go into the matter, management no longer has control, and circumstances can be revealed that are unpleasant for themselves. Maybe management launched its own investigation precisely to resolve the matter internally, irrespective of whether or not criminal offenses had occurred. Management intended to clean up its own mess in-house—with minimal noise and attention. External interference from the police could make internal problem solving difficult. Police interference may damage or delay internal problem-solving processes. These are some of the reasons why control is more important to some organizations than a fair and transparent prosecution of offenses in public courts of democratic societies.
2. *Reputation.* If it becomes known that the police are investigating the case, it could lead to negative publicity and financial loss, in line with disclosure, as described above. For example, law-abiding employees who are attractive on the labor market could choose to

leave. Qualified external candidates could choose not to apply. While a private investigation can be communicated as something positive, a police investigation is almost always perceived in the market as something negative. The company does not want the negative publicity that the prosecution of a former chief executive typically will entail. The company will not enjoy or have any benefit from the former executive being imprisoned. An internal solution to internal crime could enhance internal confidence in the company and reduce risks of future criminal activities. External interference from the police might create an impression of the company being unable to handle and solve internal problems. If a criminal case becomes known to the police, law enforcement will typically arrive with a search warrant at company premises, and soon there will be all negative news about the company all over the media. This could make customers less reluctant to continue business with the company.

3. *Exclusion.* As long as the company is under investigation by the police, the company may be put on hold for contracts in both the public and private sectors. Customers will generally be more reserved toward the company. The same can happen with suppliers because they are uncertain about the outcome of a police investigation. Both customers and suppliers may experience criticism for entering into agreements with a company under investigation. If an investigation is followed by prosecution and conviction, and if the company is sentenced to a fine or executives are sentenced to prison, then the company may be permanently excluded from business with public sector organizations such as the World Bank.
4. *Penalty.* Reaction against the company may be a reason for not going to the police. The company hopes it can keep the matter hidden and thus not lose money, as it would have to pay a potential fine. Generally, the consequences of going to the police are considered greater than keeping the matter hidden.
5. *Protection.* Shielding both individuals and the organization from police investigation is yet another reason for not disclosing evidence of white-collar crime to the police. In a police investigation, others than those who were subject to negative attention might emerge in a bad light and possibly end up being indicted, prosecuted, and convicted. This is desirable for neither board members nor executives, especially if suspicions may turn against them. They have the power and resources to prevent critical examination of their own conduct. Generally, the outcome of a police investigation can become something completely different from what the company wants. Police involvement does more harm than benefit to the business.

6. *Passivity.* Police often demonstrate passivity when approached about possible offenses. Many cases are dismissed without investigation. A survey by the Norway Security Council shows that 75% of companies that responded to the survey agreed with the statement that crime is not reported because the police usually dismiss the case without proper investigation.
7. *Effort.* In the same survey, 65% of respondents agreed with the statement that crime is not reported because it takes too much time and effort. The police will ask for all kinds of documentation and access to computers. If the police open an investigation, then key employees will have to spend time in police interviews, and executives will have to spend time explaining to police officers how the organization operates.
8. *Failure.* Just like a private investigation can fail to establish the facts, so can police investigations fail to find the truth about a negative incident. If police investigations are expected to end up in nothing, why bother involve the police, some organizations may certainly argue.
9. *Trifle.* The organization considers what happened to be an insignificant issue. White-collar offenders operate with relative impunity because of widespread apathy in both private and public contexts. The organization has tolerance and leniency toward internal criminals in trusted positions. While penalty laws tell otherwise, white-collar criminals are not considered real criminals when compared to street criminals. Secrecy of findings versus the police need not be a conscious act in the sense that something shall be hidden and someone shall be protected. It may be that the one who commissioned the investigation has a different perception of the severity of investigators' findings than the examiner or the police. An example is the military equipment manufacturer Kongsberg Group, which was investigated by PwC for possible corruption in Romania. Kongsberg Group management did not find examination results serious. They considered them to be trivial findings. That was the official explanation of Chairman Jebsen and Chief Executive Qvam. This case became publicly known after Norwegian police had learned about it from a whistle-blower.

These possible explanations all have in common that economic objectives of profit maximization could have a lot to lose by going to the police, especially if it might be assumed that the organization is able to keep crime a secret. When an unwanted injury and harm first occurs because of law enforcement taking action, however, then prestige and economic loss becomes far greater than if the organization had reported crime evidence to police in the first place. Thus, the decision to go to police or keep police outside is a question of costs and benefits, where costs are affected by risk of secrecy detection.

Secrecy to the police, however, is a far greater question in society than cost-benefit for the company involved. Private investigations are of concern because they involve a privatization of police investigations of potential punishable acts. Settlement between the suspect and the nation should always be organized by formal authorities and agencies in society. The government cannot accept a privatization of such a settlement procedure. Privatization of settlement between the offender and community is unfortunate, not least because the company does not believe it will benefit its business if it reports a person to the police who is eventually sentenced to prison.

Nevertheless, privatization of criminal justice seems not uncommon in Norway. Offenses are not reported to the police. In the Norwegian survey, 40% of respondents agreed with the statement that crime is not reported because companies have decided to treat such matters internally.

While some private investigations come up with trivial findings as perceived by the client, it happens that the business firmly believes there has been a crime and goes to the police with the case. But then the police may dismiss the case, which evokes very negative reactions from the ones who reported the offense.

Previously in this book in Chapter 4, testing of hypothesis was presented. A rather special form of testing is concerned with alternative hypothesis, or as Brightman (2009) calls it, analysis of competing hypotheses. For the Kongsberg Group example, some competing hypotheses can be formulated:

1. Kongsberg did not inform the police because the company could lose control over the matter.
2. Kongsberg did not inform the police because it could harm company reputation.
3. Kongsberg did not inform the police for fear of exclusion from contracts in the public sector.
4. Kongsberg did not inform the police for fear that the company should be punished with a fine.
5. Kongsberg did not inform the police for fear that senior management should be punished by imprisonment.
6. Kongsberg did not inform the police because the police generally dismiss cases, thus often making matters worse for the company.
7. Kongsberg did not inform the police because a review is demanding too much time and resources.
8. Kongsberg did not inform the police because private investigators did not make any findings of significance.

The last explanation was presented by senior management in the media. They could not find or prove that any unlawful acts were committed.

Chairman Jebsen and CEO Qvam thus provided empirical support for the trifle assumption for lack of disclosure to the police.

Brightman (2009) recommends testing such hypotheses by collecting data and then assigning each entry to one or more hypotheses. The information can support a hypothesis, or it may be contrary to the hypothesis. Both are important to get registered. With a sufficient number of information pieces, the most probable hypothesis can be identified. An image will emerge when many pieces of information are assigned a particular hypothesis, as plus (support) or minus (criticism) in relation to that hypothesis. Once a hypothesis has been assigned many plus information pieces and few, perhaps no, minus information pieces, it may very well be that it is likely to be confirmed.

The Kongsberg case emerged in 2014, when it became publicly known that the police were investigating the company for corruption in Romania. The year before, PricewaterhouseCoopers had found evidence of corruption, but senior management in Kongsberg decided not to disclose information to the police. It was likely a whistle-blower in the company who told police about the examination report. The defense company was charged for corruption.

Senior management at Kongsberg said it did not act on suspicions of undesirable business practices because the private investigation turned up no proof. Kongsberg and one of its employees were hit with charges related to the sale and delivery of communications equipment to Romanian authorities. Marianne Djupesland, a prosecutor for Norway's national economic crime unit, confirmed to the *Wall Street Journal* that the police had carried out a search related to the charges, but did not say where or whether they had seized any many materials. Djupesland declined to comment on the actual charges (Hovland, 2014). Later that year, Djupesland confirmed that Norwegian detectives had been in Romania to interview individuals in close cooperation with Romanian police. After the visit, Romanian police charged several executives with corruption.

The *Wall Street Journal* had an article entitled "Are Internal Bribery Probes Private? Attorney-Client Privilege Protections over Corporate Investigations Led by Outside Law Firms Are Eroding" (Schechtman, 2014):

> To tackle corporate bribery, the U.S. Department of Justice is increasingly relying on companies to turn over their own bad apples. But one former chief executive is trying to turn the tables, arguing that he should be able to use the results of the corporate investigation that uncovered corruption allegations against him.
>
> The request, argued in a motion filed last week in New Jersey federal court by lawyers for former PetroTiger Ltd. CEO Joseph Sigelman, raises key questions about the confidentiality of independent investigations. In recent years, those internal probes have played a vital role in helping the U.S. Department of Justice bring antibribery cases.

Mr. Sigelman claims that the company's internal investigation, handled by law firm Sidley Austin LLP, served as the impetus for the Justice Department's charges that the CEO bribed a Colombian official. The investigation documents could therefore "exonerate him" in the bribery case headed to trial in District Court in New Jersey in January, wrote Mr. Sigelman's counsel, William Burck of Quinn Emanuel Urquhart & Sullivan LLP.

Sidley Austin says that though it shared some of its findings with authorities, its probe was a private matter protected under attorney-client privilege. The firm is asking the court to deny the request.

Companies often hire outside law firms to conduct internal investigations after they uncover evidence of bribery. Such probes serve an increasing role in enforcement of the Foreign Corrupt Practices Act, a 1977 law prohibiting foreign bribery.

In exchange for a shot at leniency for the company, the outside counsel often turns over its evidence to the Justice Department, which can then use the findings to pursue individual executives.

Given the central role these probes can play in prosecutions, some now question whether the information gathered by these firms should be protected with the same shield of confidentiality granted other attorney work. While the Justice Department has to turn over documents to defense that are part of its own investigation, a spokesman said it doesn't involve itself in the discovery of outside counsel.

Attorneys who represent companies in these probes say that allowing subpoenas of an outside law firm would have a chilling effect on companies seeking to discover internal wrongdoing.

"On the other hand, the individual defendant, especially in a criminal case, has the need to know what potential trial witnesses have previously said in the event it's relevant to their defense," said Kathleen Hamann, a former prosecutor from the Justice Department's FCPA unit, now a partner at White & Case LLP.

An internal investigation at PetroTiger, a British Virgin Islands-based oil services company that operates in Colombia, led to bribery charges against Mr. Sigelman—who maintains his innocence—and two other executives, co-CEO Knut Hammarskjold and general counsel Gregory Weisman, both of whom have pleaded guilty to bribery charges.

A dispute with PetroTiger's board over strategy and corporate governance led to the ousting of the three executives by March 2011, according to court documents. PetroTiger then hired Sidley Austin to conduct an internal investigation, during which the law firm uncovered evidence of payments to the wife of a Colombian official at Ecopetrol SA, ECOPETROL.BO in Colombia's state-run petroleum company, according to court documents and a former PetroTiger board member.

Sidley reported the payments to the Justice Department and handed over thousands of pages of company documents. Prosecutors say the payments of approximately $333,500 to the wife for "consulting services" was actually a bribe to her husband to win a contract for PetroTiger worth around $39.6 million.

> Mr. Sigelman's counsel argues that Sidley waived its attorney-client privilege "when it divulged the investigation's findings to third parties, including officials of the United States."
>
> Sidley says that while PetroTiger's board hired the attorneys to help conduct an internal investigation, its attorneys are on neither side of the criminal case, and that it shouldn't have to help Mr. Sigelman in a "fishing expedition" that could cost the firm hundreds of thousands of dollars to wrangle the huge volume of documents.
>
> Experts say that courts have begun to erode the protections over internal probes. "We tell our clients that we will do everything we can to protect that privilege but you can't be sure what's going to happen," said Laurence Urgenson, a partner at Mayer Brown LLP.
>
> In an unrelated defamation case last year, a federal judge in New York ordered the law firm Gibson, Dunn & Crutcher LLP to turn over its interview notes from an internal investigation on financial irregularities at the hedge fund D.B. Zwirn & Co. The judge ruled that Gibson Dunn had in effect surrendered confidentiality over interview summaries and transcripts when it presented part of its findings to the U.S. Securities and Exchange Commission.
>
> Courts have become increasingly uneasy with the claim that attorneys can "selectively waive" attorney-client privilege, said Joseph McLaughlin, an attorney at Simpson Thacher & Bartlett LLP.
>
> "Courts don't want to approve the practice where a party discloses privileged information when it's in its perceived interest to share with a third party, then close the door and stop further disclosure when it's not in their interest," said Mr. McLaughlin. "The question becomes are they trying to use privilege as both a sword and a shield?"

A similar case was presented to the Norwegian Supreme Court (Høyesterett, 2014). According to the ruling of the Supreme Court, a private investigation report is included in the evidence ban in line with the dispute act because of a lawyer's duty of confidentiality based on the attorney-client privilege. It was Mr. Frank Vidar Harstad, who had been fired from his job, that wanted the report as evidence in his labor suit. The report was written by BDO partner Erling Grimstad, and defense lawyer Jan Fougner argued that the report was the private property of the client business, where Harstad had worked. The company Norsk Kylling opposed disclosure of the report and stated that the company has a client relationship with Grimstad. This interpretation was upheld by the Norwegian Supreme Court.

References

Brightman, H.J. (2009). *Today's White-Collar Crime: Legal, Investigative, and Theoretical Perspectives*. Routledge, Taylor & Francis Group, New York.

Hovland, K.M. (2014). Kongsberg Gruppen Charged with Corruption. *Wall Street Journal*, February 25. www.online.wsj.com

Høyesterett. (2014). Høyesterett (Norwegian Supreme Court), HR-2014-1775-A, September 5.

Machen, M.J., and Richards, R.E. (2004). The use of fraud examiners in the battle against occupational fraud and abuse. *Journal of Investment Compliance*, Winter, 67–71.

Morgan, M., and Nix, W. (2003). CPA perceptions of the marketability, career enhancements and quality of services of certified fraud examiners. *Southern Business and Economic Journal*, 31–50.

Schechtman, J. (2014). Are internal bribery probes private? Attorney-client privilege protections over corporate investigations led by outside law firms are eroding. *Wall Street Journal*, October 11. http://online.wsj.com/articles/are-internal-bribery-probes-private-1413157700

Wells, J.T. (2003). The fraud examiners. *Journal of Accountancy*, October, 76–80.

Stage Model for Investigations

11

Evaluation of white-collar crime investigations by fraud examiners can be carried out by applying a stage model for investigations. A stage model defines levels of maturity for private investigations. Some private investigations are carried out at low levels of examination maturity, while other investigations are carried out at high levels of maturity. Maturity indicates that fraud examiners respond to the circumstances of investigation in an appropriate manner. Some private investigations by fraud examiners are immature.

In a stage model for investigations, later stages represent greater consideration and higher maturity than earlier stages (Röglinger et al., 2012). Stages do not represent phases of an investigation. Rather, they represent alternative assessment of an investigation. A specific investigation is evaluated by assessment of maturity in terms of stage choice. Evaluation of an investigation in terms of review, audit, inquiry, and verification ends up by allocating the investigation to a specific stage in the model.

Stages of growth models have been used widely in management and organizational research (King and Teo, 1997; Maon et al., 2010). These models assume that predictable patterns (conceptualized in terms of stages) exist in the growth of organizations and in the growth of performance in organizations. These stages are (1) sequential in nature, (2) occur as a hierarchical progression that is not easily reversed, and (3) involve a broad range of organizational activities and structures.

Our unit of analysis is the specific fraud examination documented in an investigation report that is the final delivery from fraud examiners to their client organizations. Based on an overall assessment, a specific examination can be deemed immature at a low level or mature at a high level in the model.

Our stage model for investigations is a conceptual definition of examination maturity in terms of discrete levels to which it is assumed that each evaluated investigation can be assigned. We chose to define the model in terms of four stages. The stages are labeled *activity investigation*, *problem investigation*, *actor investigation*, and *value investigation*, respectively, as illustrated in Figure 11.1.

A growth model for investigation may consist of few or many steps. Here we have chosen a model with four levels, which is not an unusual number in organizational research. First, we decided what to call these steps, and then comes identification of dominant issues for each step (King and Teo, 1997;

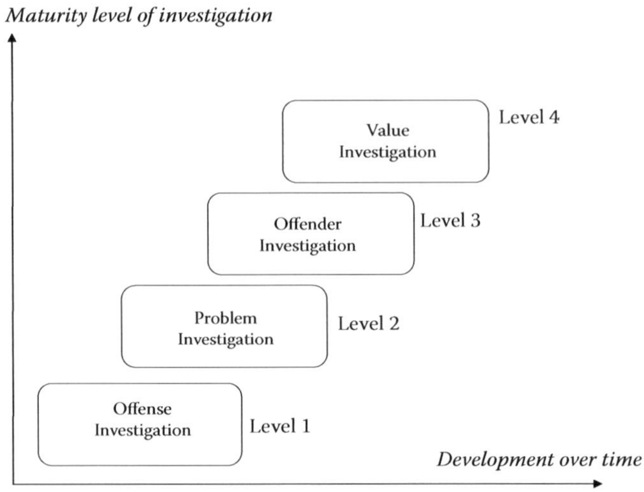

Figure 11.1 Stages of growth model for private investigations by fraud examiners.

Nunnally and Bernstein, 1994; Röglinger et al., 2012). Later, we will look at how these four levels differ in terms of start, process, result, and impact of investigation, as well as resource consumption in an investigation.

The reader might reflect on the number of stages in this model. Would three or five or six levels be more appropriate? As with many other growth models, we choose four levels. The important thing is that the steps taken together satisfy the following three criteria. First, steps are defined in such a way that it is obvious that they are different from each other. Second, it is important that every step is perceived to have the same scope as the other steps in its theme and its problems. Last but not least, a clear impression must be created that all steps in total make up the area of possibilities. These criteria imply that there should be no overlap between the steps, all steps should be similar in scope, no step shall be construed as a subset of another step, and no step should be omitted or missed.

Four Levels of Maturity

The four levels or stages or steps in our model, and illustrated in Figure 11.1, can be described as follows:

1. *Offense investigation.* Examiners investigate activities that are suspicious in the client organization. Activity mapping is at the core of the investigation to identify potential offenses. The investigation is based on activities that have been or still are performed in a reprehensible manner. Examiners are looking for activities and prepare

descriptions of these. Thereafter, investigators make up their minds about whether the activities were blameworthy or not. Here, there are typically auditors and others with financial knowledge to assess accounting transactions and management of assets.

Investigations at level 1 are usually passive, fruitless, and characterized by too much detail and unnecessary use of resources. At this lowest level, investigators are trying to find answers to the question: What happened? It is all about developing know-what concerning negative events.

2. *Problem investigation.* Examiners investigate problems that have occurred in the client organization. Problem identification and description is at the core of the investigation. The investigation is based on an issue that should be clarified. Examiners look for answers. When answers are found, the investigation is concluded. It is important to use the least amount of resources on the investigation, which should take the shortest possible time. Appraisal and management are crucial to success. The client has had an unresolved problem, and the client defines all premises for the investigation in terms of problems to be solved and questions to be answered. There is no room for investigators to pursue tracks other than those that target the predefined problem. Here, there are typically management consultants and others with rule-based knowledge to assess the problem and come up with solutions.

   Investigations at level 2 are often passive in terms of reflecting on the greater picture, as examiners focus on answering questions concerned with limited aspects of the business. Examiners tend to find answers after a restricted and low-cost investigation. At this second level, investigators are trying to find answers to the question: How did it happen? It is all about developing know-how concerning negative events.
3. *Offender investigation.* Examiners investigate suspicious persons and their potential misconduct. An offender-based rather than an offense-based perspective is at the core of the investigation. The investigation is based on the assumption that something is hidden that has to be revealed. Examiners choose their tactics to succeed in the disclosure of possible misconduct and perhaps even financial crime. Investigative steps are adapted to the terrain, especially to reactions of people in roles of suspect, witness, and stakeholder. Different sources of information and methods are used to make the most facts reach the examiners' table. Here, there are typically detectives and other private investigators to uncover possible crime. While levels 1 and 2 are focused on suspicions of financial crime, level 3 is focused on allegations toward potential criminals. Actors are identified in terms of their roles here at level 3, while lower levels can contribute evidence against possible

criminals. There are always criminal persons who commit crime. No system or enterprise commits crime. There is always a person who changed a system or abused a system. There is always a person who acted illegally on behalf on the organizations. Level 3 has a person focus, while levels 1 and 2 have a subject focus. Level 3 is characterized by the pursuit of responsible persons who may have abused their positions for personal or organizational gain. This is a more intensive investigation because suspicions and suspects should be handled in a responsible way with respect to the rule of law and human rights. Investigating invoices and bank transactions at level 1 is a task separating examiners from potential offenders.

Investigations at level 3 are much more complicated, since they have to do with people. It is also more active, where significant breakthroughs are sought. The investigation project is conducted in a professional and efficient manner. At this third level, investigators are trying to find answers to the question: Why did it happen? It is all about developing know-why concerning negative events.

4. *Value investigation.* Examiners create value for the client by identifying weaknesses and suggesting solutions. Value creation is at the core of the investigation. The investigation is focused on the value to be created through the inquiry of fraud examiners. The investigation's ambition is that the result will be valuable for the client. The value can be created in change, simplification, renewal, problem solving, and other measures for the future. Furthermore, the investigation has to be prudent in both what is achieved and how it is achieved. A number of explicit considerations are identified and practiced throughout the study. The investigation is based on explicit decisions concerning information strategy, knowledge strategy, methods strategy, configuration strategy, as well as systems strategy. Explicit strategy decisions make the investigation transparent and understandable for all involved and other interested parties. Here, there are investigators in multidisciplinary environments that will contribute to creating value for the client. Investigations at level 4 are characterized by active use of strategies, with significant and decisive breakthroughs in the investigations, which lay a foundation for learning and value creation in the client's organization. The value may be found, for example, in early detection of deviations and early closing of gaps in a satisfactory manner. Disclosure, clarification, and resolution are seen in context here at stage 4. There will be less to uncover in the future if prevention is improved. Examiners create value through proper investigation. Value is visible on the bottom line in terms of reduced costs and increased income, thereby leading to increased profit.

> Value should be created before, during, as well as after an investigation. Before the investigation starts, an understanding of risks and priorities is developed. During investigation, methodological insights occur. After investigation, barriers are constructed, gaps are sealed, procedures are improved, and evaluation for learning is established. At this fourth and final level, investigators are trying to find answers to the question: What can the client learn, and how can the organization prevent it from happening again? It is all about developing know-what concerning negative events.

At the first stage or level, it is know-what that dominates the knowledge base for investigation. Investigators find out what happened. At the second stage, the second knowledge level is needed, which is to understand how a negative event or sequence of events happened. Know-how is developed in the investigation, where investigators understand and present insights into procedural aspects of alleged misconduct and crime. At the third stage, know-why is the most demanding and often most important knowledge insight in terms of causal relationships between events and behaviors that led to these events. At the fourth and final stage, learning is important, as learning implemented in action can create value at the bottom line for the client's business.

A maturity model shows a sequential, one-dimensional, hierarchical, and cumulative development in the function of fraud examinations over time. The model moves from activity-oriented investigation, via problem-oriented and actor-oriented investigation, to value-oriented investigation. The model represents theory. A theory might be a prediction or explanation, a set of interrelated constructs, definitions, and propositions that presents a systematic view of phenomena (Colquitt and Zapata-Phelan, 2007; Corley and Gioia, 2011; DiMaggio, 1995; Sutton and Staw, 1995; Weick, 1995). Both theoretical and empirical study are concerned with practice. Theory is assumption and generalization of practice. Empirical study is measurement of practice. Using the maturity model for private investigations, fraud examination cases can be placed at a specific level depending on explicit criteria, as they are presented below on start, process, result, impact, and resource. The aim is to have a framework to discuss completed fraud examinations. At each level, stage, or step, there are some dominating themes and challenges that need to be identified.

Starting Point Evaluation

The starting point is different at all four levels, as shown in Table 11.1:

- *Level 1: Offense.* Examiners are to investigate suspicious activities where there may be irregularities and possible crime. Activities include transactions and dispositions, movements, and communications. When the Eckbo foundation in Norway was to be investigated for possible misconduct by officers of the foundation, the Eckbo board limited the investigation to examination of transactions and decisions related to asset management in the foundation to examine whether they were within the statute of the foundation. Thereby, foundation officers avoided much attention in the investigation report written by an external lawyer and an external auditor (Dobrowen and Klepp, 2009). When the City of Stavanger in Norway ordered an investigation to be carried out by PricewaterhouseCoopers, they asked investigators to find out where money from the city had ended up in Turkey. Investigators were not asked to look at the roles of city managers in money transactions (PwC, 2013b).

- *Level 2: Problem.* Examiners are to clarify issues related to possible problems such as fraud, where it is unclear whether the client firm has a solution to problems. The client may have a problem, and consultants are hired to find out whether or not there is a problem, and how the problem potentially can be solved. When the Norwegian Football Association hired law firm Lynx, it was to find out whether or not football clubs where handling player transfers in a reprehensible manner. Media suggested it, and a court case was testing it. As the court case was dismissed, the football association decided it had no problem and terminated the private investigators (Lynx, 2013). When Mentor Children, a Norwegian NGO, was accused of spending too much money on administration, the NGO hired accounting firm BDO to check if the organization had a problem. BDO found the organization had a little, but not substantial problem, and suggested some changes (BDO, 2011).
- *Level 3: Offender.* Accusations have been directed at named persons in the organization, and examiners are hired to find out whether the persons as actors are responsible for misconduct or even crime. Examiners investigate suspicious persons and potential offenders. When law firm Lynx was hired to investigate cost overrun at Briskeby sports stadium built in Norway, two named individuals were at the core of investigative attention (Lynx, 2011). When the Norwegian business empire Lunde Group went bankrupt, the bankruptcy trustee wanted to sort out personal responsibilities (Bie, 2012).
- *Level 4: Value.* Examiners are to create value for the client by pointing out weaknesses and proposing solutions. Investigators are not inquiring just for revealing neither criminal activities nor criminal actors. Nor is it good enough to confirm or disprove suspicion directed at people. Examiners are hired not only to solve a specific problem, but also to make a contribution of value to the client. Examiners are to

Table 11.1 Characteristics of the Stage Model for Private Investigations

	Stage 1 Offense	Stage 2 Problem	Stage 3 Offender	Stage 4 Value
Starting point for the investigation	Examine suspicious irregular activities *Eckbo assets* (Dobrowen and Klepp, 2009) *Turkey transactions* (PwC, 2013b)	Examine problems and suggest solutions *NGO Mentor Children* (BDO, 2011) *Football association* (Lynx, 2013)	Examine accusations and suspects *Briskeby stadium* (Lynx, 2011) *Furuheim elderly* (Dalane and Olsen, 2006) *Lunde Group* (Bie, 2012) *Norwegian betting* (Deloitte, 2010)	Create value by solving problems and suggesting improvements *Spain* (PwC, 2009) *Troms Kraft utility company* (Nergaard, 2013)
Working process in the investigation	Passive study of documents selected by client	Passive study of documents and interviews with individuals selected by client	Active study of documents and interviews with individuals in different roles	Active use of strategies for information, knowledge, systems, and methods
Work result of the investigation	Found out what had happened	Found out how it had happened	Found out why it had happened	Found out who had done what, how, and why
Impact of the investigation on client organization	No impact	Marginal changes in routines	Individuals dismissed	Complete reorganization
Resource consumption relative to benefits of the investigation	Cost overrun without benefits	Some benefits	Matching costs and benefits	Positive benefit-cost ratio

suggest how negative deviations can be prevented in the future, and how positive deviations can be achieved in the future. The focus is on cleanup and reorientation. When the Norwegian utility company Troms Kraft lost a substantial sum of money in one of its subsidiaries, a business consultant was hired to examine how the company could regain its position (Nergaard, 2013).

Work Process Evaluation

Next, the work process is different at all four levels, as shown in Table 11.1:

- *Level 1: Offense.* Examiners carry out passive study of documents that are made available from the client. The client defines the job of the examiners as going through documentation that the client has selected for examination. The client has limited the scope in terms of both issues and information sources available to examiners. Although PwC investigators in the Turkey case in Stavanger carried out active monitoring of financial flows, they showed little interest in the actors' roles in possible misappropriation of funds (welfare manager in the municipality), irregular communication (lawyers making client money transfers), and removal of the children from the parents in Turkey to foster parents in Norway (private investigator involved in smuggling children). While there were suspicions of tax evasion, misappropriation of funds, as well as corruption, investigators were in the mandate limited to a work process of identifying money transfers. Therefore, the Turkey investigation by PwC (2013b) gives an impression of passivity.
- *Level 2: Problem.* Investigators carry out passive examination of documents and interviews of people who are often loyal to the client, and therefore have been selected by the client for interviews. Selected documents and selected individuals are to be examined in the work process. While Folkvord et al. (2008) in their independent book chose a very critical perspective on asset management in the Eckbo foundation, Dobrowen and Klepp (2009) chose a less critical perspective. In the Norwegian Lottery investigation, Deloitte (2010) examined some transactions and talked to some people. But it was the Norwegian Auditor General who discover misconduct that led to the fall of the CEO. When a Norwegian rehabilitation project failed in Spain, PwC (2009) was hired to enable learning from the project, so that elderly care could be more successful in the future. Therefore, the start of this examination was at the value level 4. However, the work process was only at level 2, since a passive document review

and interviews were carried out. Unlike Folkvord (2011), who in his independent inquiry traveled to Spain on several occasions, investigators from PwC (2009) paid the location only a formal visit.

- *Level 3: Offender.* Investigators carry out active examination of documents and interviews of people with different roles. Here the examiner leaves the passive recipient role of information collection. The examiner is no longer a passive recipient of information from sources defined by the client. The examiner is no longer dependent on signals from the principal. Rather, the examiner has left the back seat and taken over the steering position. All that is presented by the client is not uncritically accepted. Still, we find the client to be the trendsetter here at level 3. But the examiners choose and dare increasingly to think for themselves. In the investigation of Mentor Children by BDO (2011), investigators from BDO released themselves from NGO views and expectations from the environment. However, BDO (2011) did not find all facts, perhaps because the client wanted to limit findings concerning transfer of funds to India. Similarly, Bie (2012) did not find all relevant facts concerning the Lunde Group bankruptcy. Although Norwegian Football Association investigators took the initiative and asked for more information, they ended up examining what the client initially had given them to study (Lynx, 2013). Nergaard's (2013) investigation of utility company Troms Kraft blew up the financial budget on the grounds that all stones were to be turned to get as close as possible to the truth in the investigation report.
- *Level 4: Value.* Private investigators make active use of information strategy, knowledge strategy, method strategy, system strategy, as well as configuration strategy. Investigators apply a contingent approach to these strategies by identifying key information sources, knowledge categories, systems, methods, and investigative work iterations that are optimal for the current fraud examination assignment. Examiners not only base their work procedure on the mandate, but also take situational factors into account, such as access to technology tracks, before strategies for achieving investigation goals are decided. During the investigation, examiners keep an open mind as to alternative paths, sources, and suspects. Although Briskeby investigators from law firm Lynx (2011) did not get to the bottom of the suspected fraud case, they sought creative ways to figure out the real roles of Kolstad and Stensrud in the affair. Lawyers Dalane and Olsen (2006) did what was necessary, far beyond the client's intention, to collect evidence that later led to the conviction of two suspects in the Furuheim case of property development.

Work Result Evaluation

The next part of Table 11.1 is about work result. How well suited were the results of the investigation? Did investigators find out what actually happened? Fraud examinations are expected to provide answers to issues about what happened, and who did what in relation to negative events. Tasks in the mandate are to be completed. An investigation's credibility is ensured partly through documentation of methods, choices, and practices. Credibility is created by work process as presented in the investigation report. The work result is what one is left with after the investigation is completed. While working process is the means, the work result is the target for an investigation.

Work results are different at the four levels in the stages of growth model, as summarized in Table 11.1:

- *Level 1: Offense.* Examiners did not find out what had happened. The investigation was a failure. Examiners did not find out who had done what. Questions in the mandate were not answered. Issues in the mandate were not solved. No solutions to problems were suggested. The investigation report is garbled and unreadable. Featured people disagree with descriptions of themselves. The investigation report contains a number of shortcomings, mistakes, and errors. Lynx (2011) investigators did not find out what had happened in the Briskeby stadium case with regard to Kostad and Stensrud. Lynx (2013) did not identify any specific player transfers that were reprehensible in the football association case. Rather, the issue remained open and the problem unresolved.
- *Level 2: Problem.* Examiners partially found out what had happened, but in a reprehensible manner; thus, the investigation was a failure. The client did not get a clear answer to the question of who had done what. The investigation report is not very understandable and useful to the client. Featured people dislike representations of themselves. As a project, the investigation was only partially successful. The investigation report contains several omissions and errors, and the report looks like a commissioned work to meet client expectations, rather than being an independent report for which investigators should be held accountable. The integrity of investigators is at stake. BDO (2011) investigators gave up finding out what had happened to money in India. Troms Kraft investigator Nergaard (2013) produces a report of more than 600 pages with a complete lack of focus.
- *Level 3: Offender.* Examiners found out what had happened, but the investigation report is in many respects unclear and ambiguous. Featured people agree with the presentation of themselves in

the report. The choice of methods and procedures is described in an understandable way, thus making the investigation somewhat transparent. Dobrowen and Klepp (2009) conducted a professional but uncritical examination of the Eckbo foundation. The Spain investigation by PwC (2009) was probably amputated in relation to clarifying responsibilities. PwC's (2013b) investigation of the Turkey case responded to the mandate, which revolved on monetary transactions, but the issue of potential corruption was never clarified. Obvious questions about participants in the Turkey action remained unanswered.

- *Level 4: Value.* Examiners found out what had happened, as the basis for action and learning. Know-what, know-how, and know-why were developed and nicely documented in the report. Investigation process and investigation report provide a basis for change and learning. It is about avoiding incidents in the future as well as improving performance in general. Examiners found out who had done what. All questions are answered. Suggested solutions to all problems are presented. All issues in the mandate are discussed in a thorough and proper manner. Investigative procedures are documented, thereby creating examination transparency. All objectives as described in the mandate as well as agreed with the client during the investigation are met. The investigation report is easy to read and very helpful to the client and other stakeholders. Featured people accept and approve representations of themselves in the report. Work results of the investigation could hardly have been better. The investigation as a project was conducted in a professional and smooth manner. There are no errors or omissions in the investigation report. Examiners document their integrity and accountability. The investigation report documents a professional application of strategies for information, knowledge, methods, configuration, and systems. Examiners Dalane and Olsen (2006) did what was necessary to prove two specific events that later led to convictions, in addition to recognizing the key role of whistle-blower Ida van der Gest. She had played a key role in the disclosure and subsequent learning of the events. Bie (2012) documented law violations clearly in his bankruptcy report about Lunde Group.

Examination Impact Evaluation

The next issue is impact. Recommendations should be followed up. An investigation should have value. Did the client or principal read the report? Did they understand it? What did they do with it?

- *Level 1: Offense.* Recommendations from the investigation were not pursued. In fact, the client did not read the investigation report. It was put on the shelf to collect dust. If there were consequences at all, the investigation had negative consequences for innocent people. The investigation had no value for the client. The investigation as a project failed.
- *Level 2: Problem.* The investigation had unfortunate consequences for some people involved. Examiners from BDO (2011) recommended that their Mentor Children investigation should lead the client to report the case to the police. The client did not do that. It did not happen, perhaps because investigators went forward in a reprehensible manner, such as the examination of remittances.
- *Level 3: Offender.* Because the investigation report was unclear and ambiguous in many respects, the investigation did not have desired effects. While the investigation had some value to the client, the potential value was much greater. Some recommendations of the investigation were pursued. The investigation project was a learning process for both examiner and client. The Norwegian betting investigation by Deloitte (2010) was correct and neat, but contributed little to solving the overall problems in the company.
- *Level 4: Value.* The investigation report is well organized and easy to read, enabling the client to take actions. The written report not only provides a record of the investigation's results, but also builds credibility for examiners' work. Recommendations of the examiners were followed up in a constructive manner. To the extent that the investigation had consequences for individuals, it was handled in a professional manner. The investigation is of great value to the client. The investigation has a significant positive effect on the organization. Whistle-blower Ida van der Gest enabled examiners Dalane and Olsen (2006) to document events that later led to convictions, as well as enabled the organization to change and learn after the incident. Bie (2012) documented law violations in the Lunde Group clearly, thereby enabling the police to prosecute Lunde and enabling creditors to recover some of their assets.

Resource Value Evaluation

The next and final issue is resource. How large was the consumption of resources in terms of money, key persons' time, and competence? What was the cost-benefit of the investigation? A resource is an enabler that makes something possible to get done. Resource consumption is not only an absolute, but also a relative measure related to the value achieved by investing in a fraud examination. The benefit-cost ratio is positive if benefits exceed costs, and negative if costs exceed benefits.

- *Level 1: Offense.* Examination did not complete within agreed cost and schedule; there was a delay and cost overrun. Consumption of resources was not at all appropriate to the results of the examination. Relevant skills were not used in the investigation. Other resources should have been applied in the form of knowledge. Resource consumption could have been reduced. The investigation by Nergaard (2013) of utility company Troms Kraft had a cost overrun that was never approved by the client. Rather than billing the agreed 30 million Norwegian kroner, examiners tried to get 44 million Norwegian kroner paid by the client.
- *Level 2: Problem.* Examiners created some value for the client, but not at all in the magnitude of examination costs. Therefore, a negative benefit-cost relationship occurs. As an investment, the examination represents a loss to the client. When Dobrowen and Klepp (2009) had completed their examination of the Eckbo foundation, only marginal changes in asset management were implemented.
- *Level 3: Offender.* Substantial value is created in the client organization in terms of solved problems, changed routines, replaced personnel, organizational effectiveness, and other benefits. However, the costs of the investigation might still have been too high, thereby creating a negative benefit-cost ratio. When BDO (2011) contributed to administrative effectiveness in the NGO Mentor Children, value was created.
- *Level 4: Value.* Compared to the costs of examiners and strain to the organization while the investigation was going on, substantial and more value was later created. As investment, the fraud examination was profitable. Dalane and Olsen (2006) enabled a revitalization of the church foundation without spending too much money.

Our stage model for maturity of fraud examinations has four levels, like many other stage models. Fewer levels would have meant that one would merge some or simplify too much. More levels could, however, be appropriate. The four levels are based on different ways to examine, from the very simple (level 1) to the more complex (level 4). Different examination cases can be placed on different levels, according to criteria for starting point, work procedure, work result, work impact, and resource consumption.

If all aspects of an investigation are at level 1, there is no thorough approach applied in the examination. Examiners only passively studied documents that were easily made available by the client. Then it is quite natural that results are not very convincing. It is not easy to find out what happened if examiners avoided digging into relevant issues. Financial crime is often well hidden in legitimate transactions. If examiners only scrape on the surface, they cannot expect to find out what has happened.

At level 2, examiners are not only scraping the surface. They are both interested and curious, and they interview people. Unfortunately, they only interview individuals who are loyal to opinions of the client. Passive examination of documents occurs at this level as well. It is somewhat easier for an examiner to figure out what has happened. First at level 3 we find examiners who conduct active inquiries and studies of documents; we find examiners interviewing people who had different roles and have different opinions and controversial views.

Interestingly enough, Table 11.1 shows that each examination case is placed at different stages when it comes to start, work, result, impact, and resource. The Briskeby stadium case, for example, investigated by Lynx (2011), has a start at level 3, which might indicate a promising result, where one can find out what has happened. However, in the course of investigation performance dropped mainly because of lack of client cooperation. The table indicates that the result of examination work ends at level 1, because examiners were not able to identify player transfers relevant to the investigation.

It is also interesting to note that the Turkey case, investigated by PwC (2013b), has a start at level 1, and work at level 1, which should imply that investigators did not find out what happened, since they did not go very deep into the matter. Yet they did find some surprising and relevant results.

The maturity model can easily be misunderstood in the sense that the model represents a development or progress of a particular investigation. It does not. The maturity model is used to place a specific investigation on a maturity scale based on an overall assessment of performed investigation phases and their impact on client organization. Maturity here means that investigators, as they carry out a number of fraud examinations over time, may become better at doing so. While untrained and inexperienced examiners can be found at level 1, the same examiners may be found at higher levels some years later.

Wells (2003) argues that becoming a professional fraud examiner takes years. The most relevant individuals are those with many interrelated skills. They are as good with people as they are with numbers, and they are inclined to be aggressive rather than shy and retiring. This helps them achieve success in adversarial situations where confrontation is endemic to their work.

Ten examination reports from Norway were applied above to illustrate the stage model. These 10 reports are listed in Table 11.2. The table illustrates how each investigation is placed by level of maturity for each of the five criteria: start, work, result, impact, and resource. For example, the starting point for the investigation into Briskeby sports stadium was at level 3, as illustrated with the number 3 in the first square. The last column shows the sum of maturity in the investigation. With this kind of calculation of maturity in

Table 11.2 Maturity of Investigations Measured by the Stage of Growth Model

Fraud Examinations	Start	Work	Result	Impact	Resource	Maturity
Dalane and Olsen (2006) investigated Furuheim	3	4	4	2	4	17
Bie (2012) investigated Lunde Group bankruptcy	3	3	4	4	2	16
Lynx (2011) investigated Briskeby sports stadium	3	4	1	3	3	14
Deloitte (2010) investigated Norwegian public betting	3	2	3	4	3	14
PwC (2009) investigated Spain investments	4	2	3	2	3	14
BDO (2011) investigated NGO Mentor Children	2	3	2	2	3	12
Nergaard (2013) investigated utility firm Troms Kraft	4	3	2	2	1	12
Dobrowen and Klepp (2009) investigated Eckbo funds	1	2	3	3	2	11
Lynx (2013) investigated player transfers in football	2	3	1	2	3	11
PwC (2013b) investigated payments in Turkey	1	1	3	3	2	10

line with the stage model for investigations, the best investigation was conducted by lawyers Dalane and Olsen (2006).

The overall stage for an investigation can be calculated by diving maturity number by number of criteria, which are five. Dalane and Olsen (2006) achieved 17 points. When divided by 5, the stage becomes 3.4.

References

BDO. (2011). Rapport til Lotteri- og stiftelsestilsynet vedr. gransking av stiftelsen Fadderbarnas Framtid (Investigation Report about the Foundation for Adopted Childrens' Future). BDO, Erling Grimstad and Morten Thorkildsen. https://lottstift.no/stiftelsestilsynet/files/2011/12/Rapport-til-Stiftelsestilsynet-fra-BDO-vedr-gransking-av-Fadderbarnas-Framtid.pdf

Bie, F. (2012). *Rapport til Stavanger tingrett* (Report to District Court in Stavanger). Vierdal Advokatfirma, Stavanger.
Colquitt, J.A., and Zapata-Phelan, C.P. (2007). Trends in theory building and theory testing: A five-decade study of the *Academy of Management Journal*. *Academy of Management Journal*, 50(6), 1281–1303.
Corley, K.G., and Gioia, D.A. (2011). Building theory about theory building: What constitutes a theoretical contribution? *Academy of Management Review*, 36(1), 12–32.
Dalane, J., and Olsen, D.L. (2006). *Granskingsrapport—ledelse og styring av Øyestad helselags boligstiftelse Furuheim* (Investigation Report about the Foundation Furuheim for Elderly). Hald, Dalane & Heimvik law firm, Arendal.
DiMaggio, P.J. (1995). Comments on 'what theory is not.' *Administrative Science Quarterly*, 40, 391–397.
Deloitte. (2010). Norsk Tipping—Granskingsrapport av 16. august 2010 (Investigation Report about Norwegian Betting Company). https://www.norsk-tipping.no/forsiden/nytt_fra_selskapet/26819.cms
Dobrowen, K., and Klepp, T. (2009). Uavhengig undersøkelse av Eckbos Legater (Investigation Report about the Eckbo Foundation). www.eckbos-legater.no/content/download/479/7915/version/1/file
Folkvord, E. (2011). *Vår korrupte hovedstad* (Our Corrupt Capital). Spartacus Forlag, Oslo.
Folkvord, E., Eckbo, A.K., and Mathisen, E. (2008). *I pose og sekk* (They Got It Both Ways). Forlaget Rødt, Oslo.
King, W.R., and Teo, T.S.H. (1997). Integration between business planning and information systems planning: Validating a stage hypothesis. *Decision Science*, 28(2), 279–308.
Lynx. (2011). *Briskebyrapporten* (Investigation Report on Football Stadium). Lynx law firm. http://www.hamar.kommune.no/getfile.php/Bilder/Hamar/Nyhetsbilder/Politikere/Briskebyrapporten,%20ikke%20sladdet_1.pdf
Lynx. (2013). *1192-rapporten. Gransking av internasjonale spilleroverganger 2007–2011* (Examination of Player Transfers). Lynx law firm, Oslo.
Maon, F., Lindgreen, A., and Swaen, V. (2010). Organizational stages and cultural phases: A critical review and a consolidative model of corporate social responsibility development. *International Journal of Management Reviews*, 20–38.
Nergaard, L.L. (2013). *Gransking av Troms Kraft AS* (Investigation Report about Troms Kraft Power Company). Norscan Partners and Grette law firm, September 9.
Nunnally, J.C., and Bernstein, I.H. (1994). *Psychometric Theory*, 3rd ed. McGraw-Hill, New York.
PwC. (2008). Granskingsrapport: Undersøkelser foretatt på oppdrag fra Oslo kommune, Byrådslederens avdeling v/Seksjon for internrevisjon (Investigation Report: Examination Undertaken on Behalf of the City of Oslo, Department of the Mayor). PricewaterhouseCoopers, Oslo, May 21.
PwC. (2009). Gransking av «Spania-prosjektet» Oslo kommune (Investigation of the Spain Project in the City of Oslo). PricewaterhouseCoopers, Oslo. http://www.oslo.kommune.no/getfile.php/Byr%C3%A5det%20(BYR)/Internett%20(BYR)/Dokumenter/Rapport%20pwc.pdf

PwC. (2013a). Utvidet revisjon av Akershus universitetssykehus HF (Investigation Report about Ahus Public Hospital). PricewaterhouseCoopers, Oslo. http://www.ahus.no/SiteCollectionDocuments/Endelig%20offentlig%20rapport%20-%20Utvidet%20revisjon%20Ahus_Rev%20OV%2022052013.pdf

PwC. (2013b). Kontrollutvalget i Stavanger v/Rogaland Kontrollutvalgssekretariat: Undersøkelse/gransking knyttet til Stavanger kommunes utbetaling av á-kontobeløp i forbindelse med den såkalte «Tyrkia-saken» (Investigation Report about the Turkey Case in the City of Stavanger). PricewaterhouseCoopers, Oslo, September 11.

Röglinger, M., Pöppelbuss, J., and Becker, J. (2012). Maturity models in business process management. *Business Process Management Journal*, 18(2), 328–346.

Sutton, R.I., and Staw, B.M. (1995). What theory is not. *Administrative Science Quarterly*, 40, 371–384.

Weick, K.E. (1995). What theory is not, theorizing is. *Administrative Science Quarterly*, 40, 385–390.

Wells, J.T. (2003). The fraud examiners. *Journal of Accountancy*, October, 76–80.

Sample Investigation Evaluations

12

The market for private investigations by fraud examiners has grown in Norway in recent years. Several reasons can be found for this growth. First, compliance by business organizations has become an important issue, especially for corporations trading their stocks on stock exchanges both domestically and abroad. Detecting and preventing financial crime has thus become critical. Second, suspicions of financial crime generally and white-collar crime in particular will harm business reputation, making it imperative to find out what actually happened. Third, Norwegian police often do not have the capacity and competence to investigate complicated business irregularities. Fourth, corporate social responsibility has become an issue on the board agenda in many corporations, where ethical guidelines, antibribery activities, and other crime-related topics are of increasing importance. Finally, innocent yet suspected individuals, especially when exposed in the media, deserve a fair investigation to prove their innocence.

Private investigations in Norway are carried out by auditing firms such as BDO, Ernst & Young, and PricewaterhouseCoopers (PwC), as well as by law firms such as Kvale, Lynx, and Wiersholm. Fraud examiners in these firms are typically trained as auditors, lawyers, and police detectives. In a country of 5 million people, there are about 100 partners and associates in these firms who have fraud investigations as their main occupation. In addition, larger banks, oil companies, and other organizations have internal investigation departments.

Twenty-One Examination Reports

An estimated 30 private investigations become publicly known in Norway per year. Out of this number, the current research was able to obtain only 21 investigation reports from recent years. Access to most investigation reports was denied by the investigation contractor where typically the investigation took place.

Characteristics of 21 publicly available investigation reports are listed in Table 12.1. First, the case name is mentioned. Adecco is a business firm, Ahus is a public hospital, Briskeby is a football stadium, Eckbo is a family foundation, Fadderbarna is a nongovernment organization for children care,

Table 12.1 Characteristics of Reports from Fraud Examinations by Private Investigators

No.	Case	Investigator	Suspicion	Pages
1	Adecco *Nursing and cleaning services business*	Wiersholm (2011) law firm	Exploitation of workforce in nursing home in terms of low wages and inhuman working hours	22
2	Ahus *Public hospital*	PwC (2013a) law firm	Buying expensive geographical information system services	15
3	Briskeby *Football stadium*	Lynx (2011) law firm	Overcharging for construction work at football stadium	267
4	Eckbo *Family foundation*	Dobrowen and Klepp (2009) law firm	Executives in ideal foundation for personal gain	119
5	Fadderbarna *NGO for children*	BDO (2011) auditing firm	Excessive administration costs in NGO	46
6	Furuheim *Church foundation*	Dalane and Olsen (2006) law firm	Executives in church foundation for personal gain	164
7	Gassnova *Carbon capture and storage*	BDO (2013) auditing firm	Irregular procurement procedures by employees	27
8	Halden Ishall *Sports ice arena*	KPMG (2012) auditing firm	Excessive cost overrun in reconstruction	121
9	Langemyhr *Construction company*	PwC (2008a) auditing firm	Fraud by overbilling city work in hours	26
10	Lindeberg *Nursing home*	Kommunerevisjonen (2013) auditing service	Outside authority of personnel	92
11	Lunde Group *Transportation company*	Bie (2012) law firm	Fraud and tax evasion for Us$30 million	86

(continued)

Table 12.1 Characteristics of Reports from Fraud Examinations by Private Investigators (continued)

No.	Case	Investigator	Suspicion	Pages
12	Moskvaskolen *Norwegian school in Moskau*	Ernst & Young (2013) auditing firm	Private living expenses for dean covered by school	38
13	Norges Fotballforbund *Football association*	Lynx (2013) law firm	Football players changing clubs without clubs paying transfer money	48
14	Norsk Tipping *Public betting firm*	Deloitte (2010) auditing firm	Financial relationships between employees and external firm	61
15	Oslo Vei *Road construction company*	Kvale (2013) law firm	Chairman and CEO suspected of fraud after bankruptcy	53
16	Spania *City of Oslo project in Spain*	PwC (2009) auditing firm	Abuse of public money intended for building local Norwegian hospital spent on friends in Spain	92
17	Terra *Cities investing in bonds*	PwC (2008b) auditing firm	Outside authority of city management	52
18	Troms Kraft *Power supply company*	Nergaard (2013) consulting firm	Accounting manipulation in subsidiary and illegal political party support	663
19	Tyrkia *City of Stavanger project for children*	PwC (2013b) auditing firm	Smuggling of adopted children out of Turkey financed by the City of Stavanger	14
20	Undervisningsbygg *School maintenance agency*	Kommunerevisjonen (2006a, 2006b) auditing service	Fraud by property managers in the City of Oslo	36
21	Verdibanken *Religious bank*	Wiersholm (2012) law firm	Investment fraud by bank executive	5

Furuheim is a church foundation with elderly homes, Gassnova is a public organization in charge of technology development for carbon capture and storage, Moskvaskolen is a local school in Moscow established by Southeast County of Moscow and Akershus County in Norway, Norges Fotballforbund is the Norwegian football association, Norsk Tipping is a government betting firm, Spania is a case of a Norwegian hospital in Spain, Troms Kraft is a power supply company, Tyrkia is a case of adopted children from Turkey, and Undervisningsbygg is a case of property management in the City of Oslo.

Next in the table, year of investigation report is listed, followed by the investigating firm. Suspicion causing the investigation is listed in the next column. Finally, the number of pages in the investigation report is listed.

Making private investigation reports publicly known—as those listed in the table—serves a number of important purposes. First, whistle-blowers receive the required recognition they deserve, and future whistle-blowers can observe that whistle-blowing matters. Next, published investigations can have a preventive effect on potential white-collar criminals and also make white-collar criminals terminate their criminal activities. Publishing enables practical focus and attention to morale and ethics, where what is acceptable and what is not become visible. Publishing increases the extent of organizational transparency. Publishing enables learning by other organizations that could have ended up in the same situation. When a corruption scandal such as the one involving global fertilizer Yara is in the media for weeks and months, the public expects to learn about the truth. Publication can generally lead to new insights about causes of financial crime, and thereby increase awareness among decision makers in society. Finally, available investigation reports can help improve teaching and research at universities. Despite all these good reasons, most private investigations by fraud examiners lead to secrecy of reports.

Investigation Performance

To evaluate the quality and performance of private investigations, a sequence of initiation, process, results, and consequences can be followed. Quality is determined by the mandate and motivation for the examination, the professional examination process, investigation results, as well as consequences of the investigation. To make it simple, a Likert scale from 1 (poor) to 4 (excellent) is applied in Table 12.2 for all available 21 investigation reports from Norway. The final column shows the total score for each investigation. The minimum total score is 4, while the maximum total score is 16.

Rather than representing a final ranking of available investigations, Table 12.2 indicates how investigations can be evaluated and compared with each other. The highest score is achieved by lawyers Dalane and Olsen (2006),

Table 12.2 Performance Quality Scores for Fraud Examinations by Private Investigators

No.	Case	Start	Process	Result	Impact	Score
1	Adecco by Wiersholm (2011)	3	3	2	2	10
2	Ahus by PwC (2013a)	4	3	2	0	9
3	Briskeby by Lynx (2011)	3	4	1	3	11
4	Eckbo by Dobrowen and Klepp (2009)	1	2	3	3	9
5	Fadderbarna by BDO (2011)	2	3	2	2	9
6	Furuheim by Dalane and Olsen (2006)	3	4	4	2	13
7	Gassnova by BDO (2013)	2	2	2	1	9
8	Halden Ishall by KPMG (2012)	4	3	1	1	9
9	Langemyhr by PwC (2008a)	4	1	3	4	12
10	Lindeberg by Kommunerevisjonen (2013)	2	3	3	2	10
11	Lundegruppen by Bie (2012)	2	3	2	3	11
12	Moskvaskolen by Ernst & Young (2013)	2	1	2	4	9
13	Norges Fotballforbund by Lynx (2013)	2	1	1	4	8
14	Norsk Tipping by Deloitte (2010)	3	2	3	4	11
15	Oslo Vei by Kluge (2013)	2	2	4	3	11
16	Spania by PwC (2009)	4	2	3	2	11
17	Terra by PwC (2008b)	2	1	2	1	6
18	Troms Kraft by Nergaard (2013)	4	4	2	1	11
19	Tyrkia by PwC (2013b)	1	1	3	3	8
20	Undervisningsbygg by Kommunerevisjonen (2006a, 2006b)	3	2	3	3	11
21	Verdibanken by Wiersholm (2012)	1	3	3	1	8

who did an excellent job in examining accusations from a whistle-blower in a professional manner, leading later to jail sentences for two key board members in a church foundation.

Here we have left out resource consumption, as it is mostly not known. At the same time, value is difficult to estimate, making cost-benefit analysis a guesswork. Finally, it is not obvious that resource consumption should carry the same weight as the other four criteria.

A number of reasons why investigation reports do not end up as publications available to the public were discussed earlier. Some reasons are related to privacy, while others are related to business conducts. Some reasons, which are not very acceptable, are related to failure by fraud examiners to succeed in their tasks. For example, detectives unable to conduct professional interviews will not gain critical insights from witnesses and suspects. Even worse, some private investigators behave like bad cops without any formal authority at all.

The business of private investigations in financial crime is only two decades old in Norway. There are concerns that the normal procedure of separation between police powers, prosecution powers, and court powers sometimes is all combined in one single private person, the fraud examiner. Although the intention by most financial crime specialists is to stop before the stage of prosecution, and only complete inquiries, there are nevertheless indications that many private investigations go too far.

A current political question in Norway is whether the industry of private detectives and fraud examiners should be regulated by the law. A regulation will limit the powers of private investigators and determine a borderline for private versus public investigations. While some police investigations fail as well, quality scores in this chapter indicate that most law firms and accounting firms have a long way to go to become professional inquiry units.

The Turkey Case

Adopted children from Turkey were smuggled out and back to Norway. There were suspicions of several kinds of crime. First, the child care manager in the City of Stavanger, on the west coast of Norway, was suspected of misappropriation of city funds. Next, Norwegian lawyers were suspected of hiding money transactions on client accounts. Then, a private Norwegian detective who helped get the children out of Turkey was suspected of both corruption and tax evasion. Finally, helpers in Turkey were suspected of being bribed.

It all started in 2006, when two children under the case and protection of city child care in Stavanger went with their Norwegian foster parents to Turkey on vacation. The children had been taken away from their Turkish parents who lived in Stavanger sometime earlier. While on vacation in Turkey, a Turkish court ruled that the children were not allowed to leave the country.

After the foster parents had returned to Norway without the children, the child care manager in the City of Stavanger transferred half a million Norwegian kroner—about US$90,000—to a client account in a law firm in Stavanger. The lawyers Nils Geir Vestvik and Atle Helljesen, who received the money from child care manager Gunnar Toresen, transferred it to the bank account of the spouse of private detective Ola Thune. The intention for the irregular money transfer was both to hide tracks to Ola Thune and to pay Thune's helpers in smuggling the two Norwegian-Turkish boys to Norway (Aas et al., 2013).

Many years later, after considerable attention in the media, especially in the daily newspaper *Stavanger Aftenblad*, the city control committee decided to initiate a private investigation by fraud examiners from law and auditing firm PricewaterhouseCoopers (PwC). The investigation was carried out by examiners Kjell Richard Manskow, Helge Kvamme, Gunnar Holm Ringen, Pål Jæger-Pedersen, Hege Oftedal, and Thor Dalhaug from PwC. They write in their report (PwC, 2013b: 14):

> The fact that part of the amount of money transferred to the attorney Vestvik's private account to a private account in the name of a spouse caregiver appears highly irregular. For this part of the money vouchers are missing that can document how the funds were allocated.

The investigators from PwC were able to trace money transactions, but they were not able to allocate responsibilities to individuals such as the city child care manager, attorneys, or detective and wife. Investigators from PwC answered the how question, but they did not answer the who question or why question for money transfer. This might be because the mandate for the investigation was focused on transactions (PwC, 2013b: 6):

> The control committee in Stavanger has decided to initiate an investigation of law firm Projure's accounting and documentation for Stavanger municipality in connection with the payment of a one-time amount from Stavanger municipality to the law firm in 2006 in connection with the so-called "Turkey case." The purpose of the project will be to conduct an inquiry, in which one looks closely at the accounts relating to payment of an amount of 500.000 NOK from Stavanger municipality to law firm Projure with potential subcontractors, and clarify/provide documentation on what these funds were used for.

The mandate thus focused on the how question and not the who or why questions. Thus, the roles and responsibilities of actors such as Toresen (city politician), Vestvik and Helljesen (lawyers), and Thune (accused of being a child smuggler) and his wife (accused of money transfer) remained unclear.

Investigators from PwC presented their report to the control committee in the fall of 2013. The committee decided to send the report to the local police. City politicians decided to close the case (Aas et al., 2013; Aas and Ergo, 2013; Berge, 2013; Grimen and Terjesen, 2013; Østebø et al., 2013).

The Eckbo Case

Eckbo's Legater is one of Norway's largest publicly beneficial and philanthropic foundations. The Norwegian registration authority responded in 2007 to information that emerged in newspapers about the foundation's management, where Finn Olaf Eckbo—a third-generation Eckbo—received

US$600,000 annually to manage the foundation. This was much more than yearly wages paid out for good causes.

Not only newspaper reports caused the registration authority to respond. An active anticorruption politician on the very left-wing side in politics, Erling Folkvord, wrote about the Eckbo foundation with the title *They Got It Both Ways*. A number of influential people in both business and politics were linked to the foundation, according to the Folkvord et al. (2008) book, and they all benefited personally from the links. This is despite the mission statement of the foundation, which is to support good causes financially.

Andersland (2008) found that the story was just so amazing that it would have been dismissed as a pure robber story if it had not been so uncomfortably well documented. In short, the book is about how significant portions of foundation funds, earmarked for charitable purposes, were used and abused for exorbitant fees, loans, and pensions to directors and business managers. The business manager for many years, Rolf Eckbo, was finally—in 1997—sentenced to 5 years in prison for financial fraud, and deprived of the right to be a lawyer.

After newspaper reports and the book by Folkvord et al. (2008), private fraud investigators Dobrowen, a lawyer, and Klepp, an auditor, were hired. They wrote a report very different from Folkvord's book. Although they found some signs of waste of funds, they found no misconduct or signs of criminal behavior. In their investigation, the investigators mainly studied documents handed over to them by foundation-loyal persons, and they only interviewed foundation-loyal individuals.

Dobrowen and Klepp (2009) concluded their investigation with the following findings:

- The organization of asset management in Eckbo Endowments is, in the committee's view, in accordance with the requirements of the organization as required by law and the articles of incorporation.
- In the committee's view, the practice of asset management in the period in question occurred in a responsible manner and has thus been in line with the foundation act and statute requirements.

The Langemyhr Case

Private investigators found Harald Langemyhr guilty of fraud of 22 million Norwegian kroner (PwC, 2008a). Police investigators found him guilty of fraud of 12 million Norwegian kroner. The district court of Oslo found him not guilty of fraud. The case against Langemyhr started when Norwegian Labour Inspection in 2008 suspected the construction company owner of misconduct and crime against the City of Oslo. Five years later, Langemyhr received a replacement of 20 million Norwegian kroner from the City of Oslo based on a new court order. Langemyhr suffered personally and socially for 5 long years. He was unable to start up his construction company again in 2014.

What went wrong? Were the private investigators wrong, accusing Langemyhr of large-scale fraud? Were police investigators wrong, maybe because they put too much reliance on the private investigation report? Or was the judge wrong, since Langemyhr was maybe guilty of fraud? We will never know.

But we may argue that the private investigators jumped to conclusions based on price estimates for construction work not verified by more than one construction consultant.

The Langemyhr investigation receives here scores of 4 (starting point), 1 (work process), 3 (work result), and 4 (report consequence). The starting point was clear based on labor inspection, and thus 4. The work process was lousy with a tunnel view in the investigation, and thus 1. The work result was quite clear, with a claim of fraud, and thus 3. And the consequence was obvious, i.e., prosecution in court, and thus 4.

Characteristics of Cases

As exploratory research, investigation reports can be studied along the time axis of (1) initiation (investigation start), (2) work process (investigation procedure), (3) work results (investigation findings), and (4) consequence (investigation effects). An investigation report should clearly state the initiation in terms of background and mandate, describe the investigation process, explain findings from the investigation, as well as suggest points for action. All reviewed 21 investigation reports satisfied these requirements, although to a varying degree.

An obvious difference among the reports in the tables is the length, ranging from 5 to 663 pages. This range does not only reflect investigation scope and workload in terms of dollars paid. Some private investigations are billed for less than US$100,000, while others cost the client several millions. Six Norwegian kroner is the equivalent of US$1, and the most expensive investigation did also produce the longest report. The investigation of utility company Troms Kraft cost 44 million Norwegian kroner and resulted in a report of 663 pages. There is a correlation between money spent on an investigation and the final report length.

Some expensive investigations result in a short report, with the argument that executives and other decision makers are supposed to read it, not only look through it. For a busy executive, more than 100 pages of reading is not always acceptable. Bie (2012) did a very thorough and probably also expensive examination of all firms belonging to the Lunde Group. Nevertheless, he shortened his report down to 86 pages.

Out of 21 available reports, 12 were produced by auditing firms, 8 by law firms, and 1 by a consulting firm. The average length of auditing firm reports is 52 pages. The average length of law firm reports is 95 pages. Although not statistically significant, this difference is interesting in the sense that lawyers tend to put more emphasis on formality and procedure, while auditors tend to put more emphasis on findings, thereby potentially producing somewhat shorter reports.

Three private investigation reports triggered later police investigations followed by public prosecution. In two cases, suspects were convicted to prison. The third case was dismissed from court, which is the Langemyhr case described above. A report of only 26 pages (PwC, 2008a) was the basis for police investigation and public prosecution in court for several weeks, but the judge criticized the investigation and declared Langemyhr not guilty.

A total of 11 individuals were sentenced to prison after Kommunerevisjonen (2006a, 2006b) public auditing service had investigated fraud by property managers in the City of Oslo. Two persons were sentenced to prison after Bie (2012) in law firm Vierdal had investigated fraud in myriad companies in the Lunde Group.

This exploratory research has introduced the empirical side of private financial crime investigations and fraud examinations. More empirical material is needed to be able to conduct research in terms of hypotheses testing and validation. Content analysis of investigation reports needs to rely on multiple raters based on criteria for classification of verbatim findings in reports.

Fraud Examination Reports

Fraud examination reports from white-collar crime investigations in Norway were the basis for evaluations as presented above. There are no guidelines in Norway for how to write a solid fraud examination report. In the United States, both the Association of Certified Fraud Examiners (ACFE) and the Association of Certified Financial Crime Specialists (ACFCS) have issued guidelines on effective report writing.

The purpose of a report is to permit informed decision making by a competent authority. A report needs to be informative—it reports back something that happened and the steps taken to reveal the circumstances and describe actions taken. It might also need to be persuasive—it might contain recommendations on some future course of action, or preventive measures to prevent a recurrence. A report should answer any questions relevant readers might reasonably have. When something can be read without effort, great effort has often gone into its writing (Knights, 2012).

A report does not serve its purpose and is not useful if the reader cannot understand it, the reader stops because reading it is too much of a chore, or if the report does not actually communicate what the author meant (Knights, 2012).

A report no one has confidence in is not useful. The report's structure—its presentation—is as important as its content. A report with inaccurate information is not useful—it could be damaging. A report with accurate information but that is written so poorly that the reader does not understand it, or misunderstands the information and makes a wrong decision based on it, is not useful (Knights, 2012).

Investigation reports are structured in many ways, but there are components common to all (Knights, 2012):

- Background—why the investigation was conducted
- Executive summary—summary of actions and results
- Scope—statement of objectives
- Approach—method and participants
- Findings—results of the investigation
- Summary—key findings of the investigation
- Consequence—effect on the victim
- Recommendations—what the client should or should not do
- Appendices—those documents that will serve as evidence later

The findings section contains the details of the fraud examination. It generally consists of several pages. Enough detail has to be provided so that the reader understands what tasks examiners performed and what they found. The reader needs to understand what occurred.

References

Aas, H.P., and Ergo, T. (2013). Professor krever etterforskning for korrupsjon (Professor requires police investigation for corruption). *Stavanger Aftenblad*, November 12, pp. 6–7.

Aas, H.P., Ergo, T., and Østebø, J. (2013). Skjulte fluktpenger fra kommunen på den private kontoen til sin kone (Were hiding escape money from the municipality on the account of his wife). *Stavanger Aftenblad*, October 26. www.aftenbladet.no

Andersland, G.K. (2008). Røverhistorie fra virkeligheten (Robber story from real life). *Bergens Tidende*, October 27. www.bt.no

BDO. (2011). Rapport til Lotteri- og stiftelsestilsynet vedr. gransking av stiftelsen Fadderbarnas Framtid (Investigation Report about the Foundation for Adopted Childrens' Future). BDO, Erling Grimstad and Morten Thorkildsen. https://lottstift.no/stiftelsestilsynet/files/2011/12/Rapport-til-Stiftelsestilsynet-fra-BDO-vedr-gransking-av-Fadderbarnas-Framtid.pdf

BDO. (2013). Gjennomgang av anskaffelsesprosessen, konsulentinnleie og habilitet i Gassnova SF (Investigation Report about Procurement in Gassnova).

Berge, M. (2013). Frp anmelder Tyrkia-saken (Frp political party report Turkey case to police). *NRK Rogaland*, January 13. www.nrk.no/rogaland

Bie, F. (2012). *Rapport til Stavanger* tingrett (Report to District Court in Stavanger). Vierdal advokatfirma, Stavanger.

Dalane, J., and Olsen, D.L. (2006). *Granskingsrapport—ledelse og styring av Øyestad helselags boligstiftelse Furuheim* (Investigation Report about the Foundation Furuheim for Elderly). Hald, Dalane & Heimvik law firm, Arendal.

Deloitte. (2010). Norsk Tipping—Granskingsrapport av 16. august 2010 (Investigation Report about Norwegian Betting Company). https://www.norsk-tipping.no/forsiden/nytt_fra_selskapet/26819.cms

Dobrowen, K., and Klepp, T. (2009). Uavhengig undersøkelse av Eckbos Legater (Investigation Report about the Eckbo Foundation). www.eckbos-legater.no/content/download/479/7915/version/1/file

Ernst & Young. (2013). Gransking—NRVS (Investigation Report on School in Moskau). Ernst & Young, Oslo, October 30.

Folkvord, E., Eckbo, A.K., and Mathisen, E. (2008). *I pose og sekk* (They Got It Both Ways). Forlaget Rødt, Oslo.

Grimen, B., and Terjesen, M. (2013). Høyre stemmer mot å få alle fakta på bordet (Right Wing Party Votes against Getting All Facts on the Table). *NRK Rogaland*, November 18. www.nrk.no/rogaland

Knights, D. (2012). *Effective Investigation Reports*. Association of Certified Fraud Examiners. www.acfe.com

Kommunerevisjonen. (2006a). *Granskingsrapport Undervisningsbygg Oslo KF* (Investigation Report on City School Maintenance Service), Rapport 16/2006.

Kommunerevisjonen. (2006b). *Granskingsrapport 2 Undervisningsbygg Oslo KF* (Investigation Report on City School Maintenance Service), Rapport 27/2006.

Kommunerevisjonen. (2013). *Oslo kommunes saksbehandling i Lindebergsakene* (City of Oslo Handling the Lindeberg Cases), Rapport 7/2013.

KPMG. (2012). *Halden kommune: Gransking av disposisjoner i Halden Ishall AS og Halden Ishall Eiendom AS* (Halden Municipality: Investigation of Dispositions in Halden Ice Hall and Halden Ice Hall Property). KPMG.

Kvale. (2013). *Innberetning til Oslo byfogdembete i bo nr. 12-197991IKON-OBYF/2 Oslo Vei AS, dets konkursbo* (Report to the District Court on Bankruptcy of Oslo Road). Kvale Advokatfirma, Advokat/Bostyrer Tom Hugo Ottesen, December 11.

Lynx. (2011). *Briskebyrapporten* (Investigation Report on Football Stadium). Lynx law firm. www.hamar.kommune.no. http://www.hamar.kommune.no/getfile.php/Bilder/Hamar/Nyhetsbilder/Politikere/Briskebyrapporten,%20ikke%20sladdet_1.pdf

Lynx. (2013). *1192-rapporten. Gransking av internasjonale spilleroverganger 2007–2011* (Examination of Player Transfers). Lynx law firm, Oslo.

Nergaard, L.L. (2013). *Gransking av Troms Kraft AS* (Investigation Report about Troms Kraft Power Company). Norscan Partners and Grette law firm, September 9.

Østebø, J., Ergo, T., and Aas, H.P. (2013). Ber bystyret avslutte Tyrkia-saken mandag (Asks city council to close Turkey investigation on Monday). *Stavanger Aftenblad*, November 13, p. 10.

PwC. (2008a). Granskingsrapport: Undersøkelser foretatt på oppdrag fra Oslo kommune, Byrådslederens avdeling v/Seksjon for internrevisjon (Investigation Report: Examination Undertaken on Behalf of the City of Oslo, Department of the Mayor). PricewaterhouseCoopers, Oslo, May 21.

PwC. (2008b). Granskingsrapport—«Terra-saken» i Rana kommune (Investigation Report—«Terra Case» in Rana Municipality). PricewaterhouseCoopers, Oslo, June 10.

PwC. (2009). Gransking av «Spania-prosjektet» Oslo kommune (Investigation of the Spain Project in the City of Oslo). PricewaterhouseCoopers, Oslo. http://www.oslo.kommune.no/getfile.php/Byr%C3%A5det%20(BYR)/Internett%20(BYR)/Dokumenter/Rapport%20pwc.pdf

PwC. (2013a). Utvidet revisjon av Akershus universitetssykehus HF (Investigation Report about Ahus Public Hospital). PricewaterhouseCoopers, Oslo. http://www.ahus.no/SiteCollectionDocuments/Endelig%20offentlig%20rapport%20-%20Utvidet%20revisjon%20Ahus_Rev%20OV%2022052013.pdf

PwC. (2013b). Kontrollutvalget i Stavanger v/Rogaland Kontrollutvalgssekretariat: Undersøkelse/gransking knyttet til Stavanger kommunes utbetaling av á-kontobeløp i forbindelse med den såkalte «Tyrkia-saken» (Investigation Report about the Turkey Case in the City of Stavanger). PricewaterhouseCoopers, Oslo, September 11.

Wiersholm. (2011) Granskingsrapport—Oppsummering: Adecco Norge AS (Investigation Report about Adecco Health Care Institutions). Wiersholm law firm, Oslo, September 23.

Wiersholm. (2012). Notat til Verdibanken ASA v/Kjell Hande (Notes to Verdibanken). Ansvarlig Advokat Knut Bergo, November 19.

Investigation Perspectives

13

The activity of private investigations by fraud examiners is a business of lawyers, auditors, and other professionals who investigate suspicions of financial crime by white-collar criminals. This chapter presents results from an empirical study of investigation reports. The available sample consists of 28 reports written mostly by auditing firms such as Deloitte, Ernst & Young, and PricewaterhouseCoopers (PwC). The blame game can occur at two stages in a private investigation. First, the mandate formulated by a client may point investigators in a specific direction. Next, investigators sometimes suffer from a tunnel view of predetermined opinions. In the sample of 28 investigation reports, more than half of them involve potential blame game victims.

Blame Game Hypothesis

My thoughts on the blame game theory, as it applies to private investigation, were first presented in the *Journal of Investigative Psychology and Offender Profiling* (Gottschalk, 2014) and are expanded in this section.

The market for private financial crime investigations by fraud examiners has grown in Norway in recent years. Several reasons can be found for this growth. First, compliance by business organizations has become an important issue, especially for corporations trading their stocks on stock exchanges both domestically and abroad. Detecting and preventing financial crime has thus become critical. Second, suspicions of financial crime generally and white-collar crime in particular will harm business reputation, making it imperative to find out what actually happened. Third, Norwegian police often do not have the capacity and competence to investigate complicated business irregularities. Fourth, corporate social responsibility has become an issue on the board agenda in many organizations, where ethical guidelines, antibribery activities, and other crime-related topics are of increasing importance. Finally, innocent yet suspected individuals, especially when exposed in the media, deserve a fair investigation to prove their innocence.

However, the blame game hypothesis suggests that suspected individuals do not necessarily become subject to a fair investigation by private examiners and financial crime specialists. In police investigations, it is equally important to prove innocence as to prove guilt. In the charter for Norwegian criminal investigations, it is stated that police officers should put just as much effort into proving innocence as into proving guilt. Even when victims and others expect public prosecution, only individuals where police investigations have found sufficient evidence will be prosecuted in court.

This may be different in private investigations. Financial crime specialists claim to have found the facts and the responsible person(s) for a negative event or incident. They may not have practiced an open mind. They may have been pointed in a specific direction by the client, and they may have only one lead, which was to be verified in the investigation. The client sometimes pays for a desired result. The client defines a mandate, and the investigation has to be carried out according to the mandate. To make a contribution in the investigation report, investigators have to describe some findings related to facts and causes.

There are two steps of looking for causal explanations in private investigations. The first step is concerned with the mandate, where investigative focus is defined. The second step is concerned with findings, where potential suspects are identified. Often, it can be perceived as a blame game by individuals who are suspected of financial crime. Investigators are told by suspects: "You should not blame me for what happened!"

Research on organizational justice and social accounts focuses on how explanations of negative events are publicly communicated to others. Explanations affect outcomes such as trust in the organization, feelings of anger, dissatisfaction, frustration, and stress. Suspects find it unfair, especially when suspicions develop into more or less grounded accusations. Of course, this can happen in police investigations as well.

A lack of causal accounts increases disapproval ratings of the harm done by placing the blame for harmful acts on others. For example, by attributing corruption to an executive in the organization as a rotten apple, the suspect will feel betrayed by other executives who, in his opinion, belong to the rotten apple basket.

External attributions place the cause of a negative event on external factors, absolving the account giver and investigation client from personal responsibility. However, unstable attributions suggest that the cause of the negative event is unlikely to persist over time, and as such mitigate the severity of the predicament. Uncontrollable attributions suggest that the cause of the event is not within the control of the attributor, further removing any blame or responsibility for the unjust act from the account giver (Lee and Robinson, 2000).

The reasons for private investigations include lack of facts and lack of accountability. Nobody will blame oneself for the negative event. The account giver, the private investigator, absolves others from the blame and responsibility for the negative event. Even in cases of self-blame, investigations are required to ensure that the self-blame is justified. Self-blame is attributing a negative event to one's behavior or disposition (Lee and Robinson, 2000).

Some are too powerful to blame (Pontell et al., 2014). Status-related factors such as influential positions, upper-class family ties, and community roles often preclude perceptions of blameworthiness (Slyke and Bales, 2012).

In a principal-agent perspective, attributions for negative events may deflect blame away from the real perpetrators. Investigators are motivated to assume power and to project control over causal relationships. This motivation to appear in control might lead the account giver to use internal and controllable attributions in his or her accounts. Such motivation might also lead the investigator to use controllable attributions in his or her accounts by deflecting blame. To blame others is simply attractive when a negative event has occurred.

The blame game includes not only internal and external attributions. Relations can also be blamed. Eberly et al. (2011) found that an employee does not solely blame her own abilities and skills for the negative event, nor does she attribute blame solely to her supervisor. Instead, she attributes the failure to the poor interaction she had with her supervisor—a feature of their relationship. Furthermore, the employee may blame being passed over a promotion on a lack of connections with key constituents in the organization or on low network centrality. In the blame game, relational attribution is problematic, as investigators will find it inconvenient to blame an individual as self in relation to other. Responsibility for a negative event is assigned to an individual or individuals, and not to a relationship or relationships.

Shepherd et al. (2011) argue that the building blocks of an informed culture are encouraging members to report errors and near misses, to apportion blame justly when something goes wrong, and to flexibly and swiftly learn by reconfiguring assumptions, frameworks, and actions. However, to protect themselves from criticism, executives and other individuals in an organization often engage in impression management that deflects blame to others.

The blame game can be explained in terms of negative events that are attributed to individuals who account givers would like to blame. People have a tendency to make sense of events by acting as naïve psychologists. When confronted with events, people seek to determine their causes. For example, couples in marriages sometimes play the blame game by determining the other spouse as the cause. Causality in terms of cause-and-effect relationships seems easy to conclude when events occur.

The blame game hypothesis can be derived from attribution theory (Eberly et al., 2011) as well as behavioral decision-making theory, which posits that decision makers are predictably biased by the interaction of the context and specific cognitive mechanisms (Hammond et al., 1998; Kahnemann, 2011). Behavioral decision making has identified an array of cognitive mechanisms that may disturb investigators' judgment. A bias can occur among private investigators based on client mandate and available resources in fraud investigations, where anchoring of suspicion can be misplaced. Furthermore, the primacy effect is a tendency for the first items presented in a series to be remembered better or more easily, while affirmation bias means to interpret information in a way consistent with existing beliefs. If the client has strong beliefs in one way or the other, this will manifest itself both in the mandate and in expectations. Similarly, the tunnel view sometimes experienced in police investigations implies that detectives go for the light at the end of the tunnel, rather than look at what is outside the tunnel.

Twenty-Eight Examination Reports

Private investigations in Norway are carried out by auditing firms such as BDO, Deloitte, Ernst & Young, KPMG, and PwC, as well as by law firms such as Kvale, Lynx, and Wiersholm. Fraud examiners in these firms are typically trained as auditors, lawyers, and police detectives. In a country of 5 million people, there are about 100 partners and associates in these firms who have fraud investigations as their main occupation. In addition, larger banks, insurance firms, oil companies, and other organizations have internal investigation departments.

This research is about criminal offenses, not civil cases. An estimated 10 private investigations become publicly known in Norway per year. Out of this number, the current research was able to obtain 28 investigation reports from recent years. Access to most investigation reports was denied by the investigation contractor, the client, where typically the investigation took place. Based on the accessed investigation reports, this chapter attempts to identify some characteristics of investigation reports listed in Table 13.1.

First in Table 13.1, the case name is mentioned. Adecco is a business firm, Ahus is a public hospital, while Briskeby is a football stadium. Eckbo is a family foundation, Fadderbarna is a nongovernment organization for children care, Forsvaret is the army, while Furuheim is a church foundation running homes for the elderly. Next in the table, literature reference to investigation reports is listed, using the investigating firm as reference. Suspicion causing the investigation is listed in the next column. Finally, the number of pages in the investigation report is listed.

Making private investigation reports publicly known—as those listed in the table—serves a number of important purposes. First, whistle-blowers receive the required recognition they deserve, and future whistle-blowers can observe that whistle-blowing matters. Next, published investigations can have a preventive effect on potential white-collar criminals and also make white-collar criminals terminate their criminal activities. Publishing enables practical focus and attention to morale and ethics, where it becomes visible what is acceptable and what is not. Publishing increases the extent of

Table 13.1 Characteristics of Reports from Fraud Examinations by Private Investigators

No.	Case	Investigator	Suspicion	Pages
1	Adecco *Nursing and cleaning services business*	Wiersholm (2011) law firm	Exploitation of workforce in nursing home in terms of low wages and inhuman working hours	22
2	Ahus *Public hospital*	PwC (2013a) auditing firm	Buying expensive geographical information system services	15
3	Briskeby *Football stadium*	Lynx (2011) law firm	Overcharging for construction work at football stadium	267
4	Eckbo *Family foundation*	Dobrowen and Klepp (2009) law firm	Executives in ideal foundation for personal gain	119
5	Fadderbarna *NGO for children*	BDO (2011) auditing firm	Excessive administration costs in NGO	46
6	Forsvaret *Army*	Dalseide (2006)	Suspected corruption at procurement of information technology	184
7	Furuheim *Church foundation*	Dalane and Olsen (2006) law firm	Executives in church foundation for personal gain	164
8	Gassnova *Carbon capture and storage*	BDO (2013) auditing firm	Irregular procurement procedures by employees	27
9	Halden Ishall *Sports ice arena*	KPMG (2012) auditing firm	Excessive cost overrun in reconstruction	121
10	Halden kommune *City of Halden*	Gjørv and Lund (2013)	Manager in department of planning and construction suspected of corruption	46
11	Kragerø Fjordbåtselskap *Shipping company*	Deloitte (2012)	Chief executive suspected of abuse of company funds	109
12	Langemyhr *Construction company*	PwC (2008a) auditing firm	Fraud by overbilling city work in hours	26

(continued)

Table 13.1 Characteristics of Reports from Fraud Examinations by Private Investigators (continued)

No.	Case	Investigator	Suspicion	Pages
13	Lindeberg *Nursing home*	Kommunerevisjonen (2013) auditing service	Outside authority of personnel	92
14	Lunde Group *Transportation company*	Bie (2012) law firm	Fraud and tax evasion for US$30 million	86
15	Moskvaskolen *Norwegian school in Moskau*	Ernst & Young (2013) auditing firm	Private living expenses for dean covered by school	38
16	Norges Fotballforbund *Football association*	Lynx (2013) law firm	Football players changing clubs without clubs paying transfer money	48
17	Norsk Tipping *Public betting firm*	Deloitte (2010) auditing firm	Financial relationships between employees and external firm	61
18	Oslo Vei *Road construction company*	Kvale (2013) law firm	Chairman and CEO suspected of fraud after bankruptcy	53
19	Romerike Vannverk *Public water supply*	Distriktsrevisjonen (2007)	Chief executive suspected of corruption and embezzlement	555
20	Samferdselsetaten *Public transportation*	PwC (2007) auditing firm	Suspicion of kickbacks from taxi owners for licenses	88
21	Spania *City of Oslo project in Spain*	PwC (2009) auditing firm	Abuse of public money spent on friends in Spain to build a local hospital for Norwegians	92
22	Stangeskovene *Private forest property*	Roscher and Berg (2013)	Board members controlling share sales	94
23	Sykehuset Innlandet *Hospital*	Davidsen and Sandvik (2011)	Chief executive suspected of employment violations	15
24	Terra *Cities investing in bonds*	PwC (2008b) auditing firm	Outside authority of city management	52

(continued)

Table 13.1 Characteristics of Reports from Fraud Examinations by Private Investigators (continued)

No.	Case	Investigator	Suspicion	Pages
25	Troms Kraft *Power supply company*	Nergaard (2013a, 2013b, 2013c) consulting firm	Accounting manipulation in subsidiary and illegal political party support	663
26	Tyrkia *City of Stavanger project for children*	PwC (2013b) auditing firm	Smuggling of adopted children out of Turkey financed by the City of Stavanger	14
27	Undervisningsbygg *School maintenance agency*	Kommunerevisjonen (2006a, 2006b) auditing service	Fraud by property managers in the City of Oslo	36
28	Verdibanken *Religious bank*	Wiersholm (2012) law firm	Investment fraud by bank executive	5

organizational transparency. Publishing enables learning by other organizations that could have ended up in the same situation. When corruption scandals such as the one involving global fertilizer Yara are in the media for weeks and months, the public expects to learn the truth. Publication can generally lead to new insights about causes of financial crime, and thereby increase awareness among decision makers in society. Finally, available investigation reports can help improve teaching and research at universities. Despite all these good reasons, most private investigations by fraud examiners lead to secrecy of reports.

The data were collected by obtaining as many investigation reports as possible. Only a fraction of investigation reports were available. This is because it was unknown to the researchers where private investigations had taken place, as only investigations somehow mentioned in the media were recognizable to the researchers. Fraud examiners denied disclosure of where they had conducted investigations. Only those disclosed by journalists were known to the researchers. When approaching both clients and examiners to get access to investigation reports, we were very often denied insight. There are indeed many reasons why most investigation reports are kept a secret, as discussed earlier. Our data collection procedure is biased toward investigations in the public sector, because misconduct in the public sector becomes more easily accessible to investigative journalists than does misconduct in the private sector.

Empirical Case Study

The blame game hypothesis suggests that individuals are blamed with a negative event—in our context suspicion of white-collar crime—after private investigators have examined facts and causes. It is interesting and relevant to study the usefulness of applying the blame game hypothesis toward an understanding of allegations and subsequent outcomes. This might help to address concerns about the potential for miscarriage of justice or even loss of job or reputation in such cases.

Table 13.2 lists individuals blamed, reasons for blame, and blame consequence for individuals investigated by fraud examiners. Not all individuals in the list were victims of the blame game. Some were real suspects and later convicted to jail sentence because of financial crime. This was the case in Furuheim, Romerike, and Undervisningsbygg. Of course, even a conviction is not necessarily an accurate indicator of guilt or innocence. Furthermore, we cannot draw conclusions on the motive of the accuser based on the outcome of the case.

Then there are six no-consequence cases. In one case, Ahus, there is no individual blamed, but rather a supplier. In all remaining cases, somebody got the blame. Seven of them had to leave their positions, even though there was

Table 13.2 Blame Game after Reports from Fraud Examinations by Private Investigators

No.	Case	Individuals Blamed	Reasons for Blame	Blame Consequence
1	Adecco *Nursing and cleaning services business*	Manager for Adecco Health	Breaking work hour laws for employees	Manager left company
2	Ahus *Public hospital*	Supplier of digital map services	Overcharge of map services	Back payment of map charges
3	Briskeby *Football stadium*	Managers of construction	Budget overruns in construction	Media blame of two managers
4	Eckbo *Family foundation*	Board members	Excessive fees and expenses	No consequence
5	Fadderbarna *NGO for children*	Management	Excessive administrative expenses	No consequence
6	Forsvaret *Army*	Managers at supplier Siemens	Corruption of army officials	Siemens executive left company
7	Furuheim *Church foundation*	Board members	Property arrangement for private gain	Board members convicted to jail sentence
8	Gassnova *Carbon capture and storage*	Nobody	Procurement	No consequence
9	Halden Ishall *Sports ice arena*	Manager of ice arena	Abuse of public money	No consequence
10	Halden kommune *City of Halden*	Manager of planning office	Corruption of planning officer	Planning manager in media
11	Kragerø Fjordbåtselskap *Shipping company*	Chief executive	Conflict with the board	Chief executive left company
12	Langemyhr *Construction company*	Manager of construction company	City officials felt overcharged by company	Prosecuted, but case dismissed

(continued)

Table 13.2 Blame Game after Reports from Fraud Examinations by Private Investigators (continued)

No.	Case	Individuals Blamed	Reasons for Blame	Blame Consequence
13	Lindeberg *Nursing home*	Manager	Breaking work hour laws for employees	No consequence
14	Lunde Group *Transportation company*	Owner	Bankruptcy	Owner prosecuted in court
15	Moskvaskolen *Norwegian school in Moskau*	Dean at school	Free lodging	Dean and vice dean
16	Norges Fotballforbund *Football association*	Club managers	No payment to previous clubs	No consequence
17	Norsk Tipping *Public betting firm*	Employees in the company	External financial relations	President left company
18	Oslo Vei *Road construction company*	Managers	Bankruptcy	Media blame of three managers
19	Romerike Vannverk *Public water supply*	President	Personal expenses paid by company	President convicted to jail sentence
20	Samferdselsetaten *Public transportation*	City manager for taxi licenses	Not equal opportunity for taxi owners	City manager left position
21	Spania *City of Oslo project in Spain*	City manager for elderly	Unsuccessful investment in Spain	City manager left position
22	Stangeskovene *Private forest property*	Board members	Shares sold within family	Board members
23	Sykehuset Innlandet *Hospital*	Hospital executive	Tough management style	Media blame of executive
24	Terra *Cities investing in bonds*	City executive	Failed investments	Media blame of executive

(continued)

Table 13.2 Blame Game after Reports from Fraud Examinations by Private Investigators (continued)

No.	Case	Individuals Blamed	Reasons for Blame	Blame Consequence
25	Troms Kraft *Power supply company*	Subsidiary executive	Manipulation of accounting numbers	Executive under police investigation
26	Tyrkia *City of Stavanger project for children*	Private investigator	Smuggling children by corruption	Media blame of private investigator
27	Undervisningsbygg *School maintenance agency*	Contract manager	Corruption	Contract manager sentenced to jail
28	Verdibanken *Religious bank*	Managing director	Ignorance of board decisions	Managing director left company

no real proof or evidence. Thus, more than half of all individuals investigated by fraud examiners became potential victims of the blame game. Nothing was proven, there was no evidence, but media speculation and job loss for some turned them into potential victims of the blame game hypothesis.

For example, Mr. Langemyhr was running a successful construction company until a customer—the City of Oslo—asked for a private investigation into some invoices. Langemyhr went bankrupt and the case against him was dismissed in court many years later.

All 28 investigation reports listed in the table were subject to case studies. Here are some examples to illustrate what the cases are about:

1. *Briskeby stadium case.* Two executives from the private sector received the blame from fraud examiner Lynx (2011), while some identified bureaucrats and politicians are the really responsible persons. However, since politicians and bureaucrats initiated the investigation, they could point examiners in the direction of two construction executives.
2. *Kragerø ferry boat case.* Deloitte (2012) investigated suspicions against the managing director, but it was all about a conflict between board members. The managing director had to leave.
3. *Langemyhr case.* Mr. Langemyhr owned a successful construction company and did work for the City of Oslo. The City of Oslo hired PwC (2008a) to investigate whether Langemyhr was charging too much. PwC concluded that there was substantial overbilling. The City of Oslo handed over the examination report to the police, which started its own investigation. The police decided to prosecute Langemyhr. In the district court of Oslo, the case was dismissed, because there was lack of evidence. Six years had then passed with massive press coverage and bankruptcy of his firm. Langemyhr sued the city, and he was reimbursed. The problem here was probably fraud examiners' too strong belief in overcharging by Langemyhr without evidence. In the mandate, the blame was already on suspicion of "overbilling, use of names as fictive hourly workers, theft of material" (PwC, 2008a: 3), and there was no mention of the city side of responsibility. PwC (2008a) confirmed all suspicions as facts in their report.
4. *Moskva school case.* A Norwegian high school (Skedsmo Videregående Skole) established a subsidiary in Moscow as a local school in a joint venture by Southeast County of Moscow and Akershus County in Norway. There was an apartment in Moscow, which belonged to a friend of the Norwegian dean, and the Norwegian dean used it for free when he was in Moscow. The Norwegian members of the school board in Moscow were investigated by Ernst & Young (2013). The Russian members of the board were never investigated. The politicians in

Norway were never investigated. Some accusations toward the Russian local leader of the school concerning private expenses covered by the school were never documented or investigated. In August 2014, the police dismissed the case, but in the meantime the school dean lost his job because investigators from Ernst & Young (2013: 52) had recommended the year before that "employee consequences for individuals" should be implemented and "police reporting" should take place.

5. *Norsk Tipping case.* The public betting firm had a CEO whose garden was taken care of by the firm. This was according to an agreement, but an investigation by the Office of the Auditor General in Norway led to the fall of the CEO. Deloitte's (2010) investigation found that there had been irregular financial relationships and transactions between three former and present employees at Norsk Tipping and the external firm EssNet.
6. *Spania case.* Politicians decided to build a home for elderly Norwegians in Spain. Millions were spent, but there was never a home built. A city manager was blamed and had to leave his job after investigation by PwC (2009).
7. *Terra case.* Some small towns in Norway had the potential of becoming rich because they have a great waterfall producing electric power. Instead of waiting for future utility income, they made investments based on future revenue. Investments were lost, and so were future revenues. The administration was blamed, not city politicians, by examiners from PwC (2008b).
8. *Troms Kraft case.* Board and management initiated investigations focused on subsidiaries and other predefined themes by Nergaard (2013a, 2013b, 2013c).
9. *Tyrkia case.* Child care in the City of Stavanger smuggled children out of Turkey by the help of a private investigator, who later received the blame by PwC (2013b).
10. *Verdibanken case.* Because of risky investments by the bank, the CEO had to leave his post after examination by law firm Wiersholm (2012), even though all of the investments had been approved by the board.

The current research is not about naming and shaming individuals and companies. It is about empirical study, where there is no reason to anonymize fraud examiners.

Qualitative Research Results

This chapter has presented exploratory research into private investigations by fraud examiners. More than half of all private investigations conclude by blaming someone who could not always defend himself or herself. The blame game seems to have occurred both when the client—who paid for the work—pointed the investigator in a specific direction, and when the investigator only had one hypothesis about causality for a negative event. Suspected individuals did not always become subject to a fair investigation by private examiners and financial crime specialists.

The blame game hypothesis is all about placing the blame for harmful acts on others. It is all about removing any blame or responsibility for the unjust from the client who pays for the investigation. Nobody will blame oneself for a negative event. Self-blame is very rare. The blame game was explained in terms of negative events that are attributed to individuals who the contractor or account giver would like to blame.

However, since this is exploratory and qualitative research, this chapter does not at all provide sufficient support for the blame game hypothesis in private investigations of white-collar crime suspicions. Rather, this chapter has contributed to insights into problems in private investigations by applying the blame game hypothesis.

Thus, there are ample avenues for future research. In terms of theoretical contribution, both attribution theory and decision bias theory should be explored in future research. In terms of practical implications, private investigators should be aware of the pitfalls discussed in this chapter. Certified fraud examiners are bound by a code of ethics that prevents them from being pointed in a specific direction by the client. The client cannot pay for a desired result. However, it may seem that these things are happening. The client may ask the examination team to investigate Person A (and not Person B), but the client may not ask for the examiners to conclude that Person A is guilty of X. Thus, even if only one idea is presented, this does not mean that a person will automatically be found guilty. However, there remains the issue whether or not it is acceptable that Person B is left out of the investigation focus. Objectivity here means that the investigator should look for the truth. If the truth about a negative event is found by investigating Person B, maybe the examiner should be entitled to investigate that person.

The research findings presented above may seem to be basically a table of raw data. More analysis is needed. Also, interviews with clients, examiners, and victims might help enrich the empirical basis for analysis. At the start of this section, two key aims were suggested: presenting the result from a study of reports and, in doing so, evaluating the blame game hypothesis. These two aims were not completely achieved. To achieve these aims, we need a more in-depth analysis of the raw data that were presented as findings. The themes that need to be drawn out of these data include how many resulted in prosecution, who were the most likely to be accused, who were the most likely to make allegations, and why did they make allegations.

An interesting question is whether the fraud examiner can be held responsible for individuals who become potential victims. Media speculation and job loss turn investigated individuals into victims of a fraud examination. Some examiners may argue that the problem lies elsewhere (i.e., media). Some examiners may argue that it is outside of the control of the investigator if other events lead to negative outcomes for the accused individual.

Future research has to explore the usefulness of applying the blame game hypothesis toward an understanding of negative allegations and subsequent outcomes. It needs to address concerns about the potential for a miscarriage of justice or even loss of job or reputation in such cases. It should study what is fair and what is unfair, what is acceptable and what is unacceptable. False allegations need to be prevented from having consequences for individuals.

Do suspected white-collar individuals deserve privacy when they are examined by private investigators? If so, do they get it? This question was one of the themes at the 36th International Conference of Data Protection and Privacy Commissioners on the island of Mauritius in October 2014.

Personal data are protected in most countries according to laws. Personal data are information that can identify a living individual. Personal data are the property of the individual concerned. Improper use of personal data is harming individuals.

Under Article 8 of the European Convention on Human Rights, a right to protection against the collection and use of personal data forms part of the right to respect for private and family life, home, and correspondence (Handbook, 2014).

Corporate Social Responsibility

Law firms, auditing firms, consulting firms, and other professional services firms have clients who ask them to investigate suspicions of financial crime (ACFE, 2014; FBI, 2014; Morgan and Nix, 2003; Wells, 2003; Williams, 2005). The task is to clarify facts and sequence of events. Fraud examinations are about misconduct and crime, which is normally a task for authorities in law enforcement, such as police investigators, state prosecutors, and court judges. Since fraud examiners are investigating issues that are related to laws in society, it is important that corporate social responsibility is practiced in firms providing fraud examination services.

This section addresses issues of corporate social responsibility in law firms, auditing firms, consulting firms, and other professional services firms that conduct fraud examinations on a contract basis for private as well as public organizations. One of several corporate social responsibility (CSR) issues is related to the finding of facts concerning violations of penalty laws.

An interesting question here is whether the investigation report is the property of the client, and thus it is at the discretion of the client to report crime to the police, or whether the fraud examiner in the professional services firm should report crime to the police, independent of whether the client wants him or her to do it.

The issue of CSR in this context is important, as law enforcement may be privatized if fraud examiners do not take on responsibility for what they are investigating and what they are finding. Law enforcement is left to public authorities in democratic societies, and not to consultants, lawyers, auditors, private investigators, or employers.

The situation addressed in this chapter is characterized by private investigators in professional services firms providing fraud examinations for their clients, where individuals associated with client organizations are suspected of white-collar crime. This situation is very different from legal or other advice often provided by these firms, as fraud examination involves the assessment of penal law violations with the potential of imprisonment for investigated individuals. Therefore, the concept of CSR is so important, as each aspect of CSR defined in this book may prevent fraud examiners from abuse of powers and instead lead them to make a contribution, rather than damage, to society.

A number of CSR issues arise from the above presentation of fraud examinations and reasons for secrecy. For example, the mandate provided by the client may point investigators in one direction, while at the same time preventing investigators from looking in another—and maybe more relevant—direction. The client may prevent investigators from digging deeper into vulnerable issues by limiting the financial budget for the investigation. And the blame game seems to be a problem in several of the studied Norwegian fraud examination reports.

Based on the current situation of professional services firms, the following evaluation can be justified in terms of the extent these firms in their fraud examinations already have CSR in place:

1. *Being accountable (business responsibility to society)*: No, as they are not sharing information with law enforcement in society even when they have clear evidence of violations of penalty law.
2. *Compensating for own negative impacts (business responsibility for society)*: No, when innocent people are subject to suspicion and investigation, and fraud examiners find no traces of guilt, examiners neither apologize nor compensate these investigation victims.
3. *Compensating for others' negative impacts (business responsibility for society)*: No, as clients have suspected individuals and created victims of investigations, their negative impacts are not compensated by fraud examiners.

4. *Contributing to societal welfare (business responsibility for society)*: Yes, in terms of professional investigations of misconduct and crime in both public and private organizations.
5. *Operating their business in an ethically responsible and sustainable way (business responsible conduct)*: No, as they sometimes take on the roles of police investigator, state prosecutor, and court judge.
6. *Taking responsibility for society and the environment in broad terms*: No, as they are into the business of making profit, and these firms do not perceive their business as part of a greater course in society. They adopt responsibility neither in the local nor in the global society, although many of these accounting firms operate globally.
7. *Managing by business its relationships with society*: Yes, this is exactly what professional firms do. They consider their relationship with society as a business issue. To relate to society has to do with advice these firms give to clients, which improves the performance of clients, and thereby improves performance in society.

There are only two yeses and five nos in this list. The next list is based on the desired situation, where several nos are turned into yes:

1. *Being accountable (business responsibility to society)*: Yes, by sharing information with law enforcement in society when they have clear evidence of violations of penalty law, and even when the client has objections against disclosure of negative information about chief executives.
2. *Compensating for own negative impacts (business responsibility for society)*: Yes, when innocent people are subject to suspicion and investigation, and fraud examiners find no traces of guilt, examiners should apologize or compensate these investigation victims.
3. *Compensating for others' negative impacts (business responsibility for society)*: Yes, as clients have suspected individuals and created victims of investigations, their negative impacts should be compensated by fraud examiners.
4. *Contributing to societal welfare (business responsibility for society)*: Yes, already in place in terms of professional investigations of misconduct and crime in both public and private organizations.
5. *Operating their business in an ethically responsible and sustainable way (business responsible conduct)*: Yes, by avoiding abuse of powers given to private investigators by clients.
6. *Taking responsibility for society and the environment in broad terms*: Yes, by defining and perceiving their business as part of a greater course in society. They should adopt responsibility in the local as

well as the global society, since many of these accounting and other professions firms operate globally.

7. *Managing by business its relationships with society*: Yes, this is exactly what professional firms do. They consider their relationship with society as a business issue. To relate to society has to do with advice these firms give to clients, which improves the performance of clients, and thereby improves performance in society.

All five CSR issues assigned no in the current situation were turned into yes for the desired situation. This means that all issues are considered relevant and important to improve corporate social responsibility of professional services firms involved in fraud examinations in private and public organizations. Given the task of finding facts about a negative event that can have been caused by misconduct and crime, it is indeed important that private investigators understand their immense responsibility in a situation where suspects and others are in a vulnerable situation. Privatization of law enforcement, as is currently a trend in many countries, represents a threat to democratic societies, as all powers toward citizens of a state should be organized and managed by the state.

Case for Discussion

How would you investigate this case? It is a case where I suggested suspicion of corruption by the national Norwegian oil company Statoil (Skarsaune, 2014a, 2014b, 2014c, 2014d, 2014e).

Statoil Employed Judge in Own Legal Dispute

The Biofuel entrepreneurs sued Statoil to clear their names of allegations of corruption. The judge in charge was offered a job by Statoil, accepted, and continued working with the case.

Erlend Skarsaune Journalist, Michael Sandelson Translator

Published: 1 July 2014

The aggrieved parties have fought to be cleared of corruption allegations for a long time. Stavanger District Court has ruled against them.

The Biofuel entrepreneurs had to go all the way to the Supreme Court in order to be granted permission to proceed further with the case. They lost.

However, Arne Helvig and Steinar Kolnes took issue with the way they were treated in Stavanger District Court. Their suspicions that something was not quite correct have now been confirmed.

This is because the judge in charge of their case against Statoil received a job offer from the oil company underway. He accepted it after a few days, but continued in his then role. The Supervisory Committee For Judges now criticises him sharply.

New Chance

The Biofuel entrepreneurs have tried to clear their names of corruption allegations Statoil passed on, and have demanded that the company either produces evidence supporting the claim or drops the case entirely.

The Norwegian legal system has supported Statoil regarding their view. Nevertheless, the case has now gone to the European Court of Human Rights (ECHR).

"What is central for us is that using undisclosed sources it is impossible to defend oneself against should not be permitted, even if one's name is Statoil. We'll now see if we want to re-open the matter, something the Supervisory Committee For Judges' decision opens for. It's also a question of cost. We've spent several million kroner, money we would rather have used for investments in Ghana," says Steinar Kolnes.

Accepted Statoil's Offer

Messrs Kolnes and Helvig became aware of the opposite party having offered the judge in charge of administering the case in Stavanger District Court for over a year a job after the court round in Norway and the Supreme Court having denied their right of appeal regarding the initial ruling.

Judge Lars Ole Sikkeland took over the Biofuel-Statoil case from District Court Judge Richard Saue.

Source: http://www.aftenbladet.no/energi/aenergy/Statoil-employed-judge-in-own-legal-dispute-3455137.html#.U7UDLr44W70

"Did Statoil Bribe the Judge?" Asks Academic

The Norwegian Business School's Petter Gottschalk thinks Statoil must come up with further information regarding employing a Stavanger District Court judge to avoid suspicions of corruption.

Erlend Skarsaune Journalist, Michael Sandelson Translator

Published: 2 July 2014

Statoil offered a job to the judge in charge in preparations leading up to legal proceedings before the Court. He accepted, continuing in his role.

The Biofuel entrepreneurs sued Statoil to clear their names of allegations of corruption. The judge in charge was offered a job by Statoil, accepted, and continued working with the case.

Biofuel entrepreneurs Steinar Kolnes, Arne Helvig, and Ove Martin Kolnes, Statoil's opposite party in the case, reacted when they subsequently became aware of the employment matter. They lodged a complaint with The Supervisory Committee For Judges. The Committee criticised the judge, who now works at Statoil, for having contravened good judge practise.

Professor Petter Gottschalk at the Norwegian Business School (BI), thinks it wrong the former judge was made a scapegoat in this matter, and thinks there is much greater cause to examine Statoil's role.

"This isn't the only case where there is major disparity between what Statoil says regarding ethics and what they do. Statoil proclaims transparency, but is one of the least transparent organisations in Norway. They won't say anything when push comes to shove," says Professor Gottschalk.

Expects Several Answers

Statoil answered in yesterday's article on Aftenbladet that they understand questions are posed regarding employing the judge, but did not wish to elaborate on the actual employment. The Professor thinks this is not good enough.

Statoil understands there are questions regarding the company employing a judge in the middle of a legal dispute, but will not answer why it happened.

"Statoil has to openly lay forth why he was contacted and which assessments they made of the fact that he was working with a case in which they were one of the involved parties. Then we can verify how transparent Statoil actually is," Professor Gottschalk says.

His thinks these questions must be elucidated.

"A suspicion of corruption will taint the case if they are not—namely that they bribed a judge."

"Victory Strengthens the Suspicion"

Professor Gottschalk underlines that a job offer can be a clear bribe. He refers to that here, the job offer came in connection with a case that Statoil subsequently one [*sic*]—the judge had begun working at Statoil by that time and another judge had taken the case over.

"Statoil having won the case strengthens the suspicion, even though it is immaterial whether the bribe had an effect or not when it comes to cases of corruption. Issuing a job offer without open competition gives an undue advantage, and that is sufficient according to the letter of the law," says Professor Gottschalk.

Source: http://www.aftenbladet.no/energi/aenergy/Did-Statoil-bribe-the-judge-asks-academic-3456219.html#.U7UDlr44W70

"We Understand Questions Are Posed Here"

Statoil understands there are questions regarding the company employing a judge in the middle of a legal dispute, but will not answer why it happened.

Erlend Skarsaune Journalist, Michael Sandelson Translator

Published: 3 July 2014

Lars Ole Sikkeland was contacted by Statoil while he was a judge in Stavanger District Court in June 2012. He was offered a job some days later and accepted. At that time, Judge Sikkeland was in charge of a private lawsuit brought by Biofuel against Statoil.

Judge Sikkeland had taken over the Biofuel-Statoil case from District Court Judge Richard Saue in September the previous year. Biofuel lost the resulting case Judge Saue had led, but lodged a complaint against Judges Sikkeland and Saue and the Court's Helge Bjørnstad with the Supervisory Committee For Judges.

The Committee reproves Judge Lars Ole Sikkeland in their ruling, criticising him for having contravened good judge practise.

Not Good Enough

The Committee refers to the Judge Sikkeland consulted Judge Saue, and they agreed that Judge Sikkeland would only handle the purely administrative tasks and not make any important decisions in the case. Nevertheless, this is unsatisfactory when it regards non-bias or ethical standards, they think. The Committee also points out that what is decisive is how the case is perceived externally when it becomes known that a judge "is employed by one of the case's partners."

Mr Sikkeland still works at Statoil. He remarks that he takes the matter under advisement.

"I refer to Statoil's communications division for further comment."

But Statoil cannot really answer regarding how you handled the case when you were a judge, can they?

"That's the answer I have, so you have to ask Statoil what they say," says Mr Sikkeland.

Source: http://www.aftenbladet.no/energi/aenergy/We-understand-questions-are-posed-here-3455304.html#.U7UD2744W70

Statoil Refutes Corruption Allegations

Experts disagree as to whether employing the judge can be counted as bribery. Statoil refuse to say why they offered the judge a job.

Erlend Skarsaune Journalist, Michael Sandelson Translator

Published: 3 July 2014

Statoil information manager Morten Eek says they distance themselves from the "incorrect allegations presented here." He would not answer the question regarding why they employed the judge who administered a case in which the company was a party.

"The way we see it, the matter concerns affairs Stavanger District Court must answer for, not Statoil. We can't check whether the Court adheres to rules applying to impartiality, even when the candidate has been open about the process here."

Statoil also find it concerning that Aftenbladet has published the name of the former judge who now works at the oil company.

"This takes place despite the Supervisory Committee having granted full anonymity in their publication. Allegations of possible punishable action are put forward, claims we perceive as serious transgressions against a person," says Morten Eek.

"Both we and the candidate have acted in good faith and with transparency. We believe Stavanger District Court must answer for whether addressing routine assessments are necessary or not."

An Explanation Is Needed

Professor Petter Gottschalk at the Norwegian Business School (BI), thinks it wrong the former judge was made a scapegoat in this matter, and thinks there is much greater cause to examine Statoil's role.

"Statoil must to openly lay forth why he was contacted and which assessments they made of the fact that he was working with a case in which they were one of the involved parties. Then we can verify how transparent Statoil actually is," Professor Gottschalk says.

His thinks these questions must be elucidated.

"A suspicion of corruption will taint the case if they are not—namely that they bribed a judge."

University of Bergen Professor of Law Jan Fridthjof Bernt thinks raising suspicions of corruption against Statoil is premature.

"Good legal professionals are sought after in an environment such as Stavanger's, and many such people sit at Stavanger District Court. So it's not surprising that that's where Statoil recruits people from. Statoil is also a large organisation, where it's not obvious what the left hand always knows what the right hand is doing," he says.

The Professor is aware that the matter looks different when the judge was in charge of a case in which Statoil was a party.

"What happened here was obviously unfortunate. First and foremost, the judge and court management should have looking out. But there's clearly a need for an explanation from Statoil's side regarding what has happened. Until otherwise stated, I'd like to believe and hope that they have a good explanation," says Professor Bernt.

Source: http://www.aftenbladet.no/energi/aenergy/article3456923.ece#.U7ZRj744W70

Supervising Judge Gave Incorrect Information about Contact with Statoil

Helge Bjørnstad claimed the energy giant offered the judge the job after he had resigned. This happened three months prior to this time, however.

Erlend Skarsaune Journalist, Michael Sandelson Translator

Published: 4 July 2014

Stavanger company Biofuel's commitment to biofuel in Ghana crash-landed at the beginning of 2009. Statoil then announced that they would still not take an ownership stake in the company after an investigation had uncovered an accusation of corruption regarding the biofuel commitment.

Statoil have neither wished to disclose the source of the accusation, nor which company carried out the inquiry—but has stated that they do not endorse the corruption allegation, just passed it on, and aided Biofuel in clarifying the matter.

Law firm Kluge investigated the matter on behalf of the Biofuel entrepreneurs. The confidential report was leaked to Wikileaks, and concludes that there is insufficient evidence to be able to link the corruption allegation to Biofuel.

But the Biofuel entrepreneurs did not gain the support of Stavanger District Court when they sued Statoil. The purpose was so that the energy giant should either prove the corruption claims, or declare the case dead and buried.

Aftenbladet's previous articles show that Lars Ole Sikkeland, one of the judges in charge of the case over a year before main proceedings began in Stavanger District Court, received a job offer from Statoil during the course of this period of time. He accepted the offer at the beginning of July, continued in his then role, resigned his position at the Court in September, and stopped working there on 9th November.

The Supervising Judge's Version

The Biofuel entrepreneurs first approached Stavanger District Court in June last year because they had heard that Judge Sikkeland had got a job at Statoil.

Supervising Judge Helge Bjørnestad answered that he remembered that "Statoil came into the picture at the very end of Judge Sikkeland's service of employment here." The supervising judge knew that Judge Sikkeland had received an employment agreement at "a completely different company", but that Statoil subsequently made contact: "He'd long since resigned his position here, stepped down according to the terms, but began at Statoil."

Nevertheless, this version does not match what Judge Sikkeland explains to The Supervisory Committee For Judges, whom the Biofuel entrepreneurs lodged a complaint with last autumn. There it is stated that Statoil contacted him before he resigned his position at the District Court, and over four months before he had his last working day.

Not to the Press

Supervising Judge Helge Bjørnestad tells Aftenbladet he is now on holiday, and that Acting Supervising Judge Thor Henning Auestad is now dealing with the matter.

But can he not comment on how you have spoken about Judge Sikkeland's contact with Statoil, which does not agree with other information in the matter? "I haven't got any more to say now, certainly not to the Press, anyway. I've said what I have to say to the Supervisory Committee," says Supervising Judge Bjørnestad.

The Committee's resolution shows that the Supervising Judge maintains he has not refused to divulge Judge Sikkeland's employment connection concerning the District Court, and refers to that he informed the Biofuel entrepreneurs of what he remembered when Statoil got involved—that Statoil got involved after Judge Sikkeland had resigned his position at Stavanger District Court.

While the Supervisory Committee criticises Judge Sikkeland for having contravened good judge practise, the Supervising Judge is cleared. The committee finds that Supervising Judge Bjørnestad was not informed about Judge Sikkeland's employment with Statoil, and points out that even though the Supervising Judge has overall responsibility, it should be "unnecessary to issue advance instructions that one should withdraw from the case and/or disclose if you engage in a job-related association with one of the case's parties. This is something every judge should understand."

Source: http://www.aftenbladet.no/energi/aenergy/Supervising-Judge-gave-incorrect-information-about-contact-with-Statoil-3456979.html#.U7eoAb44W70

References

ACFE. (2014). *Report to the Nations on Occupational Fraud and Abuse, 2014 Global Fraud Study*. Association of Certified Fraud Examiners, Austin, TX.

BDO. (2011). Rapport til Lotteri- og stiftelsestilsynet vedr. gransking av stiftelsen Fadderbarnas Framtid (Investigation Report about the Foundation for Adopted Childrens' Future). BDO, Erling Grimstad and Morten Thorkildsen. https://lottstift.no/stiftelsestilsynet/files/2011/12/Rapport-til-Stiftelsestilsynet-fra-BDO-vedr-gransking-av-Fadderbarnas-Framtid.pdf

BDO. (2013). Gjennomgang av anskaffelsesprosessen, konsulentinnleie og habilitet i Gassnova SF (Investigation Report about Procurement in Gassnova). BDO, Erling Grimstad and Morten Thorkildsen.

Bie, F. (2012). Rapport til Stavanger tingrett (Report to District Court in Stavanger). Vierdal Advokatfirma, Stavanger.

Dalane, J., and Olsen, D.L. (2006). *Granskingsrapport—ledelse og styring av Øyestad helselags boligstiftelse Furuheim* (Investigation Report about the Foundation Furuheim for Elderly). Hald, Dalane & Heimvik law firm, Arendal.

Dalseide. (2006). Rapport fra Granskingsutvalget for IKT-kontrakter i Forsvaret oppnevnt av Kongen i statsråd 6. januar 2006 (Investigation Committee for ICT Contracts in the Defense Appointed by the King in Government 6 January 2006). Submitted June 16 to the Department of Defense. www.regjeringen.no (accessed December 3, 2009).

Davidsen, E., and Sandvik, K.T. (2011). Undersøkelse av bekymringsmelding vedrørende psykiatridivisjonen, til styret i Sykehuset Innlandet HF, Oslo 21 (Investigation into Complaints about the Psychiatry Division in Hospital Inland), June.

Deloitte. (2010). Norsk Tipping—Granskingsrapport av 16. august 2010 (Investigation Report about Norwegian Betting Company). https://www.norsk-tipping.no/forsiden/nytt_fra_selskapet/26819.cms

Deloitte. (2012). Rapport Kragerø Fjordbåtselskap AS—Gransking (Report Kragerø Fjord Boat Company—Investigation).

Distriktsrevisjonen. (2007). *Rapport versjon II etter granskingsoppdrag fra styrene i Nedre Romerike Vannverk AS (NRV) og AS Sentralrenseanlegget RA-2* (Report on Water Supply Unit). Nedre Romerike Distriktsrevisjon, LIllestrøm, May 30.

Dobrowen, K., and Klepp, T. (2009). Uavhengig undersøkelse av Eckbos Legater (Investigation Report about the Eckbo Foundation). www.eckbos-legater.no/content/download/479/7915/version/1/file

Eberly, M.B., Holley, E.C., Johnson, M.D., and Mitchell, T.R. (2011). Beyond internal and external: A dyadic theory of relational attributions. *Academy of Management Review*, 36(4), 731–753.

Ernst & Young. (2013). Gransking—NRVS (Investigation Report on School in Moskau). Ernst & Young, Oslo, October 30.

FBI. (2014). Five Former Employees of Bernard L. Madoff Investment Securities Found Guilty in Manhattan Federal Court on All Counts. Federal Bureau of Investigation. www.fbi.gov

Gjørv, A.B., and Lund, A.S. (2013). Gransking I Halden kommune/Enhet for plan, byggesak og geodata (Investigation into City Function for Plan, Construction and Geodata). Hjort law firm, October 24.

Hammond, J.S., Keeney, R.L., and Raiffa, H. (1998). The hidden traps in decision making. *Harvard Business Review*, 76(5), 47–58.

Handbook. (2014). *Handbook on European Data Protection Law*. European Union Agency for Fundamental Rights, Council of Europe, Vienna, Austria.

Kahneman, D. (2011). *Thinking Fast and Slow*. Strauss and Giroux, New York, NY.

Kommunerevisjonen. (2006a). *Granskingsrapport Undervisningsbygg Oslo KF* (Investigation Report on City School Maintenance Service), Rapport 16/2006.

Kommunerevisjonen. (2006b). *Granskingsrapport 2 Undervisningsbygg Oslo KF* (Investigation Report on City School Maintenance Service), Rapport 27/2006.

Kommunerevisjonen. (2013). *Oslo kommunes saksbehandling i Lindebergsakene* (City of Oslo Handling the Lindeberg Cases), Rapport 7/2013.

KPMG. (2012). *Halden kommune: Gransking av disposisjoner i Halden Ishall AS og Halden Ishall Eiendom AS* (Halden Municipality: Investigation of Dispositions in Halden Ice Hall and Halden ice Hall Property). KPMG.

Kvale. (2013). *Innberetning til Oslo byfogdembete i bo nr. 12-197991IKON-OBYF/2 Oslo Vei AS, dets konkursbo* (Report to the District Court on Bankruptcy of Oslo Road). Kvale Advokatfirma, Advokat/Bostyrer Tom Hugo Ottesen, December 11.

Lee, F., and Robinson, R.J. (2000). An attributional analysis of social accounts: Implications of playing the blame game. *Journal of Applied Social Psychology*, 30(9), 1853–1879.

Lynx. (2011). *Briskebyrapporten* (Investigation Report on Football Stadium). Lynx law firm. http://www.hamar.kommune.no/getfile.php/Bilder/Hamar/Nyhetsbilder/Politikere/Briskebyrapporten,%20ikke%20sladdet_1.pdf

Lynx. (2013). *1192-rapporten. Gransking av internasjonale spilleroverganger 2007–2011* (Examination of Player Transfers). Lynx law firm, Oslo.

Morgan, M., and Nix, W. (2003). CPA perceptions of the marketability, career enhancements and quality of services of certified fraud examiners. *Southern Business and Economic Journal*, 31–50.

Nergaard, L.L. (2013). *Gransking av Troms Kraft AS* (Investigation Report about Troms Kraft Power Company). Norscan Partners and Grette law firm, September 9.

Pontell, H.N., and Geis, G. (2007). *International Handbook of White-Collar and Corporate Crime*. Springer, New York.

PwC. (2007). *Economic Crime: People, Culture and Controls*, 4th Biennial Global Economic Crime Survey, United States of America. PricewaterhouseCoopers. www.pwc.com/crimesurvey.

PwC. (2008a). Granskingsrapport: Undersøkelser foretatt på oppdrag fra Oslo kommune, Byrådslederens avdeling v/Seksjon for internrevisjon (Investigation Report: Examination Undertaken on Behalf of the City of Oslo, Department of the Mayor). PricewaterhouseCoopers, Oslo, May 21.

PwC. (2008b). Granskingsrapport—«Terra-saken» i Rana kommune (Investigation Report—«Terra Case» in Rana Municipality). PricewaterhouseCoopers, Oslo, June 10.

PwC. (2009). Gransking av «Spania-prosjektet» Oslo kommune (Investigation of the Spain Project in the City of Oslo). PricewaterhouseCoopers, Oslo. http://www.oslo.kommune.no/getfile.php/Byr%C3%A5det%20(BYR)/Internett%20(BYR)/Dokumenter/Rapport%20pwc.pdf

PwC. (2013a). Utvidet revisjon av Akershus universitetssykehus HF (Investigation Report about Ahus Public Hospital). PricewaterhouseCoopers, Oslo. http://www.ahus.no/SiteCollectionDocuments/Endelig%20offentlig%20rapport%20-%20Utvidet%20revisjon%20Ahus_Rev%20OV%2022052013.pdf

PwC. (2013b). Kontrollutvalget i Stavanger v/Rogaland Kontrollutvalgssekretariat: Undersøkelse/gransking knyttet til Stavanger kommunes utbetaling av á-kontobeløp i forbindelse med den såkalte «Tyrkia-saken» (Investigation Report about the Turkey Case in the City of Stavanger). PricewaterhouseCoopers, Oslo, September 11.

Roscher, E., and Berg, H.S. (2013). Stangeskovene AS granskingsberetning til Nedre Romerike tingrett (Investigation into Stange Forest Industries). Ernst & Young/Law firm Lynx.

Shepherd, D.A., Patzelt, H., and Wolfe, M. (2011). Moving forward from project failure: Negative emotions, affective commitment, and learning from the experience. *Academy of Management Journal*, 54(6), 1229–1259.
Skarsaune, E. (2014a). Statoil employed judge in own legal dispute. *Stavanger Aftenblad* (daily Norwegian newspaper), July 1. www.aftenbladet.no
Skarsaune, E. (2014b). "Did Statoil bribe the judge?" asks academic. *Stavanger Aftenblad* (daily Norwegian newspaper), July 2. www.aftenbladet.no
Skarsaune, E. (2014c). We understand questions are posed here. *Stavanger Aftenblad* (daily Norwegian newspaper), July 2. www.aftenbladet.no
Skarsaune, E. (2014d). Statoil refutes corruption allegations. *Stavanger Aftenblad* (daily Norwegian newspaper), July 3. www.aftenbladet.no
Skarsaune, E. (2014e). Supervising judge gave incorrect information about contact with Statoil. *Stavanger Aftenblad*, July 4, 2014. www.aftenbladet.no
Slyke, S.V., and Bales, W.D. (2012). A contemporary study of the decision to incarcerate white-collar and street property offenders. *Punishment and Society*, 14(2), 217–246.
Wells, J.T. (2003). The fraud examiners. *Journal of Accountancy*, October, 76–80.
Wiersholm. (2011). Granskingsrapport—Oppsummering: Adecco Norge AS (Investigation Report about Adecco Health Care Institutions). Wiersholm law firm, Oslo, September 23.
Wiersholm. (2012). Notat til Verdibanken ASA v/Kjell Hande (Notes to Verdibanken). Ansvarlig Advokat Knut Bergo, November 19.
Williams, J.W. (2005). Governability matters: The private policing of economic crime and the challenge of democratic governance. *Policing and Society*, 15(2), 187–211.

Conclusion

An abnormal outcome of an investigation is the murder of Sallie Rohrbach, who conducted an examination of accountants at Dilworth Insurance Agency. She was killed by the owner, Michael Howell. Howell's motive for killing Rohrbach resulted from her investigation of his insurance agency and detecting evidence of insurance fraud. Between March 2004 and May 2008, Howell embezzled more than $150,000 in documented and undocumented insurance premiums where drivers were driving uninsured. Rohrbach began her investigation after numerous clients began to question and complain about the insurance agency. According to Howell's wife, Howell displayed aberrant behavior such as snapping and arguing with Rohrbach as she questioned him about his finances, eventually striking her with a computer stand while she was at his agency. Her body was dumped in a wooded area near Fort Mill, South Carolina (Perri and Brody, 2011).

The UK Bribery Act is relevant to professional service firms who help prevent financial crime in business organizations: (http://www.justice.gov.uk/downloads/legislation/bribery-act-2010-guidance.pdf):

1. A commercial organisation's procedures to prevent bribery by persons associated with it are proportionate to the bribery risks it faces and to the nature, scale and complexity of the commercial organisation's activities. They are also clear, practical, accessible, effectively implemented and enforced.
2. The top-level management of a commercial organisation (be it a board of directors, the owners or any other equivalent body or person) are committed to preventing bribery by persons associated with it. They foster a culture within the organisation in which bribery is never acceptable.
3. The commercial organisation assesses the nature and extent of its exposure to potential external and internal risks of bribery on its behalf by persons associated with it. The assessment is periodic, informed and documented.
4. The commercial organisation applies due diligence procedures, taking a proportionate and risk based approach, in respect of persons who perform or will perform services for or on behalf of the organisation, in order to mitigate identified bribery risks.
5. The commercial organisation seeks to ensure that its bribery prevention policies and procedures are embedded and understood

throughout the organisation through internal and external communication, including training that is proportionate to the risks it faces.
6. The commercial organisation monitors and reviews procedures designed to prevent bribery by persons associated with it and makes improvements where necessary.

Compliance programs of organizations are aimed at assuring that the organization complies with the statutory, regulatory, and other governmental requirements that apply in a particular field. In the financial crime arena, a great deal of international and national laws and regulations have created a large set of requirements. Compliance initiatives have led some organizations to create new functions to assure obedience with the legal requirements.

Reference

Perri, F.S., and Brody, R.G. (2011). The Sallie Rohrbach story: Lessons for auditors and fraud examiners. *Journal of Financial Crime*, 18(1), 93–104.

Index

J

K

L

T

U

V

W

Y

Z